THE FURLONGS

THE
FURLONGS

The story of a
remarkable family

PAT NOLAN

Ballpoint Press

In memory of Tom and Margaret Furlong
Their sons Mickey and John
And Chloe Nolan

Published in 2014 by Ballpoint Press
4 Wyndham Park, Bray, Co Wicklow, Republic of Ireland.
Telephone: 00353 86 821 7631
Email: ballpointpress1@gmail.com
Web: www.ballpointpress.ie

ISBN 978-0-9926732-2-2

Book design and production by Elly Design

Cover photograph: Martin Furlong in action
for Offaly in the 1982 All-Ireland final. © Sportsfile

Printed and bound by GraphyCems

CONTENTS

PROLOGUE

The anxiety, the importance of this kick. Five-in-a-row they're bidding for. Mikey Sheehy to take the kick. Martin Furlong in the goal... He's saved it! He's saved it! And he gets it out to Pat Fitzgerald. Oh Martin, what a save...

Micheál O'Hehir

MARGARET FURLONG was less than two weeks past her 75th birthday but, when PJ McGrath sounded the long whistle to end the 1982 All-Ireland final, she quickly made her way from the front of the lower deck of the Hogan Stand and worked her way onto the pitch. She scurried across the field through the pouring rain with her handbag bopping up and down on her wrist with every stride she took. Years earlier she had jokingly been likened to the famous Dutch athlete Fanny Blankers-Koen, 'The Flying Housewife', having skated to victory in the women's race at a sports day in Tullamore and it was easy to see why.

She looked for her youngest son, Martin, who had earlier saved a penalty at a critical juncture in the most famous game in the Gaelic football history as Offaly dethroned a Kerry team bidding for immortality in the shape of five titles in succession. He would later be named Man of the Match and awarded with the Save of the Year for the crucial block from Mikey Sheehy that afforded his side enough impetus to stay in the game before Séamus Darby's late strike altered the course of football history. As euphoric Offaly supporters hoisted him shoulder high all the way to the steps of the Hogan Stand, Margaret's chances of a meaningful exchange with her son were shot for the time being at least.

Martin was 36 and nearing the end of a remarkable career by then. Although he was the most decorated of Margaret's four sons, he wasn't necessarily the most talented. More than 50 years earlier she landed in Tullamore from Wexford with her husband Tom, a humble man with a voracious appetite for work who dodged execution during the War of Independence, and their eldest son Micheál was born soon afterwards.

A supremely talented dual player, he left for America in 1954 when Offaly were building a forward line around his ability and looking like they might finally be amounting to something at senior level. Mickey had been home the previous year to see his county play in both All-Ireland finals but, with a large family to support back in New Jersey, another trip in 1982 was too great a stretch.

In a state of delirium elsewhere in Croke Park was John, the second of the four sons. A colossal figure of a man, there were some footballing sages around Tullamore who reckoned he could have been the best of the lot of them. But his life veered in a different direction when he contracted tuberculosis-meningitis as a teenager. He just about managed to step back from death's door during a three-year stint in hospital fighting an illness which robbed him of his hearing, not to mention the health to play football again.

The third son, young Tom, was a star of Offaly underage teams and excelled for the senior team in a variety of positions before falling foul of rule 27, which banned GAA members from any interaction with 'foreign' sports, and a belligerent county board cleric who dogged the family for years. He too left for America at 20, lit up Gaelic Park for years afterwards, was on the books of the New York Giants and then signed for the Atlanta Falcons before injury cruelly robbed him of an elite career in the NFL that was stretching out before him.

Amid all the excitement at the final whistle he had lost his mother but was determined to find Martin in his finest hour. As the crowd drifted out of Croke Park he made his way to the back entrance of the dressing rooms under the Hogan Stand. A couple of guards were there and no one was getting in.

"But I'm Martin Furlong's brother," he reasoned. The guards just smiled and shook their heads.

Someone nearby recognised him. "Come with me, Tom," he said. He followed him and worked his way into the dressing room where he found Martin, still in his shorts. The brothers burst into tears as soon as their eyes met. They embraced warmly and barely a word was said.

Mickey, John and Tom had all dreamed of winning All-Irelands with Offaly. If circumstances had been different, they might well have. But each of them, in their own way, ploughed a furrow for Martin to follow and in moments like this, as Tom and Martin wrapped their arms around each other, they exuded as much pride from his achievements as Martin did himself.

Maybe even more.

The story of the Furlong family encapsulates various strands of Irish life: Ireland's struggle for independence and the in-fighting that followed with the country torn over its new, fractured identity; the difficulties people endured just to eke out a living in the decades that followed; bewilderment at the power wielded by the clergy; families splintered by emigration; those who left making something of themselves overseas; heroism through the GAA.

Primarily, the Furlongs are identified through their sporting prowess though their lives encountered a broad range of challenges, none of which diluted their innate modesty and unflappable nature.

The Furlongs are a great GAA family. Moreover, they're a compelling family.

CHAPTER 1

WITH HEART AND HAND

AT AROUND midday on a Thursday afternoon in July 1921, up to 20 IRA members parked their bicycles not far from New Ross post office. A number of them surrounded the building on all sides while others filed inside, dressed in their civilian clothes and without any form of disguise. The staff had just finished sorting the morning mail and the town was relatively quiet. At first they didn't pay any heed to the men, presuming they were linesmen – post office officials who had charge of the telegraph system. However, when they drew out their revolvers and yelled "hands up" the innocence of the staff's initial impression was laid bare.

One of the volunteers saw a lady using the telephone in the public office and jumped over the counter, quizzing her as to the nature of her conversation. Satisfied that she hadn't been relaying any details of the raid, the phone was quickly dismantled and the telegraph wires cut.

The key of the safe was demanded from the postmaster. When he had the temerity to demur a gun was pointed at his head. The leader of the group was rather young but ran a tight ship. He barked out the orders and it was clear that the group was well organised with each man having been assigned a specific task. They spread around the building, rifling through drawers for anything of value and pocketing it; cash, postal orders, stamps, savings bank certificates.

Amid all the excitement, the entrance of the post office remained open so as not to arouse suspicion with the local RIC barracks barely 400 yards away. People continued to enter the building as they went about their normal daily business but no one was allowed to leave.

The stakes were raised though when a British Army officer strolled in with the intention of buying stamps. No sooner was he through the door when he noticed a man with his hand on a revolver in the breast of his coat. He looked around and saw the volunteers behind the counter, calling the shots and swiping what they could. He bided his time and tried to make himself inconspicuous. After some

20 minutes he made a run for the door and sprinted all the way to the barracks, quickly informing the police of the heist. Both military and RIC personnel swarmed to the scene in lorries with more following on bicycles.

By the time they mobilised themselves, however, the volunteers' work was just about done. Before the building was surrounded most of the raiders had fled on their bicycles though word hadn't yet reached one of their men guarding the back entrance. When he finally realised that he was isolated and that the crown forces were closing in, he made a run for it down Quay Street.

"Hands up," shouted a soldier who gave chase. The volunteer hesitated and reached for the revolver in the right-hand pocket of his trousers. "Hands up," the soldier cried once more. It was enough to avert a shootout which, given that he was now heavily outnumbered, the volunteer would almost certainly have lost. He raised his hands and was disarmed. He was seized and brought up to the barracks, shipping more than a few belts from officers along the way.

People on the street stopped and wondered what all the commotion was about. Margaret Moloney had travelled the few miles from Raheen into New Ross for some shopping with her mother, Anastatia, and they were drawn towards the sight of this man being hauled up to the barracks. Margaret, just 13 years of age and on her school holidays, wondered who he was. "That's a Furlong from Raheenakennedy," she was later told. The Furlong household was only a couple of miles across the fields from where she lived near Adamstown, yet she wasn't familiar with this man at all.

Tom Furlong had signed up with the republican movement four years earlier when barely 16 years of age. While Wexford was a focal point of the 1798 rebellion, it had also played its part in the 1916 Easter Rising when the towns of Enniscorthy and Ferns were taken by rebels who only surrendered once their comrades in Dublin had finally been defeated. Like many young men of the time, Furlong's head was turned by events of 1916 as support for republicanism mushroomed across the country.

After going through the usual drilling and training in the early years, his first big assignment was in connection with a raid for arms on the Clonroche barracks in April 1920. Furlong, armed with a shotgun which he wasn't required to discharge on this occasion, manned the main barricade on the New Ross road as the attack dragged on for more than five hours.

The following December, having since joined a flying column and alternated between that and the local Adamstown company, he enjoyed a more prominent role in an attack on Foulksmills barracks and fired some 50 rounds over the course of a four-hour stand off. The volunteers eventually had to withdraw having made no significant inroads and with their ammunition exhausted.

No RIC men were wounded on that occasion, though Furlong was involved in several sniping missions on the same barracks thereafter, one resulting in the wounding of a constable. By now he was on the run and in hiding from the British forces and between significant assignments would engage in activities to disrupt road, rail and electricity lines, while houses were also frequently raided for arms.

As he was the only man captured from the New Ross post office job though, it was always likely that there would be moves to make an example of him. The day after his arrest he was imprisoned in Waterford ahead of a court martial in the city less than two weeks later, facing the charge of carrying a Webley revolver. When he was arrested and disarmed, the revolver was found to be loaded with dum-dum bullets in all six chambers. The nature of his ammunition didn't do him any favours, with expanding bullets having been banned from international warfare by the Hague Convention of 1899.

As the case closed, Furlong was asked if he had any statement to make. He condemned the officers for the "brutal" manner in which they abused him on his arrest. The judge frowned and reached for one of the bullets, holding it up.

"A soldier does not feel inclined to be very kind when you find a man with this kind of ammunition on him. What did they do to you at New Ross?"

"They kicked me," Furlong replied, "in the street, before they brought me to the barracks. They struck me with their rifles and boxed me into the face."

The judge quizzed him as to whether he had reported any of his bruises to the prison doctor. Furlong replied that he hadn't, presuming it would have been a pointless exercise. Military witnesses stepped forward and, naturally, played down any rough house treatment that may have been meted out, suggesting that any thumps he got were earned for barbed responses to their queries.

It was all conjecture in any event. With the ammunition on his person when arrested and three witnesses, two military and one police personnel, testifying against him he never stood a chance of acquittal; the main issue was whether he would be sentenced to penal servitude or death. The former seemed more likely at first before the latter was settled on: Tom Furlong was to be executed.

Although the Anglo-Irish Treaty wasn't signed until December 1921, the War of Independence effectively ended months earlier when a truce was agreed, bringing about a ceasefire. Guerilla warfare had forced the closure of many rural barracks across the country such as those raided by Furlong and Co as crown forces retreated to stations in more urban centres.

The British feared that this brand of warfare would continue indefinitely and with spiralling costs given the deployment of their troops, not to mention casualties and the fierce criticism they were receiving at home and abroad for the barbaric nature of their reprisals on innocent civilians through the actions of the Black and Tans, they pushed for a resolution. A truce was eventually agreed on July 9 and came into effect two days later, paving the way for the negotiations which eventually resulted in the signing of the Treaty.

Tom Furlong and his fellow volunteers raided the post office in New Ross on July 7. His court martial in Waterford was held on July 20. At its outset he had railed against the authority of the court and refused to recognise it given the truce that had come into effect days earlier. His words fell on deaf ears initially and may have seemed like nothing more than a man bleating in desperation for his salvation but, as it turned out, there was more than a ring of truth to his assertion.

While he may have been set for execution, it eventually came to pass that the truce would grant him and others like him a reprieve. Tom Furlong dodged a death sentence and was released in January 1922, the month after the Treaty was signed, though his time behind bars wasn't finished yet as one of the murkiest and most unseemly episodes in Irish history was soon to unfold: The Civil War.

Wexford, like many other counties, was deeply divided by the Civil War. The South Wicklow-North Wexford Brigade of the IRA supported the Treaty but the South Wexford equivalent, which numbered Furlong among its membership, didn't. Having been united in one cause, they now turned the gun on each other. It has been said that Wexford was a county that saw more fighting during the Civil War than in the War of Independence. At one stage the anti-Treaty forces took control of the county before the Free State Army wrestled it back. The anti-Treaty side, for example, constantly disrupted railway lines to frustrate the Free State's ability to govern; a spate of killings was often the response by way of retaliation.

A couple of weeks after Furlong was released from prison having been granted his amnesty, he took up station full-time at the New Ross barracks, which was no longer under British control. He remained there until the Civil War broke out in June 1922 and took part in it to a small degree on the anti-Treaty side. Along with three others, he fired a few shots at Free State Army troops coming into town in a number of lorries as well as a number of attacks on posts in New Ross but none of these episodes amounted to much.

After skirmishes in Enniscorthy he was arrested in Ballyanne in July with the Civil War very much in its infancy. At first he was interned in New Ross before being shifted to Kilkenny, from where he managed to escape that winter though only made it about 600 yards from the jail before being immediately recaptured.

The time may have passed slowly but it was maybe just as well that Furlong was locked up with the number of casualties mounting on the outside. However, those who were jailed weren't always spared a bloody fate either. In March 1923 three anti-Treaty prisoners were executed in Wexford Jail having been arrested for possession of firearms the previous month, which led directly to three Free State soldiers being shot dead in Furlong's local village of Adamstown. The following day another man was shot dead in the same parish by way of response from the Free State.

The Civil War eventually concluded in May 1923 with the anti-Treaty side finally admitting defeat and Tom Furlong was released from prison, having since been relocated to the Curragh in Co Kildare, in January 1924.

He returned home to the family farm in Raheenakennedy. He was the third of four sons to Mike and Anne and, not being the eldest, would never have any chance of inheriting the farm. That would fall to his brother John and though the farm was only big enough to support one family, he and his wife Ciss never had children while the next brother, Jim, didn't marry and remained on the family farm throughout his life. The youngest boy, Mick, later opened a bar and grocery store on Quay Street in New Ross.

With no long-term prospects for him on the farm and his recent history with the IRA and time in prison having done little to promote his position in the family's pecking order, Tom reckoned he would need to be innovative and look beyond Adamstown in terms of how he would eke out a living. However, there was more to life than work.

Coming to the late 1920s Margaret Moloney was no longer a teenage girl but a strapping young woman. From another farming family in nearby Raheen, she was the second of five children. The clergy held an inordinate influence in Ireland at the time and, if a beast was sick, the priest tended to be sent for rather than anyone of veterinary expertise. As youngsters, Margaret and her friends would often jump over a ditch if they noticed a priest coming towards them on the road. If he saw them first, the expectation was that they would kneel until he had passed.

Those quasi acts of defiance apart, she remained a deeply religious woman throughout her life and it was through attending Mass at Raheen Church that she first began to exchange glances with Tom Furlong, the man she had seen carted up the street to the RIC Barracks in New Ross a number of years before. They later became acquainted and then embarked on a relationship. They were something of a peculiar couple in ways as Tom stood at just five feet seven tall while Margaret towered a few inches over him.

Nonetheless, they complemented each other well on the whole and, before too long, decided to marry and elope. They took their wedding vows at half past eight one morning in Raheen Church in front of two witnesses and immediately headed for Dublin, where they stayed for six months. Years later, Margaret would often joke of how she was treated to a "six-month honeymoon" in the capital. From there they relocated to Cavan briefly, where Tom came across a job advertisement for a ploughboy on Deegan's farm in Tullamore.

Tom Furlong knew how to work a farm better than he knew anything else. Moreover, he enjoyed it and had a flair for it, not to mention an appetite for hard work to match. He applied for the job and was hired by Frank Deegan, for whom he would work for several years to come.

Tom and Margaret initially took up residence in Puttaghaun on the north side of Tullamore before settling in a two-bedroomed house on O'Moore Street a few years later for an initial weekly rent of six shillings and sixpence a week (6/6d). It would remain the family home for 60 years from then on.

Tom didn't spare himself in terms of workload. Margaret would make her way up to the Deegan farm in Clonminch with a bottle of tea and a sandwich for him in the middle of the day. He'd pull the horse in for a few minutes, feed up on whatever she had and set off about his work again. He rented a patch of land on Church Road and kept a few bullocks and cows and chickens and reared pigs as well as having an ass for working on the bog. His livestock were always well fed and sought after at the local mart.

Margaret didn't leave her farming instincts behind her in Wexford either and picked up the slack while Tom worked during the day. When a sow was farrowing her motherly nature was always apparent, staying up at night rubbing her belly and making sure she didn't smother the offspring. Her sons still remember her hauling buckets of slop that seemed like they would pull her arms from the sockets.

In later years, Tom worked in the building trade with a local man named Larry Young, as well as the Flanagans, while continuing his own relatively modest farming activity on the side. He never learned to drive and while working in construction was a regular sight around Tullamore, wheeling his tools and materials around town on a buggy from one job to the next.

He retained a strong republican outlook though very rarely spoke of his Old IRA past with his sons or anyone else for that matter, but then Tom Furlong always was a man of few words. Most information the boys gleaned on the matter was from their mother. For years, the family would holiday at home in Wexford and the trips down there would take in many of the landmarks that dominated Tom's volunteer days. Martin remembers passing under a bridge in Macmine once when his father remarked, "That's where the train came off the tracks" in reference to the practice of derailing that was common in the war years.

When on those summer breaks in Wexford, the men would sit around and talk of the old days though the children were too carefree to take an interest at the time. If they did, they'd be sent on their way in any event.

"I remember one time we were going to Wexford," says Tom junior as his father touched ever so briefly on his escape from prison in Kilkenny once, "and we went out past Kilkenny Castle, and he said, 'There's the road that we tunnelled under, we came up in that field there'."

He also remembers his mother mentioning how his father soldiered with famed Tipperary volunteer Dan Breen and was shot in the thigh when on the run in the Knockmealdown Mountains with him one day. The wound bothered him to a degree for the rest of his life.

"He walked with a limp, when he was tired or that," adds Tom junior, "he'd be shifting weight."

Tom Furlong's anti-Treaty stance was reflected in his staunch support for Fianna Fáil for the rest of his life, with Eamon de Valera a huge political hero of his. Fianna Fáil's long-serving Laois-Offaly TD Nicholas Egan could always count on the Furlong vote. "He was a big Dev man," says Tom. "Didn't matter what Dev said, that was it." Years later when Margaret attended Dev's funeral, she was elevated to a more prominent position at the service when it was noticed that she was wearing her late husband's war medals on her chest.

So fanatical were Tom Furlong's republican beliefs that he railed against the notion of celebrating his birthday, which fell on July 12, "Orangeman's Day in the North", as he called it. Not long after he settled in Tullamore with Margaret, she gave birth to their first son, Micheál, on July 13, 1929. From then on, father and son celebrated their birthday on the same day.

CHAPTER 2

THE GOLDEN-HAIRED BOY

TOM and Margaret weren't boastful people by nature and, though they never said it in so many words, their other sons always noticed how they spoke of Micheál in a more reverential tone than they did of anyone else. The lads were never perturbed or bitter about it in any way; it was just an observation on their part that they lived with comfortably.

"Oh, he was the wonderboy," says Tom junior. "He was the number one son. He could do no wrong. He was the oldest, he was the first. They'd tell stories about Mickey, about this, about that. If Mickey killed half of New York, that'd be fine!"

"Mickey was the golden-haired boy," Martin observes. "Mickey was the man."

Naturally, as the eldest of the family, he was a pioneer in many ways and given that he was successful at many of the things he turned his hand to he set a high standard for the rest to follow. They were inspired rather than intimidated by the challenge of emulating him and, at the very least, you'd have to say they made a decent fist of it.

Mickey had his early schooling in the convent in Tullamore before moving on to the boys' school, St Brigid's, having made his First Holy Communion. There, in the school yard, he revelled in the typically boisterous kickarounds but it was in the school that he was also exposed to his first form of organised football and hurling as laid on by Bill Ennis, who taught Mickey from second class all the way to seventh before he moved on to the Christian Brothers' School.

Ennis was a crucial conduit between Tullamore GAA Club and the school and many players who won handfuls of medals from underage right through to senior credited those achievements to him more than any other individual. He was pivotal in organising the Offaly Schools League, which St Brigid's won in football in 1943 with Furlong starring. Joe Bracken, later a dual player with Offaly, was a few years behind Mickey in school but in time went on to play with all four Furlong brothers and is probably the only man alive today that retains that distinction. He reckons that Ennis was "30 or 40 years ahead of his time".

"He was one of the most forward-thinking men I ever met in my lifetime," Bracken says. "He talked about building a little centre on the side pitch in O'Connor Park so that when the break would come in the winter they could keep the lads playing maybe handball or basketball and keep them fit. He was a great teacher as well, a powerful teacher."

He helped lay the foundations for the most phenomenally successful era at underage level that Tullamore has ever known in the 1940s. The club won six out of seven minor football titles from 1942 as well as four minor hurling championships between 1941 and 1945. From 1943-45 they won three successive minor doubles with Mickey Furlong coming of age as a blue-chip forward to adorn the teams that completed that treble in '45 while still eligible for the juvenile grade.

A teammate, Billy Dowling, brother of former GAA president John, remembers playing a minor hurling game with Furlong in which an opponent drew wildly across him. When Dowling stuck up for him he got the same treatment.

"There were no sendings off in those days. Mickey wouldn't deliberately go back to get a fella. It wasn't in his nature. He was brave, go for every ball, skilful. Mostly brave. As brave as you could get."

The senior selectors couldn't wait for him to emerge from underage ranks before blooding him either. The following year he was part of the senior football team that won the county title with a two-point victory over traditional rivals Rhode in the final. A golden generation of players was emerging in Tullamore and the free-scoring Furlong was the outstanding talent among them. He had that rare combination of precocious skill fused with a hard edge, innate toughness and a fiercely competitive spirit.

And while Tullamore may have been the dominant force at underage level in Offaly at the time, other clubs were bringing through a number of useful footballers too. Offaly was a county that had never achieved anything at senior level in either code. Nothing. In 1945 they reached the Leinster football final for only the second time ever and first since 1907 but lost by five points to Wexford. To kick on they needed an infusion of young talent.

In 1946 and '47 Furlong was on the Offaly minor and junior teams in both codes. While Offaly was a county that hadn't any tradition in hurling or football back then, it was reckoned that their best chance of a breakthrough came in football. The county's main population base was in the football areas north of the county and the big ball teams generally tended to be more competitive against top ranking opposition.

In 1947, more by accident than design, Offaly were assembling a talented bunch of players at underage level and stormed to a Leinster minor final with facile victories over Carlow and Kildare by 14 and 21 points respectively. It would be Offaly's first appearance at this stage of the competition at minor level and in opposition was Dublin, who had won the two previous provincial titles after the minor championship was parked for two years during The Emergency. Among their star players was one Kevin Heffernan.

Any success that Offaly achieved in both codes at senior level in the 40 years or so leading up to the turn of the millennium was underpinned by an attitude of defiance and downright refusal to accept defeat. It's difficult to say with any great clarity when that mindset took hold but there were certainly signs of it in what turned out to be two games against Dublin to determine the destination of that's year's Leinster minor football title.

It may seem odd by today's standards but with young men having to move around for work at a younger age than they do now, the Offaly team contained a couple of non-natives. One of them, Tommy Moyna from Scotstown, had already represented Monaghan at senior level in the National League. He came to work for DE Williams distillers and wandered up to O'Connor Park one day where he fell into a kickaround with Furlong and his friend Billy Adams. The county secretary, Rody O'Brien, liked what he saw and asked would he be interested in lining out for Offaly. He partnered Furlong at midfield.

Wing-back Des Garland had played for Westmeath against Offaly in the previous year's minor championship but then moved to Tullamore, where he spent the rest of his life.

The half-back line was possibly Offaly's strongest with Paddy Casey and Archie McLoughlin alongside Garland. Casey, along with his older brother Mick, is widely considered to be one of the finest footballers Offaly ever produced. In later years he regularly represented Leinster in the Railway Cup when the competition oozed prestige, as well as being selected on the Rest of Ireland team against the Combined Universities on several occasions. His career and that of Furlong's went hand in hand to a large degree as they both starred for New York in later years. McLoughlin was a stylish, strong and fearless half-back who drew comparisons with Kildare great Jack Higgins.

Behind them, Kevin Scally was a commanding full-back while up front Seán Foran was a rangy full-forward who, along with Scally, went on to become a distinguished senior.

The drawn game was played at Croke Park as a curtain raiser to the Meath-Laois senior final and was a particularly dogged and physical affair for the grade. Fr Rory O'Brien, who has since spent decades on missionary work in Africa, was corner-back, marking Heffernan.

"I remember everybody was telling me, 'Watch that Heffernan'," he recalls, "but I didn't know who Heffernan was. He was only a name to me at the time but I think I marked him reasonably well. He didn't come across as a famous fella then. But he was a dangerous forward according to fellas who knew him."

Having played with the wind in the first half, Offaly trailed by a point at half-time. Furlong picked up a knee injury and he and Moyna were struggling against Dublin's midfield pair. Offaly started the second half well to go two points in front though Dublin pushed three ahead with time almost up. By then, O'Brien had been shifted from corner-back to corner-forward, oddly enough. Offaly had a 45 late on which seemed to be sailing wide only for him to punch it back into open play allowing sub Tommy Ennis to strike an equalising goal. There was still enough time to register a winning point though Offaly butchered the opportunity. In any event, they were grateful for the draw.

Furlong's knee left him doubtful for the replay in Mullingar though he was selected in the less taxing position of full-forward. However, a thunderous row broke out in the first quarter of the match resulting in McLoughlin being sent off. Furlong was relocated to centre half-back as a result and, despite his physical ailment, manned the position excellently, continually foiling Dublin attacks.

He couldn't repel them all, though, and with Offaly having built a seven-point lead in the second half despite having missed a penalty, Heffernan foraged deep for possession and cut through the Offaly defence before drilling a shot to the net. Casey pointed to push Offaly five clear before Heffernan set off on another rampaging run only this time goalkeeper Vincent Cowen pushed his shot over the bar. Dublin tagged on two more points to halve the deficit and pushed for a winning goal before the final whistle relieved Offaly anxiety and secured the most notable victory in the county's modest history. Up to then, Offaly's only achievements of note included two All-Ireland junior hurling titles in the 1920s and a Leinster junior football crown in 1935.

"There was great celebrations and it was appreciated by many that we won something worthwhile," recalls Ted O'Brien, younger brother of Rory, who had featured in the drawn game and would start the subsequent All-Ireland semi-final against Tyrone.

With four weeks to that game, it gave Furlong ample time to get his knee in order. His mother would have seen to it in any event. "My mother was a powerful woman for getting us back out on the field with injuries and all that," says Martin. "She'd be rubbing goose grease into you and winter green and bandaging you up. Wrapping your ankle. She was fierce good at that sort of stuff because that time you wouldn't be going to doctors."

A modest crowd had attended the Leinster final replay but the Offaly public warmed to the team ahead of the semi-final, which was staged in Drogheda. A special train was run and supporters flocked to the ground. Indeed, the start of the second half of the game was delayed by crowding on the sidelines.

By then the sides were level as Offaly had failed to make the most of their early superiority when Furlong was among the scorers as they built an early three-point lead. A dubious penalty gave Tyrone a foothold before the break and with 10 minutes to go they led by four points.

Offaly then got a penalty of their own, which Johnny Kinahan converted, before Moyna kicked the levelling point. A replay looked to be on the cards when Tyrone forced a late 45 which, somehow, floated all the way to the net.

"We were in the full-back line, myself and Scally and Jim Cloonan," says Fr Rory O'Brien, "and Mick McIntyre from Cloghan (a selector) was in telling us what to do, 'Keep out the forwards, don't let the ball go' and the next thing it was taken and it sailed under the bar and they won. They got a jammy goal. It was heartbreaking, and they won the All-Ireland. They went on and beat Mayo well. It was a great Offaly team, even though some of them scattered later on. It just so happened a great crowd of footballers came together at that time."

Despite the Tyrone disappointment, winning that Leinster title was a landmark success. The following year the minors reached the provincial final again and were undone by another last minute goal as Dublin beat them by two points to avenge the previous year's result but it was evident that Offaly were assembling a bunch of players who had the potential to make an impact at senior level.

Mickey Furlong was overage for the minor grade in 1948 and was shunted straight into the senior team. "He went onto the Offaly senior football team very quickly and he was very much a watched man in any game, you know, 'Mark Furlong!'" explains Fr O'Brien. "The in-thinking that time was, 'Take him out of it', you know. That would be football or hurling, it was in any game, take him out of it if you weren't able to mark him. He was well able for it. He had a wonderful catch and he had great skill in side-stepping people and he had great courage."

◆   ◆   ◆   ◆

As senior championship debuts go, Mickey Furlong couldn't have asked for much better. Along with Archie McLoughlin, he was promoted from the 1947 minor team and both players occupied the wing-forward positions for the 1948 Leinster Championship meeting with Kildare in Portlaoise. They scored 1-2 apiece as Offaly cruised to a nine-point win. Furlong opened the scoring with a point and quickly followed it up with a goal to put his side in command and they were rarely troubled from then on.

The next round saw them meet Wexford in a game that was referred to as "the wet day in Carlow" for years afterwards. Such were the conditions the game ought not to have been played but, that notwithstanding, Offaly looked like potential Leinster champions when leading by 10 points well into the second half with Furlong having scored a wonderful individual goal. Inexplicably, despite playing into the stiff breeze and driving rain as well as having had a man sent off, Wexford fashioned a one-point victory.

A key factor in the turnaround was the switching of one Nicky Rackard from full-forward to midfield as Wexford plundered four goals amid a typical lack of decisiveness on the sideline by Offaly, the last goal coming at the death as they clung to a two-point lead.

Furlong won his second county senior medal that year with Tullamore but even that was bitter sweet. The final between Tullamore and Rhode was fixed despite Edenderry having lodged an objection to the Leinster Council to their semi-final loss to Rhode. Tullamore beat Rhode with Furlong hooking over several points from distance. Although a natural ciotóg, kicking off the right foot was no great impediment to him either.

"He kicked them over his shoulder," says Christy Dowling, corner-back that day. "That's what I remember. We had it made if we could feed it to Furlong. What always impressed me with Mickey Furlong was how he could kick a score over his shoulder."

As it happened, Edenderry's appeal was upheld, forcing the

county board to order that a second final be played. Again, Tullamore prevailed but Furlong wasn't fit to play having been laid low by a bout of pneumonia during the considerable gap between both finals.

"He was greatly missed but he was too sick," adds Dowling. "From what I remember, the whole team would go up to the house to see him. Everybody that had anything to do with the senior team showed up."

It was a reflection of Furlong's popularity, which was considerable. He had a gregarious nature that people warmed to and a razor sharp wit, not to mention a streak of devilment. As he'd step down High Street, townsfolk saluted him as though he was something of a celebrity. To them, he probably was.

"You'd want to go to a dance and you'd see the women that would flock around him," says Mickser Casey, a former team mate and long-time friend. "I saw him do everything. I saw him ride a pony at races in Kilbeggan at the sports. The pony ran away, got out of control, and it ran through the band and knocked the band flying everywhere with Mickey on it."

An upshot of Tullamore winning the county title in 1948 was that they could nominate the Offaly captain for 1949. Furlong was only 19 and, though he wasn't Tullamore's only representative on the team, was handed the role.

A championship opener against Dublin didn't raise hopes of a long hot summer among Offaly supporters but the campaign was typical of the team's inconsistency at the time. Dublin were beaten more comfortably than the final three-point margin would suggest to set up a Leinster semi-final meeting with Westmeath. Offaly had played them twice already that year and won both times but they allowed Westmeath off the hook when only managing a draw in Tullamore before losing the replay in Mullingar. It would be Westmeath's last victory over Offaly until they finally made their Leinster breakthrough in 2004.

Interestingly, the Offaly players were addressed after the game by one of Westmeath's mentors, who commiserated with them on their defeat. His name was Fr Tom Gilhooley. He ultimately wouldn't taste success with Westmeath but in later years would be at the coalface for Offaly's most significant breakthroughs.

◆   ◆   ◆   ◆

When Tullamore GAA Club called its annual general meeting at the end of 1949, it was expected to be as unremarkable as those type of gatherings generally are. Indeed, it was anticipated that the main business of the meeting would centre around who would captain the senior footballers in 1950. Luke Lawlor was the incumbent though there were some who wished for Christy Dowling, the vice-captain, to assume the role.

Dowling wasn't canvassing for the job but thought that if there were was a groundswell of support for him, he should at least show his face and see how things unfolded. As it happened, Lawlor had enough backing to retain the role and, once that was done and dusted, Dowling slipped out the door to take his girlfriend on a date. After walking her home later that night, he met someone in town coming from the meeting. His clubmate looked aghast.

"Jesus, there was a fierce row at the meeting," he said.

"What are you talking about?" queried Dowling. "It was nearly over when I left."

The election of club officers was carried out after his departure. Jimmy Flaherty, the sitting chairman, was proposed to fill the position once again. An experienced administrator who had served at county board level, it wasn't envisaged that there would be a challenge for his position. Other nominations were sought as a matter of course before Flaherty's expected ratification.

"I propose Bill Ennis," said a young voice. People looked around to see who had the audacity to effectively oppose Flaherty. It was Mickey Furlong. He was just 20 years of age but, like his father before him, he didn't see youth as an impediment to pushing a cause he felt strongly about. Having already captained his county at senior level and being the club's star player, he had credibility too. Ennis was a heroic figure to the likes of Furlong for the grounding he had given him and others in sport, and indeed life, during their time in St Brigid's. Furlong was ambitious for the club's future and Ennis was an innovative man who made things happen rather than clinging to the status quo.

The sitting committee wasn't pleased with the opposition to Flaherty. So, they got down to it. What were the issues? Why the push for change? Furlong and others weren't happy with the facilities in O'Connor Park. There were no dressing rooms as such, just glorified huts for players to tog out in. With no adequate washing facilities, after training or a game they'd put their clothes on over a lather of sweat and off home. Furlong and his cohorts wanted the club to build proper dressing rooms with hot running water and showers installed.

It was argued that the existing arrangements in O'Connor Park were no worse than what other clubs had to offer but Furlong wasn't buying it. As the biggest and most successful club in the county, Tullamore should have been looking to set the standard and provide the best for its players. A large rump of his senior teammates agreed.

The debate didn't end with the meeting though and there were other concerns too. There was a certain amount of disquiet over access to O'Connor Park, which was the club's only pitch and was frequently used for games featuring various counties other than Offaly. There were issues with cantankerous ground staff running players off the field to protect the surface for upcoming fixtures. Over the next week or two after the AGM it emerged that there was a mass walkout on the club, mostly by playing members, including Mickey Furlong.

The majority of those who left were senior footballers though the hurlers too were depleted to a degree. The upshot was that Tullamore faced into 1950 with a vastly understrength senior football team, a scenario not too dissimilar to that which unfolded with the Limerick and Cork hurlers in recent years when their front line players refused to turn out. But Furlong and his acolytes were putting player welfare at the top of the agenda years before it became fashionable in the GAA.

At first the breakaway group resolved to form their own club in town, the All Whites. Furlong was to be the secretary but efforts to affiliate the club with the county board ran aground with the board citing a motion passed at the county convention two years previously whereby the formation of a new club could be blocked if there was one in the parish already.

Furlong corresponded with Leinster Council secretary Martin O'Neill, who had previously bestowed the 'Faithful County' nickname on Offaly, looking for advice. He reasoned that a town the size of Tullamore should aspire to have two clubs and cited how many of the players who featured on the string of successful minor teams in the '40s had no outlet to play at adult level. Ultimately the All Whites never got off the ground and the wild geese had to formulate a plan B.

Tullamore, as it happened, wasn't the only club in the parish. Outside the town was Ballinamere and Durrow, who were intertwined while retaining their independence. Ballinamere fielded in hurling and Durrow in football so the wantaway Tullamore players enquired as to the possibility of fielding a Ballinamere football team. Relations between Ballinamere and Tullamore were healthy at the time though and Ballinamere didn't want to sour that by effectively taking on the town's senior football team. So they looked to Durrow, who were going through strife at the time themselves.

They too had a fallout at their AGM when a contingent of players left in a huff as they felt that people from their end of the catchment area had a poor representation on the team. So now Durrow were somewhat depleted while there were a bunch of players at a loose end within the same parish.

A meeting was held with three Durrow representatives and three from Tullamore, one of whom was Tom Furlong, who very much supported his son's stance. They agreed to join forces but there was another road block when it emerged that their transfers couldn't be fully sanctioned until 1951.

In essence, the new brigade had to sit out 1950 before they could play club football in Offaly again. Moreover, Durrow were a struggling intermediate outfit so the chances were that when they eventually did come on board they'd have to spend a year or two trying to earn senior status.

In the meantime Durrow played challenge games with the full selection. They were captained by full-back Paddy Molloy who, today, likens Mickey Furlong to Roy Keane in many ways. Molloy is 87 now but can still vividly recall a challenge game against Rhode in Daingean one day with Furlong marking Paddy Casey, the prince of Offaly football.

"Furlong set Casey mad," says Molloy. "Casey couldn't get a kick at it and he stayed with him all day. I'd never seen Paddy Casey destroyed before but he frustrated him as well as everything else. He was lipping at him all day. We bet Rhode that evening – Furlong bet them. That was not an important match but Furlong wanted to prove a point. He was the best I have seen."

The decision of Furlong and others to leave the Tullamore club polarised opinions. Some agreed with their stance and felt that there was a need for a second club in the town regardless. There was no significant trace of animosity between the players that left and those that were left behind either but there was a knock-on effect. Tullamore won the junior football championship in 1949 with a youthful team and were looking forward to challenging strongly at intermediate level with that group.

Instead, these players were promoted to the senior grade before their time and it was a steep learning curve. Amid that backdrop, Durrow managed to win the intermediate championship against the odds and would be a senior outfit when Furlong and Co became eligible in 1951.

The older generation would have been more peeved at the split, as Molloy and others recall, and terms such as blacklegs, scabs and turncoats were used in association with the defectors. And it wasn't just in Tullamore either. There was a widespread curiosity factor attached to this Durrow team and their first appearance in a competitive fixture in the opening round of the senior championship in 1951 against St Mary's, the reigning county champions, in Daingean drew a large crowd from around the county. It was a game that would define Mickey Furlong more than any other he played.

Although many of those present didn't have an attachment to either club, few, if any, neutrals were rooting for a Durrow win given the circumstances surrounding how the team had been assembled. And, while Furlong certainly didn't act alone in bringing about the walkout, he was seen as the poster boy for all that was supposedly wrong about that Durrow team. In particular, there was a group from Rhode who wanted to make their disapproval of the team and Furlong known that day.

A stream of boos, jeers and cat calls was directed at him from an early stage in the match, which was a particularly robust affair. A nasty atmosphere prevailed and young Tom Furlong, watching the game as a seven-year-old behind the goal with friends, can remember lending some vocal support when a priest slapped him across the face.

Whatever about the jibes from the sideline, Furlong was coming in for plenty of punishment out on the field from a St Mary's side packed with colossal men that weren't afraid to make the most of their physical prowess by whatever means necessary. The match descended into chaos in the second half with Furlong in particular the victim of countless dirty blows with no protection from the referee forthcoming. But every time he dusted himself down and refused to yield, continuing to put himself in the firing line.

Then, a strange thing happened. The jeering fell silent for a number of minutes as his detractors began to warm to his efforts. The more Furlong rampaged through the St Mary's rearguard with the opposition defence climbing over each other to swing at him, the more his courage spoke to the contingent who had travelled there essentially with an agenda to make little of him. As he turned the match almost single-handedly in Durrow's favour, they gradually applauded and cheered his efforts. Effectively, those who came to mock ultimately stayed on to pray.

"They booed him at the start and they clapped him at the end," recalls Paddy Molloy. "That's a fact. The sideline was booing him for what he had done, but he played such a game of football. He won the match. There's no doubt about it. It was Furlong versus St Mary's. They couldn't handle him.

"He got kicked and bet but I'll tell you something about Furlong: Furlong had nerves of steel. You could hit Furlong where you liked and he'd get up and come for more. You'd have to kill him to stop him. And he played that evening and he gave a display of football that evening. St Mary's had some thuggerish lads, all country lads, and he wouldn't be popular in their book. They'd be all having a crack at him, every way they could get at him. He still played away and we beat St Mary's that evening. They went home very sore."

As Furlong peeled off his jersey while, ironically enough, togging down by the ditch afterwards, onlookers noticed the bruises and welts all over his front and back after the punishment he had received over the previous hour or so.

Durrow went on to meet Edenderry in the county semi-final in what was a hugely entertaining game in O'Connor Park. Unlike St Mary's, Edenderry had more of a footballing team at their disposal and midfielder and county star Seán Foran was their main man. Given the circus element that surrounded the Durrow team after the St Mary's game and their unpopularity in certain quarters, the county board sent for an outside referee to take charge of the game and Simon Deignan, wing-back on Cavan's All-Ireland winning sides of 1947 and '48, was appointed.

However, on the day something cropped up and he couldn't make it on time so he got word to his brother, Fr Jim Deignan, who taught in St Finian's College in Mullingar, and asked him to step in. He controversially disallowed a Durrow goal in the first half and when Simon eventually arrived at half-time he then took charge for the second half.

Furlong was playing centre-forward, carrying the fight to Edenderry and, with the game on a knife edge, took off on a typically rampaging run through the centre that left a host of opposition defenders trailing in his wake. Just as he rifled the ball to the Edenderry net Deignan's whistle sounded to award a free out for overcarrying. Edenderry held on for a narrow victory and they went on to win the county final against Cloghan.

It was to be Mickey Furlong's last club game in Offaly. Having worked in Salts and as a travelling salesman for Sioda minerals in the midlands area since completing his Leaving Cert, he was moving to Dublin to work in a bakery and threw in his lot with Faughs in hurling and Seán McDermott's in football.

The following year Durrow went on to win the county title without him, beating Edenderry in the final. The team disintegrated soon after that. A number of the players were non-locals based in Tullamore purely for work and were transferred elsewhere. Several of them had no real attachment to the team and, having won the championship, felt that they had made their point and achieved what they set out to do. In later years, some went back to Tullamore and reflected on their actions with regret.

Tullamore replenished themselves year on year and were the rising force as Durrow were on the way down and, naturally, took pleasure in hastening their descent on one or two occasions.

Three of the Dowling brothers, Christy, Mick and Joe, had emigrated to America and decided to purchase a cup for the county board to present to the senior football champions. The Dowling Cup was first presented in 1954 when Tullamore beat Rhode in the final to claim their first title since 1948.

Billy Dowling played at midfield for Tullamore that day and when the final whistle blew he took a moment to himself before the crowd spilled onto the pitch. Emigration had driven a wedge between him and his brothers but in their gesture they had immortalised the Dowling name in Offaly football history. It meant everything to him to be on the first team to lift the trophy, particularly after the upheaval of the previous few years. The first person to reach him on the field with heartfelt congratulations was Mickey Furlong.

"Well done, Billy, great win lad," he said. Whatever about his feelings towards the club hierarchy, it certainly didn't extend to the players.

Dowling and his team mates got showered and changed in the dressing rooms. Tullamore GAA Club had them built in 1951, the year after the infamous walkout.

CHAPTER 3

THE SACKER

THE Furlong brothers each came in different shapes and sizes. Mickey and particularly Martin inherited the Furlong genes when it came to their build but Tom and John were certainly Moloneys in stature, John especially. He was a colossal man who, in his physical prime, stood well over six foot tall with the broadest of shoulders. What's more, he had nearly attained his full dimensions by his mid-teens. A man though still a boy.

John was born four and a half years after Mickey and his elder brother always maintained that he had the most footballing talent of any in the family. Full-back was his position and, particularly given his physical advantage over his peers, he dominated the area around the square as a schoolboy footballer and cut an intimidating figure for opposition forwards. His friends, like Joe Bracken, used to call him the 'Sacker' Furlong after the famous old Wexford defender, Jim. With hands like shovels, he also drew comparisons with the legendary Meath full-back, Paddy 'Hands' O'Brien.

John's primary schooling took the same path as Mickey and he cut his teeth under Bill Ennis in St Brigid's. Bracken, who went on to represent the county at all levels, recalls an under-14 final in 1946 when, as an 11-year-old, he was hoping to nab a place among the subs for the game in Edenderry as much for the sweets and ice cream on the way home as anything else. Ennis held a trial game in advance.

"He was pairing off the fellas, who'd play on who. And he sent me down to play on John Furlong and I remember walking down towards John Furlong and I said, 'Jaysus Christ almighty, I'm not going to get a kick of the ball. That's my chance gone of going to Edenderry anyhow'. This guy was good."

There was a hugely vibrant street league programme in operation in Tullamore at the time. Though it continued all the way to senior level, it dovetailed particularly well with youngsters' football in school before they began to line out for the club at juvenile level. John won an under-14 football street league with the Dillonites when among his teammates was Eamonn Fox, another future dual county player, who remembers being paraded through town after the success.

"That was a great occasion for us," Fox recalls. "He was our staunch full-back. He was as big young as he was when he matured. You just took it that he was the bulwark behind you. Jesus, he was huge. He was a fine man."

At 15, John was on both Tullamore minor football and hurling teams in 1949 but that's effectively as far as it went for him on the field as his playing days soon came to a tragically premature end.

How good could he have been? It's a debate that will never amount to any more than conjecture. Mickey's view that he would have been the best of the four brothers isn't universally shared by all those who saw him, understandably so given the difficulty with making such a definitive judgement about a player's potential when only in his mid-teens. But, still, there is a fair constituency that hold a view similar to Mickey's, Bracken among them.

"We will never know," he says, "but I told Martin he would have been the best. I think he would have been the best of the Furlongs."

Achieving that status in a family of marvels would have been quite an accomplishment in itself but life threw down a very different set of challenges to John Furlong. He dealt with them with the the type of courage that defined the Furlongs as much as anything.

◆　◆　◆　◆

After leaving school, John began to serve his time as a plasterer with a man called Willie Martin in Tullamore. One day at work he suffered a bad cut to his hand and later went to the hospital to have it treated. When he emerged it was teaming rain. The hospital was at the opposite end of town to the Furlong home and he walked all the way. When he got in he was soaked, shivering with the cold and feeling worse for wear. His mother put him to bed and checked on him regularly thereafter. She soon concluded that this wasn't a minor ailment as his condition deteriorated.

John was rushed to hospital and diagnosed as having tuberculosis-meningitis. To save his life he had to be injected with streptomycin, a relatively new drug at the time which was found to be the first effective antibiotic when tackling tuberculosis. He was the first patient in Offaly to whom it was administered though it carried its side effects. Most, such as rashes, ulcers, sore throat and vomiting, were relatively harmless. Even the less common side effects weren't particularly debilitating, with exceptions such as blurred vision and deafness. John's misfortune was compounded by losing his hearing for the rest of his life.

When he slipped into a coma, the prognosis was grave. Tom and Margaret braced themselves for the worst, as did their other sons. It was widely anticipated locally that John wasn't going to make it. One evening there was a knock on the Furlongs' door on O'Moore Street. It was someone from the hospital who had been despatched to inform them that John had passed away. Mercifully, it proved to be misinformation, though the negligence of the hospital in this instance beggared belief.

In the meantime, it was difficult to envisage a happy ending to this episode. John spent his 16th birthday in the old St Vincent's Hospital in Tullamore. Optimism that he would see another birthday was scarce.

"I remember we had a wide open fire place in our kitchen before we modernised it and made it small," says Tom, barely seven-years-old at the time. "It was big and I remember sitting around there with my mother and father and we all crying as we were saying the rosary. All we were doing was crying. That time you'd be crying and you wouldn't know what you'd be crying about. Then there was a priest who came from Multyfarnham with miracle cures and he blessed him and all that. My mother always gave that priest great credit."

While John was in the coma, various family members and friends used to take turns sitting with him. One night Mickey was on duty and was to be relieved by his friend, Mick Drumm. As Mickey left the hospital he met Drumm arriving. He shook his head as he informed him there had been no change to his brother's condition. Drumm went upstairs expecting nothing more than a monotonous few hours at John's bedside. When he walked through the door he was greeted by John, sitting up in the bed.

"Hello Mick, how are you doing?" he said.

Although John's life would never be the same again and had veered in a very different direction to what he and others had envisaged, the siege had been lifted at least. "He was in a coma five minutes before that when Mickey was leaving," says Tom. "That brought great relief to the family."

It would still be three years before John was released from hospital, with Margaret making daily visits by bicycle while her husband saw him as often as his hectic work schedule allowed. The same with Mickey. Children didn't tend to go to hospitals in those days so Tom and Martin's glimpses of their brother were fleeting.

When he was strong enough and it was clear that his deafness wasn't a temporary ailment, John relocated to Peamount Hospital in Dublin for a period, a sanitarium which specialised in rehabilitating those affected by TB. There he learned sign language and lip-reading techniques.

He was also sent to Lourdes in 1953 in the hope of bringing about a cure. Sign language back then was cumbersome compared to now, whereby there was a different symbol for each letter of the alphabet, meaning that each word literally had to be spelt out. He retained the ability to speak though, being unable to hear himself, his voice carried an unusual tone.

One day Martin and Tom were coming out of O'Connor Park and saw John waving at them through the window of the hospital, which was across the road from the ground at the time. He beckoned them in and informed them that he was being released the following day.

"He said, 'Tell Mammy and Daddy I'm getting out tomorrow'," remembers Martin. "We decided not to tell them for a while when we went home. I think we told them later in the night alright but we didn't run in saying, 'John is coming home tomorrow!' or anything like that. Divilment I suppose."

John had a multitude of things to adjust to in his regular day to day life before his inability to continue playing football and hurling came into the equation, but the GAA would retain a central role in his existence even if the playing element had been cruelly taken from him. Despite his disability limiting his social interaction, he was popular and built a solid circle of friends over the years.

His interest in the games and his brothers' progress particularly was fanatical and his devotion to Tullamore and Offaly teams was unparalleled. He followed Wexford too and took pride in their All-Ireland hurling successes of the 1950s and '60s, as did all the Furlongs. Indeed, John often wore specially coloured socks depending on whether Wexford or Offaly were in action though there was never any question of his ultimate allegiances lying anywhere other than with his county of birth.

Over the years he taught various people the sign language as a means of communicating with them and to allow them to keep him in the loop when he struggled to pick up on conversations in pubs or goings on at club meetings and the like.

"What's he saying?" he'd often bark at close friends like Noel McGee or Martin Fitzpatrick, who would quickly twirl their fingers to relay the message. If it wasn't to John's liking, the source could be sure of a stern rebuke.

Within the family, he taught his mother, Martin and young Tom. Old Tom didn't pick it up but was able to communicate reasonably well with John given his proficiency at lip-reading, though men with moustaches or beards would cause him difficulty. Then again, there were times when John conveniently made little of his ability in that regard.

"Oh, with my father, yeah," says Martin. "'What's he saying? I don't know what you're saying.' 'Where were you last night? What time were you in at last night?' 'What's he saying? I don't know...' Then he'd look up at mother real innocent and say, 'What's he talking about?' That used to drive my father crazy.

"I would say there were a few instances where he didn't know what was going on and it was just as well he didn't know what was going on or he'd let fly at somebody. If the like of Tullamore or Offaly was getting run down or something, he'd be very defensive."

All the Furlongs liked a song and Boolavogue was "the Furlong national anthem". Singing was beyond John but he knew all of the words of the lengthy rebel ballad from start to finish. Woe betide anyone who omitted a verse. "You're wrong, you're wrong, you left out a verse!" he'd cry before quoting the missing lyrics verbatim.

Although John was popular and well known, building relationships of the romantic variety was always going to be a struggle. There was a girl he knew in hospital who had a similar disability to him and they hit it off but it didn't last. There may have been other flirtations but nothing sustainable.

While his three brothers led lives that were rich with diversity through their sporting endeavours, work, raising their own families and moving to America to experience a very different way of life, John's existence once he put his illness behind him was largely unvaried. That's not to suggest that he didn't get a kick out of life, because he most certainly did. And never did he wallow in self pity.

After emerging from hospital, his first line of work involved fixing radios but given that he was hard of hearing it was never likely to last. He retained a very limited amount of his hearing though it was sensitive to noise and people talking loudly at him, as they would often do in a forlorn effort to compensate. He used hearing aids from time to time but they were never of much help to him. Back then, part of the hearing aid apparatus had to be worn hanging around the neck and he'd often smash them while engaging in half-time kick abouts in O'Connor Park.

He served his time as an electrician with Joe Gilson, just a few doors up from the Furlongs on O'Moore St, and carved out a decent living at it for many years. Given the age difference between John and his younger brothers, Tom and Martin have no clear recollection of him prior to his illness and, after his lengthy spell in hospital, he was a grown man before they could get to know him.

"He was very good to me when I was growing up," says Tom. "He'd make a few shillings and he used to give me half a crown a week. Then I started going out and dating and he upped it to five shillings!"

John branched out on his own at times too and Martin would often work with him.

"The taxman came after him once, sending him bills," Martin explains. "John used to look at them and he'd laugh and he'd roll them up and throw them in the fire. Then he got a letter one time and it said that if whatever they were assessing him with wasn't taken care of that they'd seize all his 'worldly goods and chattels'.

"John used to have a pliers and a screwdriver in his breast pocket and he took them out and he says, 'Jaysus, they can have them if they want them, that's all that I have! My worldly goods and chattels!' He got a great kick out of that, threw it into the fire and he never paid it. I don't know what ever happened but that was his answer to that."

There was never any question of his illness affecting his mental capacity. He had always been bright at school and mastered the electrical trade with the minimum of fuss. He had a keen interest in politics and, like his father, was a fanatical Fianna Fáil supporter. He was recognised as one of the foremost authorities in Tullamore on hurling and football matters. He had an encyclopaedic mind for statistics and facts and figures though his judgement of a player was also highly valued – later in life he served as a selector on Tullamore management teams.

Once, when a player was peeved at not earning his place on the senior team, he highlighted his perceived injustice by pointing out how two of the selectors had informed him that he would indeed be starting. "Well," said John, "you were talking to the wrong selectors!"

"He was very opinionated," says Tom. "He'd argue. In any of the bars, if an argument started, 'See Furlong, see what he has to say'. He'd tell them where it was played, a junior match in Bracknagh or something like that."

He led an active social life and enjoyed his pints of Guinness. While John was no shrinking violet and could stand his ground in any company, his tight circle of friends were always protective of him nonetheless. Joe Bracken even had him stand for his daughter, Fidelma. Some of them formed a darts team and used to travel around the midlands taking part in tournaments.

"He had a very good hand at playing darts," says Sonny Lloyd, one good friend. "One thing, you could never upset him because he'd never hear it. He was capable of keeping calm whereas we'd get a little bit edgy when fellas behind you would be talking. That was one thing about him. We won a fair sight of trophies. He finished many a game."

John was also a useful snooker player and accumulated plenty of silverware thanks to his cuing action too.

He developed a knack at photography, good enough for some to entrust him with the duty on their wedding day. He made something of an inauspicious start, however. One day John was going to a match in O'Connor Park with Tom Sheeran, another former Offaly dual player who had played with Mickey, and was approached by Dolores McGee, Noel's sister, to buy a ticket for the GAA club's silver circle draw. John unwittingly played Cupid as Tom also bought a ticket before declaring, "If I don't win now I want a date!"

"And that's how we met," says Dolores. "John Furlong was responsible for that. I used to tell Tom it was the best prize the silver circle ever had!" When Tom and Dolores married in 1962, they gave John his first break in photography, though not all of the photographs materialised as they would have liked.

"It could have been a few weeks or a few months after and we had to dress up in our wedding clothes and he came out and did a couple inside and outside the house!"

The McGees were a family that John was particularly close to with Noel among his dearest friends, always a social crutch for him given his fluency at sign language. John would regularly go up to Emmett Terrace to Noel and Dolores's mother on a Monday afternoon and back a few horses with her. Dolores explains how his popularity locally was often reflected in the quality of spirits that barmen poured for him.

"John would go up the bar and he'd order three scotch whiskeys and Tom would go up and order three scotch and whatever John used to get, it'd be a completely different whiskey. His would be nicer than what Tom would get in the same bar. I could never figure it out."

His illness was something he never spoke about with friends or family and anything that Tom and Martin picked up over the years was in snippets from their mother.

When you consider the breath of sporting talent among his three brothers, it stands to reason that John would surely have had some contribution to make on the field himself had he not been dealt such a difficult hand in life. While he got great enjoyment and pride from what his brothers, and particularly Martin, achieved, on some level it must have grated that he didn't have the same opportunity. If it did, he never articulated it.

"Never heard him say a bad word about it," says Tom. "Then again, I don't know what he thought to himself, but he never said it out loud. He never felt sorry about himself."

TB-meningitis stripped John of many things. The Furlong humility wasn't one of them.

CHAPTER 4

CITY SLICKER

MICHEÁL Ó MUIRCHEARTAIGH'S legendary career, both in broadcasting and teaching, was in its infancy when in the early 1950s he took up residence in 22 St Brigid's Road, Artane on Dublin's north side. Not too far from Croke Park, naturally enough. Joining him in the digs were his friends, Kerry footballers, the Murphy brothers, Seán and Pádraig. Ó Muircheartaigh and Seán Murphy were embarking on two of the most cherished GAA careers of all time as a commentator and footballer respectively. Murphy would later be named on the Team of the Century and Team of the Millennium at right half-back.

The Kerrymen were heading out for a few kicks one evening having just moved in when they happened across another of the lodgers in the hallway. He brought his boots and joined them in St Patrick's College, Drumcondra, where Ó Muircheartaigh studied. The stranger introduced himself as Mickey Furlong. Word had come from Offaly that he had been selected for a game that weekend and he wanted to get his eye in.

Furlong quickly noticed that, with his dazzling skills and athleticism, Murphy was no ordinary footballer. He sidled up to Ó Muircheartaigh. "Who's your man? He's not bad."

"I didn't make him any the wiser at the time," says Ó Muircheartaigh. "But we got to know him very well then and he was great fun. I remember going to see him hurling and he was a stylish hurler. He was a stylish footballer as well but he was never really fit. That's why he always liked to be around the goal area. He was a scorer and he'd a great head."

Furlong had relocated to the capital at an interesting juncture in Dublin's GAA history. Dublin county teams had always been dominated by country players but the St Vincent's club in Marino were pioneers in bringing about a sea change in that regard around that time. Several club teams in the city were made up exclusively of non-locals and

Vincent's began to emerge as a serious power in both codes in the late '40s with a strictly local identity. That then extended to the county.

"They brought in a rule, Dublin players for Dublin teams," explains Vincent's stalwart Norman Allen. "That didn't mean you had to be born in Dublin but it meant you had to go to school in or be eligible to play minor for the county."

Furlong hurled with Faughs and played football with Seán McDermott's, two clubs that could hardly have been more polarised than Vincent's in terms of outlook with their legions of inter-county stars from around the country. Faughs have long had a strong connection with Offaly and, as the premier hurling club in Dublin, Furlong was only too happy to line out with them.

Kilkenny native Tommy Moore, who won two All-Irelands with Dublin, was the patriarch of the Faughs club and his pub on Cathedral Street was its unofficial headquarters. It hummed with talk of hurling on a daily basis and was a meeting point for people from all over the country on the big days in Croke Park. Naturally, Mickey Furlong was a regular.

"If you were looking for him and you felt he was anywhere around the centre of the city you'd get him in Tommy Moore's," explains Ó Muircheartaigh. "All the Faughs players used to go there. Tommy looked after a lot of them. People arriving in Dublin without a job, if they were a hurler they made off for Tommy Moore's. He got a job for you on one condition: that you played for Faughs. It worked both ways and he was very good to them."

With renowned hurlers like Tony Herbert, Jim Prior, Johnny Callanan and Harry Gray, Furlong was in good company and certainly not cowed by those around him. On his championship debut against a Dublin Junior A selection he notched 1-4 and bagged a couple of goals in the next round against the Civil Service. Herbert, who had been the last surviving member of Limerick's All-Ireland winning team of 1940, assessed Furlong as "a great man to get possession out on the wing, round his man and cut in on the byline" shortly before his death in March 2014.

The Faughs team of 1952 is considered to be one of the best in the club's illustrious history having recorded comprehensive victories over virtually every opposition they faced – with the exception of St Vincent's in the county final. The rivalry between the two clubs was keen to say the least.

"Huge, huge," says Allen. "The Dubs versus the culchies. A guy writing in the *Evening Press,* Joe Sherwood, he used to keep the pot boiling about the culchies and the Dubs and so forth. That started to draw huge crowds. There was great rivalry.

"We were a younger team and we'd be challenging Faughs and they were older and more experienced and what they'd do then when they were under pressure, they'd sit down and call a fella on and he'd be sitting there waiting to recover and get a drink and all the rest. The referee would wait till the guy got up. So when they were under pressure you'd see Tommy Moore on the sideline, 'Sit down!'

"I'll tell you, the rivalry was so much that one of the matches we played was a league final at Croke Park and there was a row in it and nine of us got suspended and nine of Faughs. We were challenging them and getting stuck into them but there was a row and I know I got six months. So that's when they say Vincent's arrived on the scene."

They were capable of competing with Faughs but not quite ready to beat them in 1952 as the Sash held them off by three points in the county final at Croke Park, Furlong chipping in with 0-2. Faughs added the league title to complete a double.

While Vincent's had yet to make a significant breakthrough in senior club hurling at that time, their monopoly on Dublin football was already established by then. Seán McDermott's had won their last county title in 1947 but their legion of stars, such as Meath pair Paddy 'Hands' O'Brien and Christo Hand and Armagh's Seán Quinn, could always be fancied to make inroads if they built up a head of steam.

"Club games that time were played at Croke Park, a lot of them," explains Ó Muircheartaigh. "I remember seeing at least 20,000 at club games with Vincent's and Seán's, and Vincent's and the Gardaí or

Clanna Gael. Everyone from the country would support whoever was against Vincent's. There was a great rivalry but it was good for both really."

In the 1952 county semi-final Allen was centre-back when Vincent's, spearheaded by Kevin Heffernan and chasing their fourth successive football title, were on the way out of the championship when trailing McDermott's late on.

"It was a gas match because Seán's were winning by a couple of points and the referee, Seán O'Neill, a Dublin referee of Kickhams, he must have played at least 10 minutes of overtime. I dispossessed Mick Furlong and kicked it down and it went out for a 45. I took it and it went straight into the net. We won. The two teams ended up in the net."

The All-Ireland club championship hadn't been initiated yet but, nonetheless, isn't required as a barometer to safely declare that Vincent's outfit as one of the greatest club sides ever. The following year they supplied all 14 outfield players on the Dublin team that beat Cavan in the National League final, won seven county titles in-a-row and added a further six in succession after that run was halted in 1956. McDermott's often struggled to blend their array of talents convincingly and didn't bother Vincent's too much after the '52 defeat, eventually folding in 1970.

Despite the fractious nature of their clashes on the field, however, Vincent's and Faughs had a strong bond off it.

"While it was terrible with rows and all that, the two clubs became very, very close friends and still, to this day, Faughs and Vincent's have a relationship now and a respect for one another that you wouldn't have with other clubs," Allen explains. "It just developed. I don't know how. The biggest enemies we had on the field were our biggest friends off it."

A unique photograph was taken of the two teams before they played in the 1953 county semi-final at Croke Park as they intermingled and stood side by side with Mickey Furlong flanked by Vincent's opponents. Vincent's won by three points and went on to claim their first Dublin hurling title. They dominated that competition too in the following years, though not with quite the same supremacy as in football.

◆   ◆   ◆   ◆

While moves were afoot to ensure that Dublin county teams were represented by local players, there was a more lax approach in that regard when it came to the county hurlers, which remains the case to this day. As a free-scoring Mickey Furlong starred for Faughs in the Dublin Championship, he was approached with a view to lining out for the county. He declined.

"He'd have been a great addition to Dublin hurling," Allen insists. "I was captain of that team for a couple of years and another huge addition would have been Heffernan because Heffernan gave up hurling and just stuck to the football. In my estimation Kevin would have made his name in hurling just as much as he made it in football."

Dublin contested four All-Ireland hurling finals in the 1940s and also reached the decider in 1952, featuring a number of the Faughs players alongside whom Furlong won his county medal that year. On the surface, he certainly seemed to have a far better shot at glory with the Dublin hurlers than either of the county teams back home.

"Well, all Offaly people were loyal," says Micheál Ó Muircheartaigh. "It would be against his nature to find himself in a situation that he'd be playing against Offaly. He had great faith in Offaly people. I remember a good friend of his, Paddy Fenlon. Paddy was a vet. Played for UCD. He played for Offaly and he used to play for the Combined Universities against Ireland. We often went to matches to cheer him on. Mickey would always go and support him playing for UCD and I often went with him and he'd be shouting his head off.

"I remember one time Paddy Fenlon was a sub for the Combined Universities and Ireland were beating them and he went down behind where the selectors were and started shouting, 'Bring on Paddy Fenlon, bring on Paddy Fenlon!'"

Bizarrely, Furlong's appearances for Offaly hurlers were fleeting.

With Offaly divided north and south for football and hurling respectively though not exclusively, the county hurling selectors didn't tend to cast their eyes too far beyond the Blue Ball in search of players. He didn't make his championship debut for the hurlers until 1951. Laois, who had contested the All-Ireland final only two years earlier and had within their ranks the evergreen Harry Gray, Furlong's future Faughs teammate, beat them in the first round. It would be three years before he lined out for the county hurlers in the championship again.

That was partly due to a daft selection policy but also the archaic rule 27, which forbade GAA members from playing, supporting or engaging with the 'foreign games' of soccer, rugby or cricket in any way, shape or form.

Naturally, Mickey Furlong's commitments with Faughs and Seán McDermott's in Dublin sometimes overlapped with those of Offaly. Several times he played with his club on a Sunday morning before rushing to a venue down the country to line out for the county.

"There was a couple of guys on the Offaly team and they'd hire a car in Dublin to come down to the games and sometimes they brought a couple of women with them or whatever," explains Tom Furlong. "Kevin Scally would have a girlfriend and Paddy Casey. Whatever their expenses were, it'd be so much for the car hire but they used to borrow a car off some friend of theirs up in Dublin and they'd figure their expenses was their drinking money. The women used to be parked up in our house, my mother knew all the women first hand. She'd put on tea and meat and the boys would be down town until their money ran out and they'd come back and get the women and go back to Dublin then.

"The women would be pissed off. My mother would be tired making excuses for the boys. But they'd still come the next day even though they knew the same thing was going to happen!"

In early May 1953, Offaly footballers had a game lined up as they prepared for the championship opener against Carlow later that month. It clashed with Seán McDermott's county semi-final with St

Vincent's. Offaly wanted Furlong's commitment exclusively on the day though he wouldn't let Seán's down. So he played against Vincent's, losing by four points, and made his way to Tullamore to play for Offaly later in the day. That night he ended up at a dance in the rugby club. He was spotted by a member of the vigilante committee, reported and suspended for six months.

Chairman of the county board at the time was Fr Edmund Vaughan, a curate based in Birr and originally from Clare. The Furlongs' was a deeply religious household but that wasn't enough to earn Fr Vaughan an amnesty in light of his run ins with the family, which started around then and dragged on for years.

Old Tom Furlong, acting as a Durrow delegate, clashed with him at a county board meeting once and was thrown out. The irony of the fact that he told Vaughan he was "nothing only a blow-in to the county" was seemingly lost on him. "I could see how he marched down the street in New Ross with a gun in his hand," says Tom junior. "He had a fierce temper."

Other counties had a more savvy approach to how rule 27 was enforced. Years before in Limerick, when it emerged that Mick Mackey enjoyed watching a game of rugby, he was appointed to the local vigilante committee to justify his presence at the matches. It allowed him to avoid suspension and attend as many games as he wished. In Offaly, seemingly nobody was safe and Vaughan's taste for enforcing his power and meting out suspensions for innocuous breaches of an outdated rule outstripped that for the county's greater good.

Furlong's team mates were outraged. Before their next game Paddy Casey led a protest as the players sat down on the field en masse ahead of the throw-in. They then got up and played the game. It may have been a simple gesture but should be viewed in the context of the time, when instances of players standing up to officialdom and particularly the clergy were rare.

Furlong saw no championship action for his county in 1953 and, on some level, must have wondered if his decision to rebuff Dublin's advances was the right one. Few could have blamed him if he turned his back on Offaly at that stage. He didn't.

He was back in the county colours in 1954, with the hurlers only too happy to enlist his services as his profile in the small ball game soared following his exploits with Faughs. In the Leinster Championship opener at O'Connor Park he led the rout of Westmeath, top scoring with 3-2 from centre-forward. "He scored a goal, I was right behind the ball and he hit it and there was like a fade on it," recalls Tom junior. "I remember well thinking, 'How did he manage that?'"

In the next round against Meath in Kilkenny, Furlong was in goalscoring form once again in a match that finished level. It's a reflection of the low ebb Offaly hurling was at back then that Meath led the replay in Portlaoise by 11 points with five minutes remaining. A goal by Furlong instigated a comeback, Ted O'Brien added another and then a third goal came when a long range delivery floated into the net after Furlong barrelled the Meath goalkeeper out of the way. It wasn't enough however as Meath held on for a two-point victory.

"Offaly senior hurling teams of the '50s rarely won any game of note," says O'Brien. "I first played for Offaly senior hurlers at 19 years of age. I didn't have a clue, I walked into the dressing room, I didn't know anybody. I knew a couple from Tullamore but there was fellas from Coolderry and all like that and you were never introduced to them, never got to know them very well. I think it was the mid-50s that Offaly put out no team in the league because they were afraid that fellas wouldn't turn up. The likes of Meath at that stage beating Offaly – Meath should never be able to beat Offaly. They were a less good team than Offaly as I saw it."

Furlong turned his attention to the Offaly footballers' participation in the Leinster Championship, not knowing he hadn't experienced his last sickening defeat at the hands of Meath.

◆　◆　◆　◆

If Offaly's useful minor teams of the late 1940s had raised

expectations of a senior breakthrough in the years that followed then they ultimately went unfulfilled. They made swift championship exits in 1950 and '51, losing to Kildare and Dublin respectively in their first outings. In '52 they beat Westmeath in Mullingar only to lose to Longford at the same venue a few weeks later. Furlong was suspended the following year as Wexford edged them out in the Leinster semi-final.

He was back in 1954, scoring the match-winning goal when they turned the tables on the same opposition to set up another semi-final meeting with Dublin in Portlaoise. Dublin didn't carry a huge reputation having not reached a Leinster final in 10 years but, backboned by the St Vincent's side that had effectively won the National League for the county the year before while continuously stacking up county titles, they were ambitious and had a number of top quality players, led by Kevin Heffernan, Ollie Freaney, Dessie Ferguson and Jim Crowley, all of whom would later win a senior All-Ireland together.

Several of the players had met in the minor final of 1947 with Offaly boasting Furlong, Kevin Scally, Paddy Casey, Sean Foran, Paddy Fenlon and Johnny Kinahan from that side while young talents like Peter Nolan, Noel McGee and Alo Kelly were also infused into the team.

The Caseys were Leinster regulars and Nolan would later assume the same status while Fenlon was no stranger to representative teams either. Furlong never quite scaled those heights, but it wasn't due to a lack of ability.

"When I started playing with Offaly," says Peter Nolan, "there was an established group containing the likes of Kevin Scally, Archie McLoughlin, Mickey Furlong, all these people that were based in Dublin. I was only starting. I wouldn't have known these people at all. First of all, I didn't drink and there was a heavy culture of drinking at that time and they weren't too fond of the fitness either.

"If I was to be honest about Furlong, in '47, Mickey Furlong was a terrific minor player. If he had the modern training facilities he could have been an even better player than he was."

Even if he didn't exhaust his full potential, Furlong's natural skill, innate toughness and bravery allowed him to excel at inter-county level though perhaps his passiveness and that of others was informed by the set up that surrounded them. Offaly's training wasn't well organised by any standards and politics played a crippling role. With each senior club having a say, the selection committee was made up of 16 individuals with no clear figurehead. While no management team can account for every possibility, it should at least aspire to minimise the variables, something that could never be achieved with the power brokers being such a disparate group with questionable knowledge of the players at their disposal and, indeed, the game itself.

It wouldn't have been so bad if this arrangement was mirrored in other counties but it wasn't. The Dublin team that Offaly played in the 1954 Leinster semi-final was bossed by Peter O'Reilly, a shrewd operator who, years later, would transform Offaly football. But up to then they were desperately inconsistent.

"They were a tough team to play against," says Norman Allen, corner-back for Dublin that day. "Hard, tough men, but not great footballers. It's a different era than now. It was more robust. Paddy Casey was a very skilful footballer and Furlong would have been up there. Furlong would have made any team."

It looked to be the same old story when Dublin carried a seven-point lead to the dressing room at half-time thanks to goals from Ferguson and Heffernan.

"I remember big Mick Casey coming soloing in," continues Allen, "and the size of him, he was a huge man, and we were backing in and Mossy Whelan says to me, 'Take him, you've got to go for him!' So I went out and he was soloing in and he put the ball a bit too far and he had to reach and I ran straight into him, into his chest. Creased him. You know when you're put into a situation, 'I'm going to get killed here, I'll have to go!' Big strong man."

Offaly limited Dublin to just a point in the second half and as Alo Kelly clipped over a couple of scores and Johnny Kinahan scrambled a goal, the deficit was down to a more manageable three points. With six minutes remaining, the sizeable Offaly crowd in O'Moore Park erupted when a Kelly free, dropping short, was punched to the net by Furlong to draw the sides level.

Dublin thundered up the field and won a couple of frees close to goal but squandered both of them. Offaly summoned one last effort to steal victory and were awarded with a free of their own from some 50 yards. Kelly stepped up and thumped it over the bar for the winning score. The Offaly supporters spilled onto the field and chaired the victors off. The county had qualified for just its third Leinster senior final and, after a display of such resilience, optimism that Offaly would finally shed the underachievers' tag soared.

They would face a well seasoned Meath team, who retained several of players that had claimed the county's only All-Ireland in 1949, in the Leinster final. Manning the full-back slot was Paddy 'Hands' O'Brien, alongside whom Furlong, Johnny Kinahan and Paddy Casey played with for Seán McDermott's.

From an Offaly point of view, the day turned out to be a complete calamity. That morning full-back Kevin Scally, a garda based in Dublin, was involved in a car crash. He was clearly shook but would start the game regardless. The sense of the occasion and all that was at stake got to some players in the build up as well, Peter Nolan reckons.

"Offaly began to make a big thing out of the Leinster final. They were going in groups and doing things they wouldn't normally do. It's only a game like the game before it. And we make too much out of it, especially people who haven't been there before. They get so nervous about that and that was a part of it with the Offaly team that time and that was a Meath team that had been on the scene for a while and they were all household names."

After the teams had been paraded around Croke Park, marching behind the Artane Boys' Band in front of the 44,109 attendance, Mickey Furlong strode into the centre-forward position, shook hands with his opponent, Meath centre-back Jim Reilly, and stood for the national anthem. This was, by a distance, the biggest day of his sporting life. Being part of the first Offaly team to win a Leinster title would ensure immortality in the county. And if Offaly could just break that duck, all sorts of possibilities would open up for them.

Disaster struck early on as Meath full-forward Tom Moriarty fielded a high delivery from Paddy Connell, sidestepped Scally and goaled in the first minute. The Offaly full-back immediately had to go off injured and was replaced by Johnny Owens, an experienced player from Rhode who was renowned for his big match temperament. He steadied the ship and proceeded to play a stormer, bringing calm to the rattled defence around him. Furlong responded with a point for Offaly, who drew level by the 11th minute but Meath pushed on to lead by a goal at half-time after Paddy Casey had seen a penalty saved by Patsy McGearty.

A pair of substitutions on either side would have a decisive impact on the game. Despite his replacement dominating at the back for Offaly, when the selectors felt that Scally had recuperated sufficiently they sent him back on and whipped Kinahan off. Elsewhere, Meath midfielder Tom Duff suffered a broken leg. The team's shrewd trainer, Fr Packie Tully, didn't have to ponder too long about what action should be taken. He turned to Peter McDermott.

The wily 36-year-old was in the twilight of a highly accomplished career and, indeed, he had refereed the previous year's All-Ireland final.

"I happened to be near there when that clash came with Myles Nugent and Tom Duff," says Nolan. "They both pulled on a dead ball. Nugent went out over Duff's head and I could see the bone coming out in his leg and that was another huge bad thing for us. McDermott came in."

Meath scored three goals in the second half, McDermott spectacularly punching one to the net and setting up another. It put them 10 points clear but Offaly had a late kick in them. Paddy Casey drilled a close range free to the Meath net and Johnny Kinahan added another goal to bring Offaly within three points. They scrambled desperately for an equalising goal but referee Willie Goodison blew the full-time whistle after playing more than four minutes of injury time. Offaly supporters cried foul, insisting that there should have been more added time given the length of the stoppage for Duff's injury, believed to have lasted up to eight minutes.

It had been a truly disastrous day. From Scally's car accident that morning, Meath's fast start followed by his withdrawal before he was restored despite his replacement excelling; Casey missing a penalty; McDermott inspiring Meath after his untimely and unlikely introduction.

The neutral consensus was that Meath were certainly not flattered by the final three-point winning margin but, by all accounts, the goals Offaly conceded were extremely soft and very avoidable.

Between the posts for Offaly that day was Joe McFadden, a 19-year-old from Tullamore who had been parachuted into goal after impressing on the Leinster colleges selection. Team mates noticed how he seemed especially nervous before the game.

Sixty years on, the frustration in Nolan's voice about what went on that day, particularly with some of the decisions taken by a rabble selection committee before and during the game, is palpable.

"It was unbelievable. They had no idea about what to do, especially in an emergency. You'll notice that Offaly could be brilliant – in the first round of the championship Offaly used to be very good and then they'd come along in the next match and they might fall apart. You had no one to look to when things began to go bad.

"I mean when we beat Dublin that day in Portlaoise we had to be twice as good as Dublin. Everything came hard to Offaly because there was no one teaching you how to do it the easy way. That was the story with Offaly. Meath were one of the clever teams before teams began to have it down. They were that way before we got clever, that's for sure.

"I hate to be talking about anyone in particular but we had a goalkeeper and it was unfair to the fella himself. It was wrong to pick him that year and it ruined what could have been a promising career.

"Then I found out later on, we had a fella Liam Moran, he played for Offaly in the goal before that. I met him a couple of years ago and

I asked him, 'Where were you in '54?' And he said, 'I had been dropped'. And this Moran came on the scene then after '54 and he was a terrific goalkeeper. He was one of the best goalkeepers in my opinion that ever played for Offaly. Now, if we had him, we had our first Leinster. When I think of it, it really rattles me what went on that day."

Meath beat Cavan in the All-Ireland semi-final the following Sunday and recorded a shock win over Kerry in the final with McDermott restored to the starting team as captain, his final act as a county footballer being to lift the Sam Maguire Cup.

A reception was held for the Offaly team immediately after the Leinster final in a tent in Clondalkin. Although he scored two points, Mickey Furlong brooded over a game that had largely passed him by. A huge opportunity had been missed and Meath's subsequent progress only served to twist the knife.

It was a young Offaly team and Furlong had only just turned 25 himself but he knew that a chance like this wouldn't present itself to him again.

He had played his last championship game for Offaly.

CHAPTER 5

THE AMERICAN WAKE

BEFORE the 1954 Leinster final was even played, Mickey Furlong had applied to the US Embassy in Dublin for a visa. He had always been bright academically and completed his Leaving Certificate when in school but there was never any question of him attending college. Few families could afford that back then and the Furlongs weren't one of them.

After a couple of years working in Kennedy's Bakery in Dublin, Mickey began to get itchy feet. He enjoyed the social life in the city and his football and hurling had benefited from being exposed to playing with and against some of the games' elite players on a more regular basis than he had previously been used to.

However, more practical factors had to be considered too. By and large, money was scarce in Ireland and wages were small. And, of course, American wakes were taking place all over the country as streams of young people left. Stories would come back of how Uncle Sam was good to them. They were earning far more money than they could dream of in Ireland. Virtually all of them left with the intention of spending a few short years over there to make enough money and then set themselves up back home again. Only a minority followed through on that. After all, how much money is enough?

If you were a prominent GAA player, the path to America was cleared considerably. In the bigger and more successful counties, plum jobs could be found for some, though not all, of those considering emigration. Offaly was a small county that lacked that sort of infrastructure and, though the ESB power stations that sprouted up around the county at that time helped to bring about some mass employment, the scent of America was almost wafting through Furlong's nostrils.

The narrow defeat in the Leinster football final notwithstanding, Offaly weren't doing well enough on a consistent basis to be confident that a bright future was on the horizon. Maybe Mickey would have felt differently if they had won that Leinster title or even the All-Ireland in 1954. It could have opened all sorts of doors for that team and sticking around to defend those titles would certainly have been tempting.

In any event, contact was made between Mickey and Paddy Grimes in New York. Grimes was a Birr native who owned the thriving *Irish Echo* newspaper in the city. He was heavily involved in the Offaly club in New York, which hadn't won the hurling championship since 1945 and had yet to win the football title. The New York championships carried a great deal of prestige back then and by enticing someone like Furlong, one of the deadliest marksmen in Leinster in both codes, to America, Grimes was significantly bolstering both teams in one swoop.

While the games in Ireland weren't for the faint-hearted back then, in America they could be particularly brutal. Furlong had always been tough, unflinching and brave, attributes that carried a higher premium than they did back home and would serve him well in Gaelic Park.

In the meantime, he still had a few loose ends to tie up with Offaly while he ticked the boxes and assembled the particulars necessary for visa clearance. In the run up to the Leinster final Furlong had taken on a monk-like existence by his standards. Lengthy drinking bans for county teams were unheard of back then but not a drop of alcohol passed his lips for weeks before the game. Then he went out and played the biggest game of his career and failed to influence it like he wanted to or felt he could. Like many of the Offaly team, he drowned his sorrows in the aftermath.

A few weeks later, Offaly took part in the inaugural O'Byrne Cup competition, facing Wexford in the first round in Tullamore. That morning Furlong played a club game in Dublin before making his way down. Offaly cruised to an 11-point victory with Furlong pulling the strings in a dazzling display, crowned when he rattled in a goal late on. "I'll never give up the drink again," he said wryly afterwards.

He played a few O'Byrne Cup and National League games before leaving for America. In his penultimate appearance against Roscommon in Castlerea he scored three points and won a penalty in a five-point victory, the *Offaly Independent* describing it as his best game for the county for a couple of years. Two weeks later he played his last game for Offaly in the National League against Louth at O'Connor Park, a three-point defeat. The players had a collection for him and after the game he was presented with a wallet stuffed with notes on behalf of the team by none other than Fr Vaughan.

The following March Offaly beat Louth to win the O'Byrne Cup at Croke Park. The celebrations afterwards were boisterous to say the least. It was the first trophy the county had ever won at senior level.

A week before he left, Sean McDermott's held a farewell function for him at the Lansdowne Hotel on Pembroke Road and made presentations to both him and Paddy 'Hands' O'Brien, who had just got married on the back of winning his second All-Ireland medal with Meath, it could be argued, at Furlong's expense. O'Brien penned a note on Mickey, outlining how sorry he was to see "the most popular player in Dublin" leaving.

Furlongs' little house on O'Moore Street heaved with people on the night of Mickey's American wake. Young Tom and Martin were mesmerised at the spectacle and glided through the crowd, picking up discarded bottles of ale and stout and draining the last few drops from them for devilment. Martin was just eight years of age and had never seen his parents cry before but their eyes filled with tears that night.

Mickey liked a song and Boolavogue got an airing or two. His flight was the following morning but there was no question of going to bed as the party trundled on. Tom Flanagan, the agricultural advisor to Offaly County Council at the time, would drive Mickey to Shannon. With no sign of proceedings grinding to a halt he feared he'd missed his flight. Peering through his thick glasses, he repeatedly cried like a pub landlord at closing time, "We're tied for time, we're tied for time, we have to be moving along now."

Eventually Mickey got himself set. It was October 27, 1954 and he went into his brother Tom in bed, planted a kiss on his cheek, wished him a happy 11th birthday and said goodbye before climbing into Tom Flanagan's car along with his mother.

Old Tom Furlong was nowhere to be seen. He disappeared out to the fields, unable to summon the will to bid farewell to his pride and joy, returning to the house only when he was sure Mickey was gone.

◆ ◆ ◆ ◆

Mickey hadn't completed his first day in New York before he sat down to write to his mother, the first of many eloquent, detailed and entertaining letters he mailed to Ireland over the years, all noteworthy for his wonderful penmanship.

"Dear Mammie..." they would all begin.

After making landings en route in Newfoundland and Boston, he was met at Idlewild Airport by Mick Martin, Joe Redican and Des Dooley, a former Offaly hurler whom he stayed in digs with in the Bronx initially. Their landlady was from Tullamore.

Coming from Offaly, Furlong was naturally mesmerised by New York as Dooley showed him around town in what Mickey described as a "tremendous big car". They went to Van Cortlandt Park with their hurleys and pucked around while the Cork hurlers and Mayo footballers, who would play New York that weekend, trained nearby. Furlong and Dooley moved on to Gaelic Park that evening where Mickey was shocked to discover just how many Offaly people there were in New York. They did their utmost to make him feel welcome.

He rounded off his first day with a visit to the home of Paddy Naughton, another Tullamore native, who held a prominent position with the Transit Authority.

He wasn't there long when he came across Christy Dowling, who had left Tullamore for America two years earlier. Dowling won county medals with Furlong in 1946 and '48 but was one of the players left stranded after the fallout. He sensed a nervousness on Furlong's part as he approached him. "He said to me, 'I made a mistake'. And I said, 'Mickey, it's all finished. That's long gone'. He was probably expecting me to turn my back on him."

That weekend he togged out in the New York colours for the first time though, having only arrived two days earlier, didn't feature against either Cork or Mayo. He did hurl against Cork for a Boston selection at Fenway Park, home of the Boston Red Sox, the following weekend, however.

Mickey spent the first two weeks in holiday mode getting to know New York before starting work as a bartender. It was, and is, a very different trade in America to what it is in Ireland. Bartenders' wages were meagre and it was through tipping that they really made their money. Furlong's bubbly personality and gift of the gab was tailor made for the profession as the notes stacked up on the bar day after day, several of which made their way back to Tom and Margaret in Tullamore.

He threw himself into the GAA, playing hurling and football for Offaly in Gaelic Park while being an automatic selection for New York in both codes. For a few years in the early 1950s, New York teams would play in the National League final against the 'home' winners of the competition, a practice that was resumed in the 1960s but in the meantime it was replaced by the St Brendan's Cup, appropriately named after the navigator, which was run on the same premise. The games would alternate between New York and Ireland year on year. Additionally, All-Ireland champions would often travel to take on the exiles in exhibition games at the Polo Grounds and Gaelic Park.

Most people who emigrated to America from Ireland in the 1950s didn't get home to visit for years. Tom and Margaret Furlong didn't know how long it would be before they would see their son again but, as it happened, he was back within 11 months for the St Brendan's Cup matches at Croke Park.

On October 9, 1955 the New York hurlers and footballers played Tipperary and Dublin respectively in a double header in front of 33,750. Furlong lined out at right corner-forward for the hurlers, which meant being marked by none other than John Doyle, the most celebrated member of Hell's Kitchen. Tipperary hadn't won the All-Ireland since completing the three-in-a-row in 1951 but they still had a stellar line up containing the likes of Tony Reddin, Mickey 'The Rattler' Byrne, Jimmy Finn, Liam Devaney, Pat Stakelum and, of course, Doyle. Furlong would never have been exposed to such elite opposition as an Offaly hurler in the '50s.

New York limbered up for the game with a run out against Faughs the week beforehand and made light work of Furlong's former teammates. On each of his trips home to play with New York teams, he always caught up with his old clubmates in Tommy Moore's pub.

New York's hurlers hadn't lowered the colours of a county team in National League or Brendan's Cup finals but a huge shock was on the cards when they led at half-time. Two goals in quick succession, the second by Furlong, helped them to a 2-5 to 0-7 interval advantage and a third goal on the restart by Frank McLysaght stretched the advantage to seven points. Tipp thundered back and wiped out the lead within 10 minutes as New York, almost inevitably, struggled to maintain their early pace given their relative lack of exposure to top class opposition. Goals from Larry Keane, Seamus Bannon, John Hough and Gerry Doyle helped Tipperary to a convincing 4-17 to 4-7 win in the end.

Furlong then immediately readied himself to play against Dublin in the football final. It was a robust affair and New York were forced into replacing seven players over the course of the game, one of them Furlong, who was knocked out cold in the first half. Bill Carlos, the former All-Ireland winner with Roscommon, and Seán Brennan excelled at the back for New York though with Kevin Heffernan running the show up front for Dublin they always had that little bit extra as the exiles again ran out of steam against a side that had only been in the All-Ireland final two weeks previously, losing by three points to Kerry. Jim McGuinness scored a late goal to seal a 2-9 to 0-10 win for the Dubs.

It didn't dampen the spirits of the New York lads too much. They were determined to make the most of their time back home as they popped up all over the country. Tom and Margaret carried a spring in their step for those few weeks. Having made strenuous efforts to see Mickey play as often as they could in various parts of the country while he was in Ireland, his departure had left a void in their lives in that regard as well as others. Going to see him hurl in Croke Park for New York against Tipperary was some form of recompense. But just hearing his voice in the house again was enough in itself.

"I remember having my hand out to him when he was going back and, the poor divil, he didn't have a pot to piss in," Martin recalls. "They were after partying for the two weeks they were home and he wouldn't have had a hell of a lot of money in the first place but I remember him putting his hand in his pocket and giving me whatever loose change he had. He was combing his hair at the mirror in front of the fireplace, I remember that."

Shortly after he returned to America, Furlong was compelled to carry out military service in the US Army for a couple of years, much of which he spent in Japan. He underwent training in Fort Bragg, North Carolina. He was entitled to a three-day pass every two months and would use it to get back to New York to play a big game. Furlong was never a fanatical trainer but it wasn't optional here and he shed a stone and a half while surviving fitness tests that required him to run for 21 minutes continually. He was fascinated by the sizeable 10-gear trucks they drove and, if he could get away with it, would slip into one of them for a snooze while his colleagues worked on their marksmanship in the pouring rain on the firing range.

When it came to going overseas, a week-long train ride was taken to California where, after a couple of days, they boarded a ship bound for Tokyo. Following World War II, an Allied occupation of Japan continued until 1952 as a democracy was successfully implemented. US military personnel still retained a presence in the country, however, and do to this day.

Furlong was based in Camp Drake initially. He had always led an active social life and found the long nights looking at the walls particularly cumbersome. The food wasn't great but it was always plentiful and Furlong, coated with a nice tan, felt he was in the shape of his life. The women weren't bad either and he regaled about them for years afterwards!

Not long into his stay in Tokyo, word reached him that Offaly had dished out a nine-point hiding to Meath in the Leinster Championship, just two years after his own heartache at the hands of the same opposition. He was delighted for the lads, but homesick all the same and wondering what he might be missing out on. Offaly's preparation for the Leinster semi-final against Kildare descended into a shambles amid indiscipline among some players, however, and they were well beaten. With Dublin having been shocked on the other side of the draw by Wexford, another golden opportunity for a first Leinster title was blown.

To maintain his fitness while in Japan, Furlong formed a soccer team that had a league of nations feel to it with four Germans, two Poles, a Scot, a Czech, a Japanese and a handful of Americans. They trained a couple of times a week and arranged games with teams from around Tokyo. Furlong smiled at the thought of Fr Vaughan getting wind of it back in Ireland and slapping him with another suspension.

Once he completed his service he was back in action in the St Brendan's Cup in October 1957 when the Galway footballers and Tipperary hurlers came to the Polo Grounds. Once again defeat was New York's lot, but only by five points in both games with Furlong firing two goals for the hurlers.

That same year Furlong won his only New York Championship as the Offaly footballers claimed the title for the first time. The competition had a two-pronged structure at the time with the winners of the league playing the victors in the knockout format. Offaly won both, beating Cork and Kerry respectively, to take the championship outright.

By then Furlong had been joined in New York by Paddy Casey and winning that championship justified Paddy Grimes' efforts to bring them across the Atlantic. The Offaly hurling team in New York was highly competitive too but, just like back home, they couldn't break the stranglehold of Tipperary, Kilkenny and particularly Cork at that time.

Kilkenny, All-Ireland hurling champions in 1957, visited in 1958 and played New York in June of the following year. They were among the first games that Brendan Hennessy played for New York. Although a Kerry man, hurling was his first game having hailed from the small ball stronghold of Ballyduff. A wonderful hurler that would have been comfortable playing in any company, he was inducted into the Munster Hurling Hall of Fame in 2003 alongside Mick O'Dwyer for football.

"When I came out here first I was only 19 and Mickey was a big influence on me," he explains. "He was always encouraging me. He'd be one of the best men I played with and a great teammate.

"He was a fantastic man, you wouldn't meet a nicer guy than Mickey Furlong. Mickey was the lead man in the forward line. You could always depend on him. When you needed that score, nine times out of 10 he'd be the man that would get it for you. And he didn't go around you, he went through you.

"He was not a dirty player but, I tell you, whatever way you wanted it, you got it if you were on Mickey. When the game was over then you would never meet a nicer man and everybody wanted to be in his company."

Against Kilkenny, Furlong clashed with Ollie Walsh early on, as the legendary goalkeeper made a save, before prodding the loose ball to the net.

"That time you could go in and hit the goalie," Hennessy explains. "Mickey didn't hit him with the hurley or anything. Being a footballer Mickey knew how to get around a corner-back with the hits and stuff. He was on John Maher. He was the softest man he ever played on. Anyway, he got inside him and Ollie was making one of his brilliant saves and Mickey stuck him to the post. He got a goal; he got a couple of goals actually. Ollie went off, he banged his head off the post."

New York went on to win comfortably and beat Kilkenny again the following Sunday in Gaelic Park. When word of the Walsh incident filtered back to Ireland, old Tom Furlong couldn't resist stopping into a favoured bar of his in Inistioge en route between Tullamore and Wexford to chew the fat with the locals about the goalkeeping great being laid low by his eldest son.

◆　　◆　　◆　　◆

Mickey was working in Mickey O'Sullivan's bar in the Bronx one night when he saw what looked like a young couple walk in. He liked the look of the girl, tall with dark hair, in her early to mid-20s and made it his business to talk to her. Her name was May Widger from Lacken in Co Waterford. She'd been in New York for a couple of years having spent some time nursing in England, where she struggled to settle.

Furlong was playing a game that weekend in the Catskill Mountains and asked if she'd come up to watch. She declined and left soon afterwards with her companion, a chap from Dublin. There was nothing going on between them but he warned her that she was "too nice a girl" to get mixed up with guys like him.

May thought no more of him in any event. She was living with a young Irish couple in Astoria at the time and they asked her along to the St Patrick's Night Dance in the Manhattan Centre. She didn't have a date and was a little uncomfortable at being the third wheel but tagged along in any event. She was sitting at her table when one of her friends came over to her.

"There's a fella over there that wants to meet you," he said, "he thinks he's met you before."

She turned around and it was Mickey Furlong. "Do you want to dance?" he asked.

"And that was it," says May now, with a glint in her eye. "We started going out together.

"His smile, his eyes. It was just a mutual attraction between the two of us. It was just meant to be. And we always got along, we could chat no matter what and, honest to God, I would never want anybody else in my life, I could never meet anybody else in my life.

"We went out together for two years and we decided to get married and we planned a wedding out here. God, he was a great planner. At that time we had a nice big wedding, we had 80 people and we went to Atlantic City for our honeymoon. At that time there was no casinos or anything, it was just this Irish pub down there and he knew about it so we stayed in Atlantic City for the weekend and we came back."

A more expansive honeymoon was in the offing in any event. Mickey and May were married on August 30, 1958, just weeks before the St Brendan's Cup games back in Ireland. John 'Kerry' O'Donnell, the chief of New York GAA, added May to the entourage as a wedding present to her and Mickey. They arrived back at Shannon Airport to meet their new in-laws for the first time, with young Martin among those present in his short pants.

Mickey would captain the football team against Dublin but that fixture was played three weeks after the hurling game, which was against Wexford. They weren't All-Ireland champions at the time but their victories in 1955 and '56 marked that Wexford side out as one of the greatest ever, a status they retain to this day.

New York were no slouches either though and boasted a team of players who had all excelled for their native counties before emigrating. The game was chaotic, however, and Furlong was an early casualty with a broken hand. "The corner-back for Wexford, he pulled right across Mickey, a dirty stroke, and Mickey went off," recalls Hennessy. "It was the first five minutes." His new wife, listening on the radio while with her family in Waterford, was aghast.

New York absorbed his loss and rolled up their sleeves but mayhem ruled for much of the game. A melee broke out in the 20th minute which resulted in New York full-back Jim Carey being sent off along with Wexford's Tim Flood. Norman Allen, a serial opponent of Mickey's when playing for St Vincent's in Dublin years before, had since relocated to New York and was now a teammate.

He was marking Willie Rackard and explains, "I hit him a shoulder, caught him in the chest and he went out cold actually. When they were resuming the match Rackard was up and he was walking back over to his position and he shortened the hurl and he gave me a belt across the knee. So I gave it back with interest. I was looking at the ref, Gerry Rosengrave, he was from my own club, St Vincent's, and I just winked at him. I put him in an awful position. There was several incidents in that match."

New York were seven points clear at half-time and pushed further ahead in the second half before a late flurry of goals flatteringly brought Wexford within a point, 3-8 to 3-7, but the St Brendan's Cup was won by the exiles' hurlers for the first time. It was the highlight of several players' careers, with New York or otherwise. Hennessy and his brother Michael played at midfield and were jointly named as Sports Star of the Week in the *Irish Independent*.

Not all the press comment was complimentary, however. "Pulling on the ball first time is the secret of the visitors' success" read the *Irish Times* editorial. "They 'pulled' far more recklessly than can be relished by Irish referees however."

"It got a bad press and John 'Kerry' O'Donnell took offence and the GAA in New York," says Allen. "They banned the press from coming to Gaelic Park for a couple of years afterwards."

Mickey Furlong was immediately ruled out of the football equivalent with Dublin back at Croke Park three weeks later. But, as captain, he was having none of it. He resumed his honeymoon with May and limbered up for a crack at the Dubs, who were crowned All-Ireland champions just a week before and named 14 of their All-Ireland winning side to play New York.

They came mighty close to completing a double but goals from Johnny Joyce and Dessie Ferguson helped Dublin to a 2-6 to 1-7 victory. Eddie O'Sullivan and Furlong probed most effectively for New York up front and the Dublin goal led a charmed life at times with Paddy O'Flaherty bringing off a string of saves while seeing the ball rebound off his upright three times.

It didn't get much better than that in Furlong's New York career though Hennessy insists they'd have been a force to be reckoned with if they were permitted to compete for the Liam MacCarthy Cup. He can rattle off the team that beat Wexford in 1958 without pausing for thought and says, "That team would have won an All-Ireland. They wouldn't let us in because we were sponsored by a beer company. Waterford were All-Ireland champions in 1959 and they came out here and we beat them in the first game and the second game was a draw."

In the 1959 St Brendan's Cup games, Furlong captained the hurlers but they were surprisingly well beaten by Tipperary while Kerry, including Seán Murphy, with whom he had shared digs with in Dublin years before, had six points to spare at Gaelic Park.

In 1960 he suffered a terrible leg injury while playing with the Offaly team in New York which effectively ended his career. "The two best men on the Cork team, he dominated the both of them," says Henessy. "The second guy that came on him, he gave it to him right across the ankle. He told me that himself now. That finished him."

Furlong underwent surgery in 1961 and '62 but couldn't get himself right. He played a couple of games in 1963 and, at 34, called it quits.

By then, Mickey and May had three young children, Michelle, Thomas and Michael, all under the age of four, and were expecting a fourth. Social unrest was rising in New York as muggings and murders dominated the newspapers day after day. A young girl was raped in their neighbourhood in Rockaway and they wondered was this the climate they wished to raise a family in. May had struggled with homesickness ever since she came to America. She thoroughly enjoyed the honeymoon back in Ireland a few years before and it had left a nostalgic notion of the old country in her mind.

Back home, Tom and Margaret had acquired a site around the corner from their house in Tullamore. They offered it to Mickey and May to come home and build a house and they gleefully accepted. Mickey wrote to his mother outlining how he had never fully settled in America and was happy to leave it behind.

The plan was that May would go home to Ireland first with the children and move in with Tom and Margaret initially with Mickey working on in New York to save money before joining her at a later stage. That proved to be a critical error. The Furlong home was a small two-bedroomed house that already had five people under the one roof. That number doubled when May arrived and then gave birth to another son, Johnny. Relations inevitably became strained.

John F Kennedy was assassinated in Dallas while May and the children were in Tullamore. Being one of the most significant events of the 20th century, it fundamentally changed America but the country took on a different complexion in her mind while she was away in any event.

"I think I was home for about six months and, do you know, it took that trip home," says May, who came to appreciate what she had in the States for the first time. "It was the winter time and it was freezing cold over there. I had Johnny and he got pneumonia, it was just a mess and, you know, the little house in Tullamore there that they had, it was just a small place and it was just crazy. I said, 'What have I done here?' And it took that trip for me to realise what I had in this country. Then I decided to come back.

"If I had waited and built the house and then come home it might have been a different story. This way I would have had my own place. It wasn't meant to be that way. I truly believe that that was the way it was to happen. I came back and I was never so glad to see America. I needed to do that."

The romantic notion of coming back and rearing a family in Ireland had always tugged at Mickey. Now he knew it would never be realised.

CHAPTER 6

THE SECOND FAMILY

AS Tom junior puts it himself, the Furlongs were like two families in one. Almost 10 years separated the second and third sons and then there were three years between Tom and Martin, who was over 17 years younger than Mickey. "It's a pity I couldn't have traded one of ye in for a little girl and I'd have a bit of help around the house," Margaret would often tell her sons. She would always welcome the company of Dollie Harris, the little girl from across the road, who was regularly in and out of the house, helping her with chores such as churning butter and providing her with an outlet for girly talk.

As youngsters Tom and Martin were always likely to be closer to each other than to their elder brothers. Neither brother has a clear recollection of John prior to his illness while Mickey left the family home for Dublin when they were both quite young and then he headed to America a couple of years later. Still, Martin can recall Mickey occasionally taking him out in the van when he worked as a travelling salesman for Sioda minerals. Sometimes he'd stop by the side of the road to allow his little brother to take a pee and feign to drive off, prompting squeals from Martin as he gave chase.

When Tom and Martin were little there was a fancy dress aspect to a carnival held in Tullamore. Two of the biggest employers in the town at the time were DE Williams and P&H Egan, rival drinks companies. Margaret styled Tom in Williams' green and white and Martin in the red and white of Egan's and between them they carried a sign reading 'Competition is the life of trade'. They reluctantly settled for third prize.

Competition was rife between the two of them and they pushed each other as young lads without really being aware of it. Kickarounds in the back yard were fiercely competitive and the old wooden gate they used for a goal was nearly withered to nothing by the time they grew out of it. Three goals gets in was their game of choice. "That's how we made goalkeepers out of each other," says Tom.

They honed their reflexes playing table tennis in the house too. With space at a premium, the table would be shoehorned into the living room, right up on top of their father as he'd stretch out in front of the fire after a long day's work with his feet up on the mantelpiece, the smell of his smocks scorching hanging in the air. At times a stray ball would catch him on the head as he slept. Within seconds the ball could be melting in the fire and the lads might get a clip of their tennis bats from him.

They had a dart board as well and Tom Sheeran, while waiting to collect staff from Salts on his bus run, would regularly stop by to play with John, Tom and Martin for the prize of a paper crown.

When the weather grew cold they and their friends would throw buckets of water down the slope at the corner across from their house. Once it froze they had a slide and endless hours of fun. "You'd have a pair of boots with protectors and studs on them," explains Martin. "You'd start back on a run and get up speed and then you'd hit the ice and go sliding all the way down and you could go 30 or 40 yards down the hill. There was often 15 going down on a train together. Crazy. Cars coming up then, some of them would be getting it hard to come up the hill and they'd be giving out hell about us having the slide. We had a lot of fun at that. A lot of sore spots too, banging your ass and your head. What harm were we doing? There was only so many things you could do with your time that time."

Tom and Margaret were the quintessential Irish couple of that era. She ran the household but he was the boss. They didn't socialise together; women generally weren't seen in pubs back then. Tom might have a few drinks down town on a Friday evening after his week's work and Margaret would have the odd glass of sherry at home. Every Sunday they went to O'Connor Park to take in whatever games were on regardless of the teams involved. He was a stickler for time. "Come on woman, we'll be late," he'd say, before nipping out the door, leaving her to catch up with him well down the street, sometimes as she pushed a pram. There used to be a sports day at O'Connor Park that contained a women's race in which Margaret skated to victory once. "Bejaysus Mrs Furlong," said one wag, "you're a real Fanny Blankers-Koen!"

With Wexford and Kilkenny regularly meeting in Leinster hurling finals in that era, Tom and Margaret would travel to the games with Matt Tyrrell, a Kilkenny native who had a shop down the street from them, and bring a couple of the lads with them. Niceties would be exchanged all the way up to Dublin but once the match started all bets were off. After a few glasses of stout on the way home, a sort of sing off would break out; Matt with the Rose of Mooncoin, Tom belting out Glory O To Our Bold Fenian Men.

Tom and Margaret never showed each other any affection, at least not in front of others. "I don't know how any of us were ever born as far as that goes," smiles Martin. "She was a great oul' skin. There was an oul' sofa there and you could be lying on it and she'd start tickling you and she'd have you laughing so hard you'd get the hiccups. She supplied that end of it."

Tom never had any deep and meaningful conversations with his sons but always commanded their respect. It would be wrong to say he ruled by fear but he certainly had a short fuse and the lads were aware that minimising the current was in their best interests. He insisted on a roaring open fire when he came in from work in the evenings, for example, and was seldom disappointed.

Young Tom and Martin dabbled in a bit of soccer as youngsters but concealed their interest in the "garrison" game from their father by throwing their boots over the back gate of the house before walking out the front door to collect them so as not to arouse any suspicions.

In later years, when a television came into the house, Tom and Margaret would watch various sports keenly. The Olympics was always a favourite and they particularly liked tennis. He, oddly enough, also had a fondness for Monica Sheridan's cooking programme, *Home For Tea*, and always smirked when she licked her fingers yet again.

A brief interest in greyhounds was pursued at one stage after John harangued his uncle Patsy in Wexford into giving him a pup. The dog got off to an inauspicious start after emptying its bowels in the back of the car en route back to Tullamore. When the novelty wore off for John, his parents and the rest of the family would walk the dog. He took part in some coursing events and won a couple of races in Mullingar, a decent achievement given that his preparation wouldn't quite have been cutting edge.

The house was a hive of activity at times with a broad spectrum of people coming and going. Across the road was Hurst's Garage and various parts or machinery would be left in Furlongs' to be collected outside of working hours.

Given where their house was situated just on the outskirts of town, it was an ideal spot for people to park their bicycles as they came in for a dance or the cinema. Scores of bikes would rest against their wall sometimes and, if there was a big game in O'Connor Park, the lads would open the back gate and maybe get a couple of pennies for their efforts. Frequently they'd get knocks on the door looking for a pump but after a few weren't returned old Tom's response became, "Oh no, you'll get no bloody pump here!"

While Tom and Margaret took great pride in their sons' sporting abilities, they were loathe to articulate it. It came across in their demeanour rather than through their words. Doling out criticism was a different matter. They could be guaranteed a stern critique from their father when they arrived home after a game, "a fireside inquest" as Tom junior calls it. "Why did you do that? What were you thinking that time?" Eventually Tom would leave it as late as he could before going home after he played a game and Martin later adopted the same approach.

"You always accepted that he was the boss but Tom didn't always accept that," says Martin. "Tom would give him a smart answer or something and he'd get a few belts. If you did it now you'd be put in jail but it didn't do us one bit of harm. It was the right thing to do. It's a pity it was ever stopped. You wouldn't have as much hooliganism as you have now but my father was hard on Tom alright."

"That was one of my faults I suppose," Tom admits now in relation to his ill-advised quips. "What do you want to rise a row with your father for?"

They weren't always at loggerheads though. When word game to the house that old Tom's father had died in Wexford at 94 years of age, Margaret couldn't summon the will to tell her husband. So she sent young Tom in to impart the news. He hugged his father as he shook with the tears.

◆　　◆　　◆　　◆

Despite Mickey's fallout with the club, there was never any question of Tom and Martin playing for anyone bar Tullamore. The 'once a blue always a blue' adage mightn't have applied to Mickey but it certainly did to Martin: He was already turned out in the club's colours literally as he emerged from the womb after some difficulties during Margaret's labour.

With Mickey having left for America and John's sporting career effectively stillborn, a vacuum was finally filled by Tom's emergence. It was obvious to all who saw him from an early stage that he wasn't a run of the mill player.

"Oh no, he was special," says Martin, a man with no weakness for hyperbole. "He was special. I mean, he was very talented. He had a tremendous turn of speed and a good pair of hands. He had a good catch. He had a very good football brain. And he could score. And he could play in goal. He was a brilliant goalkeeper, when we were young and even after.

"Of course, there was a lot of pride there to see him coming up and continuing what Mickey had started. They always said they were two different styles anyway: Tom would go around you whereas Mickey would go through you. That was something that was commented on a lot of times."

Tom credits much of his football development to his time in Tullamore CBS. Br Jeremiah Murphy and Séamus O'Dea ran the football teams in the school during his time. A native of Templemore in Co Tipperary, O'Dea's teaching career had taken him to various parts of the country and he had experienced a broad spectrum of schoolboy football before he settled in Tullamore.

"Maybe I'm seeing it through rosy glasses," he says, "but I would rank him with the best schoolboy I ever saw play, and that would be Seán Purcell from Galway. I always reckoned he was the best schoolboy I ever saw play but I saw Tom Furlong as a schoolboy, playing in school matches, and judging him on that, he was as good a footballer as was in Ireland."

Br Murphy, a Kerry man, had astute football intelligence and he and O'Dea dovetailed nicely together.

"He had a great football brain. He'd place fellas and I often said, 'Why are you putting him there?' He'd be nearly always right. At that stage he'd be at all the preliminary matches in the minor grade. I was around with him at a lot of these matches. He'd see a good footballer, he recognised fellas that would have potential. That was Tom.

"Tom was a very clever fella. He wouldn't be what we'd call a swat or anything like that but he was good enough. In the modern times now, he'd be capable of getting a good many points in his Leaving Cert. He was intelligent, very much so."

Tom had a different personality to Mickey and wasn't quite as outgoing and engaging, but then few were. He was more laid back. Among his closest friends in school were Gabriel Hayden and Joe Wrafter, the three of them highly rated footballers who would all line out on a fancied Offaly minor team in 1960.

"He was never in bad humour," says Hayden of Tom. "No matter where you met him. Even now, but I'm going back now to school times. At that time we were 18 years of age and the women would say, 'Lord, Tom Furlong's never in bad humour'. He always had a smile on his face."

In his formative footballing years Tom was best known as a goalkeeper. At just 14, he was between the posts when Tullamore won the county minor football title in 1958. He won a minor hurling medal the same year as a sub. Tullamore won the next two minor football crowns with Furlong in goal once again in 1959, when he also manned the position for the Offaly minors, who lost the Leinster final to Dublin.

He had dabbled in a bit of soccer with the local club in Tullamore and picked up a few useful tips when they had an expert goalkeeping coach over from England to give a course once.

His goalkeeping technique would have been seen as unorthodox for Gaelic football in that era. Diving around the goal to make saves, as they did in soccer, was, bizarrely, seen as flamboyant. Furlong was cat-like in his agility and could read forwards' shooting action extremely well. He wasn't passed over in regard to one of the family's chief characteristics, bravery, a imperative trait in any goalkeeper.

But, at 16, he experienced a growth spurt and quickly shot to over six feet tall. "I was all back and no legs," he says. "My legs were short, my back was long." With his size, handling ability and skill, pigeon-holing Tom Furlong as a goalkeeper wasn't sustainable in the long term. Br Murphy moved him out of goal for the school team and he was involved in the Offaly minor team management in 1960 when he persuaded the other selectors to do the same.

The Offaly minors struggled past Carlow in the first round that year with Furlong in goal. For the semi-final against Dublin, who had won five of the previous six All-Irelands at that grade, he was selected at full-forward.

"Joe Flanagan was the masseur for Offaly," he explains. "He used to do it in his own time. He had been down in Galway the week before and he came back with a pile of poitín. I remember he used it as a rub on me at half-time and I ran out and ran up to the full-back and stood beside him for the throw-in and he was (feigns sniffing) and he looked at me and he must have said, 'What's these bog men doing, having shots of whiskey at half-time...' He never came near me in the second half."

He gave the attack a focal point as Offaly romped to victory thanks to a storming last quarter with Wrafter's goal, brilliantly set up by Furlong, driving a decisive wedge between the sides. "Furlong was always the man that made things happen," says Pat Heffernan, captain of that Offaly minor side. "It always seemed to be easier for him than anyone else." The Offaly seniors saw off the same opposition in Portlaoise that day meaning that the county would be represented in both games on Leinster final day at Croke Park.

For the seniors, it was their first appearance in a provincial final since that ill-fated day in 1954. They retained a number of players from that game, the likes of Mick Casey, Seán Foran and Mick Brady. Like the minors they had struggled past Carlow in the first round and there was nothing to suggest that the provincial hoodoo would be broken in 1960.

Peter Nolan played in that game but had already resolved to follow his girlfriend, Patsy, now his wife, to New York. At that stage he didn't feel like he was leaving much behind from a footballing viewpoint at least. But the arrival of Peter O'Reilly from Dublin as trainer transformed the team. This was surely their best chance yet of winning the Leinster Championship.

Like the seniors, the minors would face Louth in the final. At the time Furlong had a summer job in London working in construction to help fund his schooling and ease some of the financial burden on his parents. "I figured, well, Offaly will fly me home to be full-forward against Louth. So by Wednesday I got word, 'If you're in Croke Park on Sunday you're playing and if you're not, you're not'."

After a tight first half, Offaly pulled five points ahead in the second half and when Furlong palmed the ball to the net with 11 minutes remaining they were out of sight. Offaly had won just their second Leinster minor title, following on from the pioneering side on which Mickey starred 13 years earlier.

All through his youth Tom Furlong had listened to people tell him he'd never be as good as his eldest brother. Now that he had his Leinster minor medal, he had no need to be cowed by Mickey's reputation any longer.

"Oh, that was the big thing," he admits. "I was as good as Mickey now. I felt tremendous about that. And Offaly winning the senior then, Jaysus, the whole county went mad."

It was a truly momentous day in the history of Offaly GAA with the seniors scoring an edgy one-point win. Standing shoulder to shoulder with the game's elite had rarely been anything more than a pipe dream for success-starved Offaly followers. Now they had two Leinster titles in the space of a couple of hours.

Peter Nolan, Paddy Casey and Mickey were together in Gaelic Park when news came through. Naturally they were delighted that the duck had been broken, but rueful that it hadn't happened during their several years of service.

There was a reception for both teams at the Spa Hotel in Lucan before they finally made their way back home in the early hours. Tom remembers meeting a local man in the Spa who for years had chided him that he would never be as good as Mickey; he withdrew those comments as soon as he saw him. "We got the morning papers before we left Dublin," says Tom, "and we even checked the small print in the minor game. That was a big thing, to get your name on the paper the same day."

The minors failed to progress beyond the All-Ireland semi-final, just as they had in Mickey's time. However, there was no shame in losing to what would prove to be a star-studded Galway team featuring names like Johnny Geraghty, Noel Tierney, Enda Colleran, Séamus Leydon, Seán Cleary and Christy Tyrrell, all of whom would feature on the county's famous three-in-a-row senior sides of 1964-66.

The seniors drew with Down, denied victory by a hugely controversial late penalty, and lost the replay to the eventual All-Ireland winners amid disgruntlement at the fact that Peter Nolan wasn't flown home from America. It was all the more bewildering given that Nolan came over to play for New York against Down a few weeks after the All-Ireland final.

"Me and Fr Vaughan never got on," he says, reflecting on the flimsy red tape that prevented him from coming home to play for Offaly. "From my own personal point of view, I had a huge personal satisfaction when we went over to play Down. I was playing on Jim McCartan and they took him off me. McCartan had done a job on Offaly. And the first man to congratulate me after the game that day in Croke Park was Mick Brady. He had been playing on McCartan for Offaly."

While he was home, Nolan decided to stay around for a few weeks as Clara, bidding for their first title, had qualified for the county final against Tullamore. Tom Furlong was only 16 but was too good to be restricted to underage football only.

"There was a lot of controversy about that, being a youngster, playing senior football at that time," says Tom. "I think my mother was worried. Jaysus, I thought it was the greatest thing that ever happened, to get picked on a Tullamore team."

Clara employed Mickey's old Offaly team mate, Johnny Kinahan, better known as a forward, at full-back to police Furlong. He limited the damage to manageable proportions from a Clara point of view as the game ended in a draw with Nolan in imperious form at midfield.

"Kinahan was an old wily campaigner," Tom observes. "The thing about that game was I wanted to be moved out on Peter Nolan. He was catching every ball in sight. He had a great game. Physically Peter Nolan would have kicked the shit out of me, I guess, looking back on it. I felt I could have knocked him off his game, which you could do sometimes."

Nolan opted against returning to America until after the replay, which fell a fortnight later. He trained maniacally in between and was untouchable as Clara strode to a historic eight-point win. For many, the game was equally memorable for a goal scored by Furlong, reckoned to be one of the best ever in O'Connor Park, a most unorthodox strike that borrowed from his goalkeeping background. As Kinahan was about to fly-kick a dropping ball to safety, Furlong dived headlong through the air and punched it past goalkeeper Willie Nolan.

"If Johnny Kinahan wasn't playing full-back that day against Tullamore, Furlong would have destroyed us," Nolan insists. "Kinahan was one of these Meath-type cagey footballers. If we had the usual full-back like the big fella that we had before Kinahan, we'd be in bad shape. Kinahan was a different story.

"Furlong scored, I would safely say, the best goal I ever saw scored that day. I'll never forget it. He gave a full length dive and he hit the ball just off the ground with his fist and, this is not just talking, our Willie was in the goal and he never saw it. And he would have done a job on us that day only for Kinahan. You needed a good footballer to play on him and we happened to have him that day."

◆   ◆   ◆   ◆

Furlong was studying for his Leaving Cert at the time and the CBS team contained a number of players from the successful Offaly minor side of 1960. The school had little tradition of success and was operating in the Leinster Colleges 'B' Championship.

"In one particular match we were four points down I think after 10 minutes and he scored a goal and a point just like that," explains Séamus O'Dea. "A leader. He had this thing in him. He came out the field for the kickout and he caught the ball and he soloed his way in, a point, we were in the lead now. Now he says, 'Lads, come on, we have these fellas'. We hadn't of course, but the other fellas believed him and so did our own lads. They couldn't fathom him. Any ball that went down he was capable of scoring."

They qualified for the Leinster final against Portlaoise CBS, a side spearheaded up front by the highly rated Danny Delaney. One of their mentors commented to O'Dea before the game that "we have the man to mark Furlong". "Well, if you do," O'Dea replied, "you'll win."

Tom credits Br Murphy as having the single biggest influence on him as a footballer. He knew how to coax the best out of him by pulling the right strings at the appropriate time.

"He came and told me, 'Listen, I know you're good but this Portlaoise full-back is the best there is. If you can manage to just break the ball, that'll be the most we'll expect of you'. Of course I went out on the field and I was fuming. I was going to get this guy. Reverse psychology. I got two goals and Liam Boland got three goals. I was in this guy's face the whole day."

He was still eligible for the minor grade in 1961 as Offaly returned to the Leinster final only to be beaten by Dublin. His team mate, Gabriel Hayden, remembers pleading with the Offaly sideline to move Furlong from full-forward to midfield. By the time the switch was made it was too late for it to make any difference to the outcome as they lost by three points with Furlong dizzied by the selectors' indecisiveness by the end of it all.

"We were behind a lot," he says. "They moved me out to centre-field, centre-forward, moved me back in to full-forward, moved me everywhere, moved me back out to centre-field. I was popping up all over the place."

He also played for the Offaly minor hurlers that year, losing the Leinster semi-final narrowly to Dublin. Again, he was full-forward but was struggling. Having Fr Vaughan in his ear didn't help either. "He came down behind the goal and started yelling at me. 'Pull on the ball!' When I pulled on the ball he says, 'Block the ball down!'"

Eventually Vaughan came in and told him to go down so that he could be taken off. "I says, 'There's the hurl, go hurl yourself or fuck off and leave me alone', or something like that. Then he disappeared and Joe Dooley (a selector) appeared. I knew Joe well and I laughed at Joe and says, 'I'm not going off, don't be a yes man for Vaughan'."

He swapped with KK Kenny at centre-forward, a move that benefited both men, and looked to have won the game when striking a late goal with Offaly two points down only to be pulled back for a free in which was missed.

Tom was always more of a footballer than a hurler and that game marked the end of his county hurling career. However, his stern rebuke of Fr Vaughan on the field that day wouldn't be forgotten and played no small part in his county football career later coming to a hasty conclusion too.

CHAPTER 7

BOOTLESS WONDER

THE Offaly senior footballers surfed the momentum from 1960 and it carried them all the way to their first All-Ireland final in '61. There, defending champions Down were waiting for them once again, looking to enshrine their immortality ever further having become the first county to take the Sam Maguire Cup across the border the year before.

The emergence of two new counties like Down and Offaly on the footballing landscape captured the imagination nationwide. A crowd of 90,556 packed into Croke Park for the 1961 All-Ireland final, which still stands as the record attendance at GAA headquarters and certainly won't be broken as long as the current model, which boasts a capacity of 82,300, is retained. Tens of thousands were turned away as the gates closed almost two hours before the throw-in.

Once again, narrow defeat to the Ulster kingpins was Offaly's lot, going down by a point amid claims that Tommy Greene was denied a certain penalty by Cavan referee Liam Maguire. That Down side is widely considered to be one of the greatest in the game's history, yet in successive years they had enjoyed more than a slice of fortune to see off an Offaly team forever condemned to live in their shadow. A widely held view of that Offaly side is that while they were hugely formidable in defence, particularly with the fearsome full-back line of Paddy McCormack, Greg Hughes and John Egan, they lacked something up front.

Although not bringing Peter Nolan back from America is rightly identified as a critical reason for Offaly's failure to cross the All-Ireland threshold back then, the decision not to add Tom Furlong to the senior panel in 1961 is glossed over by comparison. With the Offaly minors' interest ended at the Leinster final stage that year, Furlong was nominated to join the senior panel ahead of the All-Ireland semi-final against Roscommon. It was a move which was blocked by Fr Vaughan.

Furlong may have been only 17 but he was a strapping young man standing in excess of six foot tall. He was already terrorising opposition defenders in Offaly club football and, while there was and is a sizeable gap between the minor and senior grades, his displays for the county at underage level at least suggested that playing on big days at Croke Park didn't faze him. They only lost by a point in the end. Would he have been worth that much, even as a trump card and unknown quantity off the bench? Instead he was among those squashed into the old ground like sardines that day.

"I would have scored a point, yeah," he maintains. "They didn't have enough forwards that could score. They had some great workers, but they weren't scorers. They had a great back line and a good centre-field but they didn't have a really good forward line."

Two weeks after the All-Ireland final Offaly played Kerry in the inaugural Grounds Tournament in O'Connor Park. It was a competition which ran for several years between the four provincial champions with the All-Ireland semi-final pairings from earlier in the year alternated. Furlong was selected at centre-forward and was marked by Tom Long.

"The first ball I won I tipped it on my toe and I showed it to him and then I went around him and tipped it over the bar. Jaysus, that was great. I did the same thing again. This is great, this is easy. The third time I did it, the side of my jaw... I was down on the ground and Tom Long was looking over me and he says, 'Don't you pull those schoolboy tricks with me!'

"I got into the second half and I pulled the same trick again and went around him and who did I meet only Kevin Coffey. He was a fierce strong man altogether. He do-barred me so that was about it for me solo running."

The boy was raw but the boy was good. Offaly won the game by eight points in what was their first ever victory over Kerry. The game marked the start of the hectic schedule for the team with National League and O'Byrne Cup fixtures also in the offing. Furlong was also the key man on the Tullamore minor team bidding for a fourth consecutive county title a couple of weeks later.

They played St Rynagh's in the final in Birr and lost by a point having had a number of goals disallowed by the referee, Johnny Nolan, brother of Peter and Willie. "I remember getting the ball and I saw a guy coming from this side and I saw a guy coming from that side and I just put the brakes on and I stood there with the ball. The two guys just crashed right in front of me and dropped on the ground. I took the shot and it was rising and just went over the bar."

Furlong was immediately whisked to Tullamore where Offaly were playing Louth. He was introduced as a sub in place of Tommy Cullen for his league debut. The following week Offaly gained some measure of revenge for the All-Ireland final defeat when beating Down in the final of the Grounds Tournament at Croke Park but Furlong was at home in bed having been laid low by a bout of mumps.

By then he had an O'Byrne Cup medal as Offaly beat Longford in the final, a nice momento to take from 1961 after losing a Leinster minor final, a county minor final and missing out on the Grounds Tournament final due to illness. As well as that, Tullamore seniors lost another county final after a replay, this time to Gracefield, meaning that Furlong had played in four senior county finals before he had turned 18 and won none of them.

He had completed his Leaving Certificate and started work in P&H Egan's in Tullamore earning £3.10 a week with Br Murphy having put in a good word for him, years after his mother had decked him out in the company's colours. "I was a clerk in the office making out invoices and taking orders over the phone. I knew every bar in Longford, Westmeath and Offaly. They bottled Guinness and ales and the minerals they made themselves."

He made his championship debut in the opening round of the 1962 Leinster Championship at full-forward in a five-point win over Carlow and was shifted to centre-forward for the semi-final against Kildare. He was back on the edge of the square deep into the second half with the game drifting away from Offaly as Kildare led by five points. Furlong forced opposition goalkeeper Kieran Dockery to spill possession, resulting in a goal by Mick Casey. When Peter Daly sent in another delivery around the Kildare square shortly afterwards Furlong produced one of his trademark mid-air dives to outwit Dockery and punch the ball to the net at the Hill 16 end.

"I thought it was the greatest goal I ever scored," he says. "It hit the ground and I hit it at the same time, just as it bounced. It went like a bullet into the net." He was somewhat peeved to open the *Irish Independent* the following day to read John D Hickey describing the goal as a fluke. Offaly were steeped to win by two points but remained on course for a third successive Leinster title with Dublin next up in the final. Maybe Furlong was the x-factor up front that could drive them to All-Ireland glory this time.

However, he sustained an injury in the first half of that Kildare game that turned out to be a broken wrist on his left hand. The team doctor, Brendan White, strapped it up at half-time and adrenalin carried him through the rest of the game. He went to the Mater Hospital afterwards for an x-ray but they couldn't set it as his wrist was still too swollen. Either way, time was against him with the Leinster final only two weeks away.

The next day in Tullamore he ran into Jack Whelan, a staunch local GAA man who enquired about the wrist. He told Furlong to call to his house at six o'clock that evening and they'd go to a bonesetter in Moate. They eventually caught up with him in a pub in Athlone. He prodded around Furlong's hand and identified the area where it was broken.

"Do you drink?" he asked.

"No," Tom replied.

He gave him a shot of brandy anyway and pushed his thumb into his hand until there was a click. Another shot of brandy was administered at that point.

"That's when I started to like brandy," he smiles. "He wrapped it in a regular gauze bandage and he gave me this bottle of rub. That's what he called it – rub. It was the foulest smelling thing you ever had. He said, 'Put this on three times a day before an open fire'. God bless my mother, she used to put it on."

When he returned to the bonesetter two days before the final the bandage was removed and Furlong asked him would he be able to play.

"That's up to yourself," he said.

"That's it, I'm good," Tom replied, before he scurried back for training that evening. Fr Vaughan, of all people, would carry out the fitness test.

"This is how much influence this guy had. He got the ball and he started throwing it at me. I knew well he was going to throw it at my left hand. Being a goalkeeper, wherever he threw it I stepped to the side and caught it into my chest. I'd move over and throw it back to him. So he pronounced me fit."

Dr White strapped both of Furlong's wrists before the throw-in in a bid to throw his marker, Lar Foley, off the scent though he aggravated the injury again during the game. Offaly struggled throughout and a switch from full-forward to centre-forward for Furlong wasn't enough to turn the tide in their favour. The near misses of 1960 and '61 had seemingly taken too much of a toll on the team as they struggled to find the form of those previous campaigns. The late raid against Kildare was only a stay of execution; Dublin won by four points and wouldn't have been flattered by a more comprehensive victory.

Still, Tom Furlong wasn't yet 19 and with the minors having annexed another Leinster title that year the production lines were still spitting out talented footballers. He reasoned that, unlike Mickey after his Leinster final defeat eight years earlier, he'd have more opportunities for provincial and All-Ireland glory.

However, his first Leinster senior final also proved to be his last.

◆　◆　◆　◆

Immediately after Offaly's harrowing loss to Down in the 1961 All-Ireland final, Paddy Grimes, who had brought Mickey to New York, entered the team dressing room and invited them to come to New York. Grimes was a big-hearted man and his gesture was more than a meagre consolation to the players. Back then it was the trip of a lifetime. Furlong and Larry Coughlan weren't involved when they reached the All-Ireland final but were regulars by the time the trip came around in October 1962. There was a little consternation about the personnel that should travel but the two lads got the green light and never looked back.

The team stayed in the Hotel Manhattan near the old Madison Square Garden and Tom was mesmerised by the views from his room on the 44th floor. They stayed for a fortnight and received $80 a week in expenses. This was the life. Tom hooked up with Mickey and spent several evenings with him at Mickey O'Sullivan's bar, where he worked. Mickey was made up at the fact that his younger brother was in New York with the Offaly team and took to celebrating it one night while putting Tom on the other side of the bar. He made a killing on tips.

They went to the races at Belmont Park and had an evening at City Hall where they met the Mayor of New York, Robert F Wagner Jnr. There would also be two matches against New York. Old Tom Furlong had heard through Mickey of how rough the games were over there and asked that his son not be played. He was introduced as a sub in the first game which New York won by a point thanks to a last minute goal and started the second instalment, in which Offaly came out on top to claim overall victory. But, while he enjoyed that trip, he didn't see himself coming back any time soon.

"I didn't think when I was leaving that I'd ever come back to it. I told my mother I couldn't understand them being out till four o'clock in the morning drinking, it was terrible," he says, laughing at the more sheltered lifestyle he led at that time.

However, Offaly goalkeeper Willie Nolan took such a liking to New York that he decided to stick around and he settled in the city for many years afterwards. In the meantime, there was a National League game against Louth the Sunday after the team came back and Offaly needed a goalkeeper. Furlong was thrown the No 1 jersey. He was called on to make a number of stops, including a smart double save, before eventually being pushed up to the half-forward line. The Offaly attack badly malfunctioned on the day with just 0-2 registered by the end of a bad tempered game.

"We had to get a police escort out of Dundalk," says Tom. "It was a dirty game, a fierce dirty game. We got a penalty in the second half and Mick Casey was running up to take it and the guy took the two legs out from underneath him. The referee wasn't giving anything against Louth."

Furlong was left in goal for the rest of the league campaign and was very much a natural in the position. Although he preferred playing out the field, he enjoyed goalkeeping, with cross-channel soccer 'keepers like Harry Gregg and Gil Merrick among his idols. He largely settled in well between the posts for the Offaly seniors, though he had his moments too.

"We played Roscommon in the league and there was a fierce gale," he explains. "This guy kicked a ball in when we were playing with the wind. It was looking like it was going over the bar but it was coming down under the posts anyway. Next thing the ball keeps going back out and I'm on the 21-yard line. So I knew I was dead. The ball fell to a Roscommon forward and he stuck it in the net and I had to go all the way back, 21 yards, to pick it out of the back of the net.

"I got home anyway and my father and Tom Sheeran were telling me I shouldn't have gone out after the ball and all that shit. I was pissed off with myself and I didn't need to be told I was wrong. So I said something about Tom Sheeran, some game he played down in Carlow for Offaly, he kicked the ball out and it nearly went into the net. 'Jaysus, where did you hear that?' My father was so mad at me for saying it."

In Offaly's final league game he put in a blinding display against Dublin in a resounding 13-point victory, albeit both teams' interest in the competition was at an end regardless of the result, and was named Sports Star of the Week in the *Offaly Independent*. In the first round of the 1963 Leinster Championship they had little trouble in seeing off Longford to set up a semi-final meeting with Laois.

Offaly were bidding for a fourth successive Leinster final

appearance but with the team struggling, Furlong was pulled out of goal and placed in midfield in the second half. He kicked a point but Offaly lost, 2-7 to 0-9, and the window of opportunity for many of the players that were so close to All-Ireland glory a couple of years earlier was closing.

With the county team's activity at an end for the summer Furlong turned his attention to club duty as he sought a change of luck in his bid to win a senior county title with Tullamore. In August he went on holiday with his close friend Gabriel Hayden. Ballybunion was their intended destination though they bided their time about getting there as Hayden caught up with his girlfriend Kathleen in Nenagh before they all moved on to Shinrone. They inevitably got lost on the windy roads to Kerry with Furlong having to climb up a pole and strike a match to see where the road signs were pointing them to.

Hayden too was a prodigious young talent whose career went hand in hand with Furlong's from their days in the CBS and with the Offaly minors. Both were on the Tullamore senior team that had an upcoming county quarter-final against St Rynagh's. They played soccer on the beach that week with Hayden's brother Mick and Paddy Larkin, another friend from home, before tipping up from Ballybunion to Birr to play for Tullamore in the middle of their holiday. They won 3-9 to 2-6. Incredibly, Furlong accounted for 3-7 of his side's total.

It put him in a strong bargaining position when he, along with Hayden, asked team trainer Alo Kelly for some expenses after making the trip from Kerry. He threw them a few pounds and they pointed the car for Galway on the next leg of their tour of the country. Within a few days they'd blown the last of their money and pondered their next move.

There was enough petrol in the car to get down to Tom's parents' place in Wexford and young Martin was on holidays down there already having cycled that far from Tullamore. Tom figured he'd have a few bob to tide them over. The Freshmen, a popular showband from Ballymena, were gigging down there and provided the highlight of the Wexford leg of the trip before they finally landed back in Tullamore.

MAN AND BOYS: Tom Furlong with sons John (standing), Mickey (seated), Tom (right) and Martin (left) in 1948.

FIRST STEPS IN O'CONNOR PARK: A young Martin Furlong in 1949.

FAMILY VALUES: Margaret and Tom Furlong at the rear of their home on O'Moore Street, Tullamore.

GOAL-DEN YEARS: Martin and Tom pictured in front of the gate which they used as a goal when youngsters. It took quite a battering in their formative years.

THE CLUB: Tullamore minor football team, 1949. John Furlong is circled above, and to his left is his lifelong friend, Noel McGee.

OUT WITH A COLD: Tullamore, Offaly senior football champions, 1948. Mickey Furlong (circled), was unable to play in the rearranged county final having been struck down by a bout of pneumonia.

AMERICAN DREAM: The Offaly team narrowly beaten by Meath in the 1954 Leinster final, which proved to be Mickey Furlong's (circled) last championship game for the county before he left for America later that year.

TOM'S TURN: Offaly's Leinster minor winning team of 1960. It was just the county's second success in that grade following the pioneering breakthrough in which Mickey starred in 1947. Emulating that feat was no small feat for Tom Furlong (circled).

STEPPING IT OUT: The Tullamore team, including Tom Furlong (circled), parades before the 1960 county final against Clara.

OUT OF PUFF: Teammates and friends Joe Wrafter, Tom Furlong, Gabriel Hayden and supporter Martin Furlong (flag in one hand and fag in the other) photographed in 1961.

OUT FOR A STROLL: John Furlong on William Street, Tullamore, in 1957.

CATCH IT: A very important catch by Phil O'Reilly during the 1963 Offaly county final. Martin Furlong was ready to pounce.

WINNING WAYS: Martin Furlong (circled) winning his first Offaly Senior Football Championship with Tullamore in 1963. Tom was suspended for the final having fallen foul of the GAA's Rule 27, which hastened his move to America.

ON THE BRINK: The Offaly minor team, with Martin in goal (circled), pictured following their 1-10 to 1-8 victory over Mayo in the 1964 All-Ireland semi-final.

SAVING GRACE: Martin Furlong tries to get to his feet as a goalmouth scramble ensued following his match-winning save in the final minute of the 1964 All-Ireland minor final.

RIGHT: Martin Furlong and Liam Duffy (in background) receiving presentations from Bill Ennis following Offaly's historic All-Ireland minor win.

QUARTER MILE: Two Furlongs tie the knot. Martin and Katie on their wedding day in June 1969 (left); and Tom and Yvonne on their big day in October 1970.

PUT THE BOOT IN: Tom Furlong in his prime – a classic picture of his place-kicking skills with the New York Giants from 1966. Inset: Famed American football coach Vince Lombardi with his long-time assistant Norb Hecker, who signed Tom Furlong for the Atlanta Falcons.

START SPREADING THE NEWS: Mickey Furlong (centre) pictured with fellow former Offaly footballers Paddy Casey (left) and Mick Drumm ahead of the St Brendan's Cup game for New York against All-Ireland champions Dublin at Croke Park in 1958.

LOVE BIRDS: Mickey and May on honeymoon in Tramore, 1958. Mickey sports a bandage on his hand having shipped a blow while hurling for New York against Wexford in the St Brendan's Cup final victory.

BOMBS AWAY: "Would you like one of these landing in your back yard?" wrote Mickey to his mother while on duty in Japan, October 1956.

TOGETHER AGAIN: Martin, Tom Snr, Tom Jnr and Margaret.

COMING TO AMERICA: Martin took his first trip to visit his brothers in America in 1966. Here he is at Mickey's home in New Jersey. From left, Tom, Michelle, May, Mickey, Thomas, Mary and Martin.

GOOD FRIENDS: John fooling around with Carmel Smyth; Margaret is ready to pounce.

RISING SON: Tom Furlong taking to fatherhood with his two-week old son Tommy, October 1971.

GONE FISHING: John Furlong casts a line.

THE BIG CUP IN THE BIG APPLE: The Sam Maguire in the Tower View Ballroom, Queens, New York following Offaly's success in 1972. Included in the picture is Yvonne and Tom Furlong and on left, Offaly county secretary and future GAA president John Dowling.

PAST MASTERS: John (circled) lining out for Wrafter's over-40s pub team in 1975.

ALL SMILES: John, Mickey, Tom and Margaret Furlong at O'Connor Park with Ricey Scully (right).

Not long afterwards, Tom answered the front door to be handed a letter by a young boy. It explained that he had been suspended for six months for contravening the GAA's rule 27. Furlong wondered what on earth it was for. Then it struck him. Some weeks before, there was an internal soccer match in P&H Egan's between the brewery staff and the transport workers. He didn't intend to play and even loaned his football boots to a colleague. He went to watch the game, which soon turned into something of a free for all. He wandered out onto the field in his civvies and booted in a goal. The brewery staff won 1-0. However, a report of the game somehow ended up in the local paper.

Furlong immediately appealed the suspension. Ahead of his hearing, he got his hands on a rulebook for association football from a local anorak and brought it along with him. He was pinning his defence on the fact that that rulebook stated that an official game of soccer consisted of two teams of 11 players each. "Sure, by the time the match was finished it was maybe 15 on one side and 18 on the other side," he says. Fr Vaughan's ears were typically unsympathetic.

"You take the word of the vigilante committee over me?" Furlong queried. "I'm a practising Roman Catholic and so are you and you won't take my word on the Bible that I didn't play in a soccer match?"

"No," said Vaughan sternly, "we take the word of the vigilante committee."

"Well," Furlong replied, "some priest you are."

He turned and stormed out. Football was essentially what made Tom Furlong's world go round. Now it had been cruelly taken away from him. He had a girlfriend at the time, Chris Naughton, who had emigrated to New York. So too had his good friend Joe Wrafter. And, of course, Mickey had already blazed a trail. His job in Egan's didn't have great long-term prospects and the wages were meagre. But the suspension effectively made his mind up for him; he started filling out the forms for an American visa.

The Furlongs weren't the most communicative family and sitting down with his parents to outline his plans to leave the country wasn't high on Tom's agenda. When letters started dropping in through the door with the US Embassy's stamp on the envelope their suspicions were naturally aroused. His father only found out for sure when Donal Carroll, previewing the 1964 contenders in the *Evening Herald*, wrote that Offaly's chances would be hindered by the 20-year-old Furlong's impending emigration to America.

The thought of losing another son to America tortured old Tom. He was too set in his ways to sit him down and try and talk him out of it. Instead he thought a grand gesture might do the trick. Old Tom never learned to drive and the family certainly wasn't well off but he assembled whatever money he could and forked out £568 on a brand new car for his son, hoping the allure of it would be enough to keep him at home. Like most Irish men of his generation, he never showed affection to his sons or openly professed his love for them, but a gesture like that said it louder than words ever could.

And yet, it wasn't enough. In fact, one of the few journeys young Tom took in the car was up to the embassy to get his papers in order. Just like when Mickey left 10 years before, old Tom couldn't bear to wave his son off, opting to walk the fields once again until he was well on the way to Shannon.

Funnily enough, Martin wasn't too perturbed about Tom heading away. "I was hoping he'd go for selfish reasons!" he smiles. "I was going to fall in for the car. It was a brand new Austin Mini, a red one."

There were attempts to secure better employment for Tom in a bid to keep him at home. Br Murphy got him an interview with Clerys on O'Connell Street in Dublin. He accompanied him to the interview which was conducted by the managing director, Denis Guiney.

"What will you do," he asked Tom, "if you don't get this job?"

"I'm going to America," he said.

"Take my advice, son," he replied, "go west."

His suspension had elapsed before he was due to go and Tom fancied one last outing in the Offaly jersey before leaving, to prove a point if nothing else and show the county board bureaucrats, and particularly Fr Vaughan, what they'd be missing out on.

In early March 1964 Galway were coming to Tullamore for a

National League game. Offaly couldn't progress any further but Galway were on the cusp of the home final and that was no small matter: the winners of that got to go to New York to play the final proper. Galway had lost the previous year's All-Ireland final to Dublin and were a team going places. They fitted the bill in terms of giving Tom the opportunity of signing off on a high. He was selected at midfield.

"He was a brilliant footballer, really, really good," says Pat Donnellan, a Galway stalwart of that era, of Furlong. "He made a huge name for himself in New York as well.

"Any time we went to Tullamore to play Offaly, we'd be bloody lucky to beat them, even if we were All-Ireland champions. They were a good strong, physical team. But the problem with Offaly in the '60s was they hadn't the forwards. It's only when they got Tony McTague and these boys later on that they started winning."

Furlong was the star of the show. Five minutes into the game he showcased all his brilliance, encompassing lightning pace, power and accuracy in one breathtaking move. He took a pass from his old pal Gabriel Hayden in his own half and set off up the field like a gazelle.

"My boot came off on my own 50-yard line and I kept going. I was looking for somebody to pass the ball to. I kept soloing on and everybody kept running away from me like there was something wrong with me. Then I got about 30 yards out and I said, 'Fuck it, I'll let fly'."

Struck with his stockinged right foot, the shot flew past Johnny Geraghty and in off the post. Ask any of the old sages in Tullamore to this day what their outstanding footballing memory of Tom Furlong is and the reply will more than likely include reference to that goal.

Offaly trailed by a point at the break and Furlong kicked the equalising score on the restart. They limited Galway to just 0-2 after that and ground out a one-point victory. Furlong can remember his midfield opponent Mick Reynolds decrying their efforts with time almost up. "Why are ye doing this to us?" he kept saying.

Dublin beat Roscommon that same day to leapfrog Galway and

qualify for a National League home final against Down, which they won to earn the trip to New York. Furlong would be there before them but, ironically, he wasn't allowed to line out for the exiles in their victory over the Dubs as he had already represented his native county in the competition on that fateful afternoon at O'Connor Park.

On foot of his display, he was invited to appear on RTÉ's midweek television sports show, hosted by Seán Óg Ó Ceallacháin. Straight after the game, Fr Vaughan swept into the dressing room and hailed the result. This, he stressed, could inspire a return to football's top table with Offaly's standards having dropped in the three years since 1961.

Furlong let Vaughan have his say and then peeled off his jersey and held it in front of him.

"That's the last time I'll wear one of these while you're around," he bellowed.

Soon he was in New York and Offaly had lost quite possibly the best footballer they never really had.

CHAPTER 8

MINOR MIRACLE

ONE day in 1959 Eamonn Fox and Pat Heffernan, two young players in the Tullamore club, were engaging in a kickaround in O'Connor Park, where it was customary for young lads to race behind the goal and kick the balls back out to them. A ball hopped between two youngsters aged about 12 or so. One of them put his foot over it and jostled the other out of the way before claiming the ball.

"By Jaysus," said Fox. "Mickey Furlong will never be dead while that young fella's alive, whoever he is."

Heffernan looked at him.

"Do you not know who he is?"

"No?"

"That's Mickey Furlong's youngest brother."

◆　◆　◆　◆

There are two ways you can go if you're the youngest in a line of talented sporting brothers: feed off it or be intimidated. Martin Furlong largely chose the former, though he did have to put up with the usual "you'll never be as good as your brothers" spiel.

"You'd have to say Mickey started the Furlong thing," says Martin. "He was a good footballer and hurler so as it came to pass down along the line, well, Tom was a brother of Mickey so he couldn't have been too bad. 'The breeding is there', or whatever. Then I came along and I was a brother of Mickey and Tom's so I had a name before I ever had a name."

Martin may have outstripped his brothers in terms of his medal haul but emulating them academically wasn't high on his agenda. Both Mickey and Tom sat their Leaving Cert and John started an apprenticeship shortly before he fell ill but as soon as full-time work presented itself to Martin he was happy to leave the books behind. While on the way to school one day he saw a notice in the window of

Wakefield's, a local grocery store, advertising for a messenger boy. He expressed an interest and Dick Abraham gave him the job which paid 10 shillings for working four days a week after school plus Saturdays.

He wasn't attending the Vocational School in Tullamore very long when the opportunity to work there full-time came up. His wages tripled and his mother got 10 shillings a week, another 10 shillings was lodged in the post office and the rest he kept for himself. Séamus Morris lived up the road from the Furlongs in Spollanstown and Martin later started working a couple of nights a week in his chipper, the Capri Café.

"Séamus Morris and his wife Josie had a huge influence on me and so did Dick Abraham. They were a big guidance, no doubt about it. Séamus Morris was like a second father to me. He was very good to the family as well."

Work may have kept Martin out of trouble as a youngster but so did football and hurling. Beyond his exchanges with Tom in the back yard and out on the road, his first introduction to the games came through the usual channels: school and playing for the Dillonites in the local street leagues. He wasn't pigeon-holed as a goalkeeper from the off and, indeed, was centre-back on the Tullamore under-16 team that won the county title in 1962.

Despite his family background, however, self belief was never something that coursed through Martin's veins.

"No, not really, no. Confidence wouldn't be in abundance. I just never felt that confident really. I don't think any of us had any big ideas about ourselves or anything like that."

Martin dabbled quite a bit in soccer in his youth and it was through that he suffered a harsh lesson in the formative years of his playing career. Early in 1963 he played for Tullamore in the FAI Youth Cup against Athlone Town, who had Turlough O'Connor in their ranks. O'Connor was an up and coming name and represented the Ireland youth team against West Germany at around the same time. Come the spring he was on the Westmeath minor team that would play Offaly in the first round of the Leinster Championship.

102

Furlong was chosen in goal for Offaly but no sooner was he handed his first Offaly championship jersey but it was taken away from him. Fr Tom Gilhooley, a Westmeath native and curate in Tullamore, was head of the management team. He proved to be an immensely popular man over the years but not on this particular day.

"Just before we went out on the field Fr Gilhooley came to me and said, 'I'll have to take the jersey back. We're not going to play you because if Westmeath play Turlough O'Connor, which I think they're going to do, we can object'. So I was broken-hearted, cried me eyes out."

The game was played as the curtain raiser to the Offaly-Longford senior tie, in which Tom was to play in goal. He arrived early to watch his brother play but when he saw no sign of Martin as the teams emerged he went down to the dressing room to look for him. He found him in floods of tears. Tom was enraged and initially refused to line out for the senior team. Bizarrely, the game started without him before he finally took his place in goal. Although Fr Vaughan didn't appear to have a direct involvement with Martin's omission, Tom wasn't in any doubt that his finger prints were daubed all over it. As it happened, O'Connor played in the minor game, Westmeath won and went all the way to the All-Ireland final with Offaly's objections amounting to nothing.

Martin's dalliance with soccer threatened to go further than that too. Séamus O'Brien, manager of Athlone Town, got in touch wondering would he sign for them. He was picked to play against Drumcondra one Friday night in Tolka Park. However, he was struck down by flu and had to pull out. He didn't bother going back after that. It's not a decision that keeps him awake at night.

"The same camaraderie wouldn't have been in it that you would have with the Gaelic. That was the end of that anyway. I preferred playing GAA. It was more natural to me I guess."

Sadly, Tom and Martin never got to play championship football together for club or county. Tom's 3-7 haul against St Rynagh's in the 1963 quarter-final proved to be his last senior football championship game in Offaly prior to his suspension and Martin would make his debut in the semi-final against St Mary's. They did play together in a few challenge games before that though, one of them against Ballinasloe. A row broke out around the Tullamore goal and one of the Ballinasloe forwards got stuck into Martin. Tom raced from full-forward and barely broke stride before flattening the aggressor with a box. The match was quickly abandoned.

Alo Kelly, the former Offaly star, was team trainer and still played up front but had filled in as goalkeeper in the St Rynagh's game. Joe Bracken, a long-time team mate of all the Furlong brothers, went to Kelly and insisted that he promote Martin to the goalkeeping position.

"We needed a goalie," says Bracken, "and I had seen Martin Furlong playing about three weeks before that for Tullamore minors and he was great. I got down on my knees and I asked Kelly. We were playing the army up in the Curragh in a challenge match and I said, 'Give this lad a feckin' run because I think he'll be great'. I could see the potential in him and he'd been on the Offaly minor team as well and if he was good enough for the Offaly minor team in them years he was good enough for Tullamore."

With Tom having accounted for all but two points of Tullamore's 3-9 against St Rynagh's, people wondered where the scores were going to come from against St Mary's in the semi-final. It was a game that was unique in Martin Furlong's career, not just for the fact that it was his senior championship debut for the club, but that he and his defence didn't concede a single score as Tullamore bizarrely won by 2-9 to 0-0.

He had only just turned 17 and wasn't exactly a commanding figure in the physical sense, say, compared to his brother Tom before him. In an era when goalkeepers were a hunted species by burly forwards, who could let them catch the ball and then plant them in the net, there was potential for carnage.

"You were open season," says Martin of the goalkeeping trade back then. "You weren't supposed to be but you were. It didn't bother me, sure I had the finest of men outside me. I had good backs; I had

Brendan Dagg, Dickie Conroy, Dermot Keegan. Outside that you had Phil O'Reilly, Tom Hayden and Gabriel Hayden like. There was nobody going to hit me too handy and get away with it."

Like many of Tullamore's county titles, they overcame indifferent form for much of the year to transform themselves come the business end of the competition. They beat Gracefield comfortably in the final. Having played in four county finals and won none before reaching the age of 18, Tom at least got a medal for the 1963 success even if he was suspended for the final. The seven-year gap to Tullamore's previous senior football title was the longest in the club's history and the team toasted the success in Jack Digan's pub on the Kilbeggan Bridge.

Club football wasn't the limit of Martin's ambitions, however. More so than when his brothers were emerging, there was an allure to playing for Offaly when he was coming of age on the back of the '60/61 teams. He was still eligible for the minor grade in 1964 and would play a central role in one of Offaly's most important and treasured successes.

◆　◆　◆　◆

From the late 1950s Offaly were producing consistently good minor teams. Indeed, from 1957 onwards, they reached eight out of 10 Leinster finals in that grade, winning four. Offaly may have been a small county but the competition for places on the minor panel was stiff.

Fr Gilhooley was in charge once again and Martin quickly put the previous year's experience behind him. "He wasn't a man that you could hold a grudge against. He was a great priest but, number one, he was a great person."

There may have been plenty of quality around the county at that time in the minor age group but Gilhooley was determined to exhaust every corner of Offaly rather than limiting the search to the more traditional footballing strongholds. The fact that he wasn't a native of the county was no harm in that regard.

"He used to go out to different areas in Offaly, out to Cloghan, over to Croghan, over to Walsh Island, PJ Mahon's, to Dinny Kelly's in Geashill and he'd say, 'Is there any young lad you think now, if you knocked the corners off him...' and he did that all over Offaly," explains Mick O'Rourke, a member of the '64 minor panel. "That's where he picked up his few extra players. I often heard him saying, 'There's a player in every corner of Offaly, bring him in and give him a chance'. You'd be watching to see were you going to get a jersey. If it was number 30 you were delighted. Now the lads would be huffing and and puffing about not getting starts."

"We used to have trials and there was well over a hundred that started out and then you were nibbled down and I was the only one from Walsh Island," says Willie Bryan. "You'd know no one and I was always a fella that, if I could, I'd pass it. Anyway, I was told if you don't start playing your own game rather than all this passing that it mightn't work out for me.

"I was serving my time in Bord Na Móna and I went to school up in Kildare town, it was a six-week course. And Kildare town was a thousand miles away from Walsh Island. I felt, 'Well, I'm gone up there now, that's the end of it'. I wanted an Offaly jersey so much that I took a jersey at the training.

"John Dowling came in and said, 'Lads, there's an awful lot of jerseys going missing so we'll have to search your bags'. I thought, 'Whatever hope I had of getting on this team I have no hope now'. And he never searched my bag and I got out with the jersey anyway. I would have jumped over the moon. If I ever was to get on that team I was getting on it."

Bryan was only a first year minor on that side and not as influential as some might have thought given the huge impact he later made at senior level. Another who would later be crowned Footballer of the Year, Eugene Mulligan, was only 15.

"We had some tremendous players," says Mulligan. "We had probably half a dozen exceptional players, starting with Martin

Furlong. You had Mick Ryan, John Smith. Willie, at the time, wasn't. Sean Grogan, Tony McTague and fellas like that, literally down the middle. The fellas like me then, I don't mean filling holes, but we were way behind those type of fellas. They were exceptional players then."

A bond was formed among that minor team that would prove to be the catalyst for so much success. O'Rourke, Bryan, Mulligan, Furlong and others from that side soldiered together for many years and became the firmest of friends. Straight away, Furlong stood out as he drove the spanking new car that his father had bought for Tom to training and matches.

"I was just saying to myself, 'Jaysus, we hardly had a bad bike' and he had a Mini car. That's my initial memory of Martin," says Mulligan.

They swept past Louth and Kildare to reach the Leinster final with "the footballing genius of their gum-chewing centre-forward Tony McTague", as the *Midland Tribune* described him, boring holes in the opposition defences. "As I've said, many times, a lot of people associated McTague with free-scoring," says Furlong. "He'd take two or three little steps up and tap it over the bar but he scored an awful lot from play as well."

Martin had developed a ritual of climbing Croagh Patrick on Reek Sunday, which falls on the last Sunday in July, over the previous few years but that was the weekend the Leinster minor and senior finals were usually played. For the next couple of decades he would more often than not find himself playing in Croke Park on that particular day as toiling his way up Croagh Patrick became a distant memory. Offaly beat Laois by a point and he became the third Furlong brother to win a Leinster minor title.

Each of Offaly's three previous provincial wins at that grade had seen them drop out at the All-Ireland semi-final stage but this time they went one step further, seeing off Mayo with two points to spare. Their final opponents would be Cork, who boasted four players – Tim Murphy, Con Roche, Charlie McCarthy and Liam McAuliffe – who were part of the minor hurling team that had won the All-Ireland earlier that month.

Eric Philpott was the star turn in their attack. He was a dashing forward with pace to burn who excelled on Coláiste Chríost Rí teams in both codes. When he was a small boy he broke his right leg and while it healed his father would toss a football at him. He'd kick it back with the left and remained a ciotóg for life. He was a deadly accurate free-taker to boot.

He started the final like a train and had the Offaly defence in all sorts of bother early on. The Offaly players were in a tizzy after getting delayed at the Spa Hotel in Lucan, where they had their pre-match meal. By the time they got to Croke Park they jumped into their playing gear and ran out onto the pitch. Furlong had his palms reddened a couple of times in the opening minutes when making what proved to be crucial saves. The game was refereed by future GAA president Mick Loftus and in the ninth minute he was a central character in the game's first big turning point. Philpott takes up the story.

"I remember clearly what happened," he says. "I opened up the game and I was really flying now. I remember Martin was coming out with the ball having saved some ball that came in and Charlie McCarthy just gave him a token foot trip, nothing kind of spectacular, nothing very violent, but you know Martin like. Martin got up and threw the ball at Charlie having got his free. He proceeded to make a bit of a shape and Charlie made a bit of a shape back and Charlie was the same club as I was, St Finbarr's, so there was a bit of handbags stuff and a bit of a shemozzle and Loftus ran in and I remember him putting his hand on the back of my jersey, pulling me aside and Johnny Coughlan as well.

"We just thought he'd more or less have a word with us, the match was only on a few minutes. He then just took our names and sent us off. We couldn't believe it. I couldn't believe it anyway. The match was only on a few minutes and to send us off without warning? It was very rare that a fella was sent off, it was really rare that a minor would be sent off a few minutes into a game."

Coughlan was a useful corner-back but there was no doubting the fact that his loss was much less of a blow to Offaly than Philpott's was to Cork. Offaly took control of the game from there and seemed to be out of sight when leading 0-11 to 0-3 by half-time.

Cork got themselves organised at half-time and, with the wind at their backs, started to eat into the Offaly lead with their cause given significant impetus by a goal scored within two minutes of the restart. With 10 minutes to go they were level. They pushed two points ahead with four minutes on the clock. Oliver Kilmurray kicked a long range point to halve the deficit before McTague kicked a free which he had earned himself to draw the sides level.

With a minute remaining, Offaly captain and centre-back Seán Grogan kicked a free long into Cork territory. It broke for corner-forward Eddie Kennedy, who lobbed over his fourth point of the day to put Offaly back in front. History was within touching distance. Quite literally, as far as Martin Furlong was concerned.

By now, most of the 76,498 crowd that would watch the senior final was present in Croke Park as Cork thundered up the field one last time. Playing into the Hill 16 end, they won a sideline ball over by the Cusack Stand. Midfielder Jim Downing arrowed the ball in the direction of the edge of the square, where Tim F Hayes, the big centre-forward, and full-forward Liam 'Barney' McAuliffe were lurking. Hayes rose highest and punched the ball goalwards. Fleetingly, it felt like the winner as far as he was concerned. The ball seemed destined for the bottom right hand corner of the net but Furlong sprawled cat-like across the goal to smother it on the line.

"I got up the highest to punch it down into the net. It was a great save because I thought we had the goal got," says Hayes.

Goalkeepers weren't the protected species they are nowadays. Hayes and McAuliffe descended on Furlong bidding, essentially, to score a pushover try. Offaly full-back John Smith barrelled McAuliffe into the goal, where they got to know each other, while Mick Ryan grappled with Hayes.

"He was brilliant the way he had the ball covered," Hayes continues. "I was on my knees right in front of him and when he went to get up I gave him a bit of a shoulder and I thought it was over the line. I was looking at the umpire and there was no flag going up. I must have been the only clown that ever did what I did anyway, but I went over and got the flag and put it up myself. It was right on the line. I got a photograph sent to me some time after."

"I saved it well outside the line," Furlong insists. "There's a photograph somewhere of it well outside the line and they tried to pull me in over the line."

While Hayes waved the green flag, Loftus opted to give a free out as a result of the onslaught on the goalkeeper. No sooner was it taken but he sounded the long whistle. Offaly were All-Ireland minor football champions. Essentially, it boiled down to that last gasp save and proved to be a critical victory in the county's GAA history.

Paddy Fenning, who would win several major honours with Furlong for club and county in subsequent years, was an impressionable 13-year-old in Tullamore who had begged his grandfather to allow him to rent a television that weekend so he could watch the game.

"That, to me, was as important a save as the penalty in '82 and any other saves he made," says Fenning. "I'm not saying we were losers, but we weren't achievers until then. I'll never forget looking at the team coming home in O'Connor Square and I saw these guys, you can imagine, 13/14 years of age, heroes."

"It would have been horrific if it didn't work out," says Willie Bryan. "There was a huge effort made that time and, I would say, a lot of money spent on that particular minor team."

It helped transform the county's mindset. Eight of the players involved that day would go on to win senior All-Irelands. One of them, McTague, finished the game with 0-9. He was born in Rosscarbery, Co Cork, only a few miles from Tim F Hayes. If his father's work as a guard hadn't taken him to Ferbane he would surely have been starring on that Cork team instead and Offaly mightn't even have got out of Leinster.

The minor victory of 1964 spawned so much success which followed. For Martin Furlong, the win ranks as the best of his career. Better than Offaly's eventual breakthrough at senior level and the iconic victory of 1982, when he was a central character.

"It was hugely important," he says. "In Offaly football I'd say it was the most important because it broke the duck, that Offaly could win an All-Ireland. I still believe that if we hadn't won that there's a fair chance it wouldn't have happened. I'm not saying it wouldn't have happened but it set the road for '71 and '72, and '71 and '72 set the road for '82."

When the Offaly hurlers finally emerged as a credible force in the early '80s, the footballers' success in previous years had ploughed a furrow for them to a degree with the county's famed belligerent fighting spirit already well established. Maybe all those subsequent senior successes would have happened regardless of 1964. But, at the very least, they came easier on the back of it.

The difference in the subsequent fortunes of the two sets of minor players that took part in the curtain raiser at Croke Park that day is stark. Some of the Cork players went on to play senior and others, like Charlie McCarthy and Con Roche, starred for the hurlers but none had stellar football careers.

Philpott was on the senior team that reached the All-Ireland final in 1967, losing to Meath, but that sending off hung over him like a cloud. To a certain extent, it still does. That minor football final was the first to be broadcast live on television. The semi-finals and finals at minor and senior level were the only county games shown live all year round back then. Sendings off were few and Philpott's stuck in a lot of memories.

"It had a fierce effect on my future career because I played in two further All-Irelands, the under-21 in '65 and the senior in '67. I was more or less finished then by '69 and I missed out on the '73 win. It did affect me big time because I was never sent off up to that and I was never sent off after.

"Down in Cork here, when people talk about me they never say, 'You were the fella that played in the '65 under-21 final or the '67 senior final', they always say, 'You're the fella that was put off in the minor All-Ireland', because it was on the telly.

"Even the family, like. My brother and my father, Lord have mercy on the two of them, they're dead. Jaysus, my father particularly was devastated for a good number of years in fairness. I kind of got over it to be quite honest with you after a while but he spoke about it for a long time after it."

Philpott has never met Loftus since but in the summer of 2012 he was on holiday in France on the same weekend that Cork and Kerry played in the Munster semi-final. There were a number of Irish people staying in the complex and one of them engaged in a bit of banter with him about the game. They got to talking and he revealed that he came from a family in Mayo steeped in the GAA.

"Really?" said Philpott, "what's your name?"

"Michael Loftus," came the reply.

"Your father was a referee?"

"Yeah."

"He put me off in the '64 minor All-Ireland!"

"What did you do?" he asked.

"The funny thing about it," Philpott replied, "was that it was nothing. I didn't do anything."

A lot of the aftermath washed right over Martin Furlong. Grogan hoisting the Tom Markham Cup is a blur at best. When they settled in to watch the senior game, in which Kerry beat Galway, he remembers a kerfuffle in the crowd around half-time and seeing a man carried out, seemingly dead. It turned out to be Michael Donnellan TD. His son John lifted the Sam Maguire Cup alongside his brother Pat later that afternoon following Galway's victory and was then informed of his father's passing.

The Offaly team repaired to a reception at the Spa Hotel that night. "I remember being in bed, I don't know whether it was my own room or not," says Furlong. "Somebody had commandeered some alcoholic refreshments and they were up on the top shelf of the wardrobe and I remember partaking of some of that alcohol!"

A raucous reception awaited them in Tullamore the following evening. The players were piled up on the back of a truck as St Colmcille's Pipe Band led them through the town and into O'Connor Square. Martin's family didn't toss any garlands at him but they passively exuded huge pride in what he had achieved. John would willingly contribute to the conversation when the minor success was brought up for years afterwards down in Wrafter's pub. "I'd say John was the proudest Furlong of the whole lot of them," says Martin. "That was how he got to express himself."

Mick O'Rourke can remember seeing grizzled veterans like Noel McGee and Martin Fitzpatrick, two of John's closest friends, in floods of tears as they were paraded to the crowd.

"The homecoming was unreal for us, coming down the town in a truck from the railway station," says Eugene Mulligan. "You'd be lucky if you nearly got on it. It was incredible. That time the whole thing of safety, people weren't as concerned then as they would be now. People were literally in on top of you."

The captain, Seán Grogan, addressed the masses.

"We won't rest until we have the Sam Maguire Cup here in Tullamore," he declared.

CHAPTER 9

FALLEN FALCON

LIKE with Mickey a decade before, Paddy Grimes was a central player in Tom Furlong going to New York. Back then, immigrants needed a sponsor with $10,000 in the bank and Grimes fulfilled the role for Tom. Helping Offaly to win back the New York Championship would be his end of the bargain. Mickey was living in Rockaway at the time and Tom spent his first couple of weeks in New York with him and his family.

Three days after he landed he lined out for the Offaly footballers against Kerry at Gaelic Park. Kerry won by a point but Tom scored 0-5 from midfield and was named the Player of the Week. For that he was presented with a watch inscribed by Ballantine Brewerys, who sponsored New York GAA at the time. Although Offaly lost the game, Mickey was bursting with pride. Years in America meant that his glimpses of Tom playing football were fleeting. The third Furlong brother had only fully come of age as a footballer in the previous couple of years and this was Mickey's first opportunity to see him in that respect.

"He ran out on the field after it was over and grabbed me and gave me a big hug," says Tom, "'The only difference between me and you,' he said, 'is that I used to go through them!'"

He eventually moved in with Joe Wrafter, his long-time friend from Tullamore, and Johnny Nolan, whom they chided about his refereeing performance when they lost the 1961 minor county final to St Rynagh's. It wasn't the first time that Tom was slotting in for Willie Nolan, Johnny's brother, who had stayed in New York two years earlier while on tour with Offaly, which saw Furlong placed in goal for the county team as a result. Willie had been called into the service, thereby creating the vacancy in the lodgings. Tom was due to follow him shortly afterwards but was fortunate or unfortunate, depending on how you look at it, to pick up an injury which ruled him out.

One night he was training in Van Cortlandt Park and was chatting to Kevin Woods, a first generation Irish-American who played with the Offaly team in New York, about American football. Woods took to demonstrating the tackle from behind in this strange and exotic game with Furlong the subject. He landed awkwardly, suffering a compound fracture of the elbow, and was whisked straight to St Joseph's Hospital in Yonkers. The upshot was that Furlong couldn't pass the medical when he got called for the service, meaning he wouldn't have to spend a year or two in a far flung part of the world like Mickey did years before. Indeed, he still has something of a crooked arm to this day as a result of the injury.

Having initially worked at laying carpet, he then began bartending in Eddie O'Sullivan's on 230th Street and Bailey Avenue. The arm put him out of action however, though he got an interview with the Manhattan and Bronx Surface Transit Operating Authority and secured a post working in building maintenance. It was early August but Tom Furlong was already in his third job since landing in New York barely four months previously. He earned $250 a week in the bar but MaBSTOA paid just $100. However, it offered him long-term stability away from the mayhem of bar work and decent benefits over time.

The New York team embarked on a world tour in the late summer of 1964 but the injury ruled Furlong out for virtually all of it. Their last match would be against Offaly in Birr and his arm had healed sufficiently by then. He was flown over to play. Tom was looking forward to the game for obvious reasons but, by now, was taking a drink. He ran into a friend, Mickey Bracken, at 12 o'clock mass in Tullamore on the day of the game. They went for a couple of quick pints of cider across the road in Wrafter's and Tom sold him the American dream.

However, when he got to Birr, he wasn't picked to start after someone got the whiff of alcohol off him. One of the New York players got clobbered after a couple of minutes, though, and he was thrown into the fray. New York won and Furlong acquitted himself well.

"It was a very good New York team and he was playing very well that time," says Pat Heffernan, centre-back for Offaly that day. "Peter Nolan was at the height of his powers. It was a pity, like. Tom was magnificent in America for years after it."

It was only a flying weekend visit though as he had to be back in work on the Tuesday morning, meaning that he missed Martin's day of glory with the Offaly minors in the All-Ireland final just five days later. He brought his transistor radio into work and received word of Offaly's famous victory when he finally got a signal after climbing up on the roof of the building on 132nd Street and Broadway in West Harlem.

In New York, Furlong had a reputation before he settled in the city on foot of his exploits when Offaly were on tour two years before, not to mention the fact that his brother had already blazed a trail.

"He was the talk of the town," says Mickey Moynihan, an exceptional New York player of that era who, by all accounts, would have slotted in seamlessly with his native Kerry back home. "He was so talented. Tommy was a great place kicker. He had the speed of anybody in Gaelic football at that time as well. There was a lot of good forwards I saw but they were a little bit slow, including myself. But he had that speed that very few guys had and great control. Great ball control and a class player. I never saw him involved in any fight. He wouldn't back away from anybody but it wasn't his game to go out and beat anybody. He could beat you just playing football, he didn't have to hit you."

Nevertheless, the football in New York was as unflinching as ever but Furlong had his guardian angel in the shape of Paddy Casey. In one of his early games in New York for Offaly, playing against Cork at centre-forward, they were winning well at half-time and Cork changed their centre-back for the second half. Casey knew the player in question and wasn't in any doubt that he was detailed to rough Furlong up. He immediately strode from his centre-back position.

"Furlong, come here," he said. "Go back and play centre half-back."

"I never played in the back line in my life," he replied.

"Go back and play centre half-back," Casey barked.

He may have been coming towards the end of a distinguished career at that stage but you didn't argue with Casey. Certainly not if you were Tom Furlong, who rates him as the best footballer that ever came out from Ireland. The laws of the jungle applied in the games in New York then and Casey was very much a lion who wasn't easily tamed. The first ball that broke between him and his new marker saw Casey win possession while leaving his opponent sprawled out on the ground. After he played the ball away he hovered over the Cork player and spat out a few choice words. He stayed down initially before going off.

"Now," Casey said to Furlong as he trotted back to his original position, "you go back centre-forward."

Offaly footballers hadn't won the New York Championship since Mickey's time in 1957 and, like the Offaly team at home, they had a formidable defence but lacked scoring power. That's where Tom Furlong came in. They won the 1964 title, albeit the final wasn't played until March 1965. The three main contenders in the competition in that era were Kerry, Offaly and, oddly, enough Kilkenny, who, admittedly, had just one native county man, Seán Brennan, in their ranks. The Offaly team was largely made up of natives and those that weren't generally had strong links to the county.

"If any of that three were playing each other in Gaelic Park, you'd have six or seven thousand people in the park on a Sunday," Tom explains. "They were the three top teams."

Just like in '57, there was a knockout competition and a league format. The winners of both played in the championship final unless the same team won the two. Offaly won the knockout and lost the final of the league to Kilkenny, meaning they had to play them to determine the champions overall. Offaly then won an unmercifully robust and physical encounter by 1-4 to 0-4.

"It was one of the toughest games I ever played in that I remember," says Furlong, though admittedly his memories of the game are hazy at best. "I got a belt in the first half and that was lights out for me, I didn't remember anything else in the game. Peter Nolan came up and took a 50 and it was sailing wide and I was looking up at it like an idiot and Séamus Nugent pole-axed me. I remember bits and pieces. I got three points, Peter Nolan kicked a magnificent 50, and Eamon England from Killavilla, he played hurling for Offaly, but he was a strong man and he scored a goal. I guess I had a concussion. I came to at about 11 o'clock that Sunday night in Paddy Casey's house."

When Galway won the National League home final in 1965 they travelled to New York for a two-legged final proper. Oddly, Furlong was only a sub for the first leg. It's extremely doubtful that New York had six better forwards than him at that time though an apparent reluctance to train may have been at the heart of his exclusion.

"He was a brilliant player and he had speed to burn," says Peter Nolan. "He was like a deer. But then, we used to train and we had a fella from Monaghan training us. He was a very hard trainer. He wasn't anything to do with tactics but he was a very tough trainer and we were very fit. That type of training didn't suit Tom."

"Maybe it looked like I wasn't taking it serious but there was a method to my madness," says Tom.

After Furlong had denied Galway a trip to New York before he left Ireland in 1964, they were happy enough to see him on the sideline. They were at or near the peak of their powers at the time having won the All-Ireland the previous year, the first of three in succession.

"They came out here in '65 and they were very, very worried about where Tom was going to be playing and Tom wasn't even on the team," says Joe Wrafter. "On the day of a game he'd step up to the plate like you wouldn't believe though. He was incredible like that."

Played in late June in the middle of a heat wave in New York, the Gaelic Park surface was typically dusty and patchy and the game wasn't one for the purists. Furlong was eventually sprung from the bench and kicked the winning point in the last minute for a 0-8 to 1-4 victory. He started the second leg a week later but Galway had figured New York out by then. They won by 3-8 to 0-9, with Furlong accounting for all of the exiles' scores, to take the National League title by seven points on aggregate.

◆　　◆　　◆　　◆

Tom Furlong was a relatively late developer when it came to

kicking frees. Although he was the chief scoring threat on the successful school and minor teams that he played on, others were entrusted with place-kicking responsibilities. It was only by chance that he fell into it. Noel McGee took the frees for Tullamore but was having an off day once and passed responsibility to Furlong. Similarly, when he got to New York, Paddy Casey was struggling one afternoon and told Furlong to take over. He practised in Van Cortlandt Park and quickly became proficient.

He'd bring an American football too and enlisted the help of friends to hold the ball and kick it back to him. He found it easier than kicking a Gaelic football. It was lighter for a start and given that he kicked 'soccer-style', with the side of his foot, rather than the straight-line toe-poking method that was widespread among field goal kickers at the time, he had more accuracy and distance in his kicks. American football grew on him once he moved to New York. Getting tickets for the New York Giants' games was rather difficult so he started following the Jets along with his house mate at the time, Mike McCormack.

A member of the New York Giants staff was at that National League final when Furlong put on a flawless display of place-kicking against Galway. The Giants were going through an underwhelming period at the time and failed to make the play-offs in the 1965 season having won only half of their Eastern Conference games. As the season was winding to a conclusion, some of the coaching staff would pore over the team's shortcomings in Jim Downey's Bar on 44th Street and Eighth Avenue.

Working there was a chap called Eddie McDwyer from Daingean in Co Offaly. When McDwyer heard them moaning about the difficulties they were having with goal kicking he mentioned Furlong's name to them. One of the coaches, Emlen Tunnell, a legendary former player for the Giants and the Green Bay Packers who was now the assistant coach, was intrigued. He told McDwyer to bring his friend down to Yankee Stadium the following Tuesday morning at eight o'clock for a trial.

It was a bitterly cold morning and they were just pulling the tarpaulin off the pitch when Furlong arrived. He was introduced to Tunnell and other members of the coaching staff, who instructed him to start kicking into the open end of the ground. He took pots at the posts from a range of distances. As he took one kick he lost his footing as he struck; the ball split the uprights regardless. After taking 30 kicks he had converted 27. When he turned around he saw the co-owner Wellington Mara, head coach Allie Sherman and kicking coach Ken Strong.

"What I didn't realise at the time was word had spread into the big boys inside so they had all come out and they were standing behind me. I turned around then and they were all there and they were shaking their head. They had never seen a soccer-style kicker.

"There were still four games to go in the season. So I figured they'd sign me. Tunnell said, 'You had a great workout, tremendous, you should be kicking against the Chicago Bears next Sunday'. Sherman didn't want to sign me. He had never seen a soccer-style kicker and he wasn't putting his faith in it. But they signed me to a contract to keep me on."

Furlong was put in the taxi squad which meant he effectively sat on the bench in his civvies for the remaining games of the National Football League season and was paid $200 a week. They told him to report to the training camp ahead of the following season but then things changed when they signed Pete Gogolak.

Gogolak was Hungarian-born, his family having fled their native country during the revolution in the '50s to settle in the US. He was contracted to the Buffalo Bills in the rival American Football League and his signing for the Giants is credited with sparking the 'war of the leagues', eventually resulting in an AFL-NFL merger. Gogolak had the same kicking style as Furlong given that he had played soccer in Hungary before leaving as a teenager. Sherman may have been dubious about that style but, unlike Furlong, Gogolak had proven pedigree in the game having come through the college system and played in the AFL.

He starred for Cornell University before putting down a couple of good seasons with the Bills. Such was his success in the game as his career progressed that he is credited with revolutionising field goal kicking to the point where virtually every elite kicker now approaches the ball at an angle and kicks on the instep rather than the straight-line and toe-poking style that was prevalent back then.

Furlong was undeterred, however. He'd got a sniff of a career as a professional athlete in the biggest sport in America and he wanted more. Paddy Lenihan, an influential Cork native who was a former president of New York GAA, penned a reference for him which he included with letters that he wrote to more than a dozen teams. Ten of them replied expressing an interest. He effectively narrowed it down to two – the Boston Patriots (now the New England Patriots) of the AFL and the Atlanta Falcons.

There was always going to be a pull from Boston given the strong Irish community there. They were owned by Bill Sullivan, an Irish-American businessman. "I didn't think I'd have much of a chance with them because they had a guy, Gino Cappelletti. He was the field goal kicker and he was also a wide receiver and he had a damn good year the year before. He was selected on the All Star team. I said there's no way I'm going to beat him out. But what I didn't know was he was retiring so meanwhile I had gone down and made three trips down to Atlanta."

The Falcons were a new franchise and the 1966 season would be their first in the NFL. Furlong felt they offered him the best shot at making an immediate breakthrough. They decided to sign him. At first he was offered a salary of $10,000, which was the minimum wage in the NFL at the time.

"Of course I wouldn't take that," he smiles. "So he upped it to $11,000 and I wouldn't take that and he offered me $12,000. Now I was beginning to get a bit worried because when was he going to say, 'Forget about it'? So I signed for the $12,000."

Micheál O'Hehir had gotten wind of Furlong's flirtation with American football back in Ireland and asked him to keep him abreast of developments. When he told him that his salary worked out at roughly $800 per game, O'Hehir was aghast.

"He says, 'You mean you're getting $800 a game for just running out on the field and kicking a free and running off to the sideline?' I says, 'Yeah'. The highest paid player in England that time was Denis Law. He says, 'Denis Law is only getting £200 a week!' Micheál O'Hehir couldn't believe it."

Furlong wasn't the only Gaelic footballer catching the eye of American football scouts around that time. Kerry footballer Donie O'Sullivan was studying in St John's University in New York for a year. While there he kept his hand in by playing for the college's American football team as a field goal kicker. The New York Jets were training at the college for a period and liked what they saw of O'Sullivan.

"I had a few try outs with them at Shea Stadium," explains O'Sullivan, who also observed Furlong's field goal kicking at the time. "This was going on towards the end of the year, early December 1966, and I was supposed to join them the following year. That isn't saying I was going to make it, but they'd sign you on, give you some contract.

"I didn't show up to the camp. I told them; they were very good. There was a coach there, he was very famous. I didn't know. He was a very good individual called Weeb Ewbank. I didn't know he was that outstanding until afterwards.

"Joe Namath, he was the famous quarter-back. And their kicker at the time was a fella called Jim Turner. They were getting rid of him because his distance wasn't good enough. But he was a lovely individual, most helpful to me when I was there.

"I was good for distance but so would so many Gaelic footballers. Tony McTague would be very good. No doubt about that. Mick O'Connell, Maurice Fitzgerald and these people. Matt Connor. Any of those. If you have good distance and a bit of accuracy.

"Tommy was playing soccer as well. He was an all-rounder. He was a complete athlete. I'd say he was more accurate than I'd be."

O'Sullivan decided against hooking up with the Jets again and has no regrets. He went home and won a further two All-Irelands with Kerry, captaining them to success in 1970.

"I'm so glad. I'm always grateful because of the enjoyment. If you're kicking, there was a downside to it and Tommy Furlong would say the same thing – you're sitting down on the sideline and you're called in to kick so you're kind of out of the game. The attraction of football, there was no comparison."

The newly appointed coach of the Atlanta Falcons was Norb Hecker, who had come from the Green Bay Packers. When the legendary Vince Lombardi was appointed head coach of the Packers in 1959 he immediately installed Hecker as his assistant. Together they won three NFL Championships and when the Falcons were looking for a coach they initially tried to prize Lombardi away. He was thought to be keen but negotiations ran aground when he apparently wanted part ownership included. Owner Rankin Smith wouldn't concede that but asked if he'd have any other recommendations for them. When Lombardi didn't put Hecker's name forward, Smith effectively took it as an endorsement and appointed him.

"Eight guys came for try-outs during our three days of work-outs," Hecker told *The Gadsden Times* as he settled into his new job. "We signed three of them and may sign another, so I think that is pretty good." The three were Furlong and halfback pair Don Porterfield and Harold Hurley.

However, just because he had been signed on by the Falcons didn't necessarily mean that Furlong had made it. A total of 104 players were brought to camp at Asheville, North Carolina in early July, 1966. Only about half of them would be retained for the season proper. So, although he had signed professional terms, Furlong was effectively still on trial and it was a cut-throat business. "Everybody's an enemy there," he explains, "you're fighting for a job."

Still, if he kept nailing the kicks as he had been then he had every chance of being retained. A reporter from the *Atlanta Constitution* was intrigued by the kicking Irishman and wrote glowingly about him. However, he had handicaps to overcome that his competitors in camp didn't have to contend with.

"They were all college guys and I wasn't a college guy and I wasn't American. As a guy told me before I went down there, there was still a lot of bigotry at that time. I remember I kicked balls in behind the goal and I was going down looking for them in the undergrowth and one of the coaches came along and said, 'What are you doing down there? Get your ass up out of there, that's full of snakes'. He turned around and he says to one of the ball boys, 'Hey you, nigger boy, get down here and get those balls'."

In the profiles that the club collated on each player, "none" was written for where Furlong attended college. He didn't want people thinking he was ignorant and asked them to insert the "Christian Brothers" instead. "Then I thought Christian Brothers sounds like a distillery! There was Christian Brothers brandy out in America so I didn't know whether that was great or not either."

The training camp in Asheville was testing. "You got up in the morning at six o'clock, got down to breakfast and then you had practice and meetings and then you had lunch and then you went practising again and then you had dinner."

Naturally, field goal kicking took up a large part of Furlong's day, though it was a limited role that didn't allow you to get into the thick of the action. With his speed, size and handling ability, he felt he had the potential to make it as a wide receiver. He mentioned it to one of the coaches but got short shrift.

"They wouldn't listen to me. I could catch the ball as good as any of them. They figured I was a real dumb Irishman, didn't know where my Xs and Ys were.

"Field goal kicking is very complicated in a way. The three components in a kicking game is the snapper, the holder and the kicker. The guy that snaps the ball, he's got to snap the ball back, the holder is seven yards behind him. That ball has to come back seven and a half spirals and he's got to catch the ball and put it down with the laces facing the goal. From the time the guy snaps the ball I start moving because I've got 1.4 seconds to get to kick the ball."

One of the holders in the playing group wasn't too enamoured with the Irishman. They were going through the routines one day when he fumbled the ball as Furlong ran up to strike. Having already started his kicking action, he kicked through fresh air and fell flat on the ground clutching his knee. He suffered what proved to be ligament and meniscus damage. He knew he'd be out for a few weeks at the very least. There is never a good time to sustain a serious injury but the timing in this instance was particularly disastrous.

Hecker, at that time at least, wasn't a very hands on coach and didn't speak directly to Furlong at any stage until then. But he called him into his office that evening, told him he was releasing him and asked him for his play book. Given his background and kicking style, which was perceived as unconventional back then, Furlong was on the back foot right from the off. At the first sign of adversity they cut him loose. He went back to New York and had to look after the injury himself.

"I was shell-shocked. I don't remember saying a word to him. I got shit canned right away whereas if I had gone to the Patriots I reckon they would have given me a chance to get my knee back in shape.

"Later on, when the agents came in and all that, you signed a contract and you were guaranteed X amount of money or something like that but back then it was just the players and the general manager that did the signing and you had nothing. You weren't protected at all."

Within a few months he was back on his feet again. He hooked up with the Brooklyn Dodgers, a newly formed semi-professional side that played in the Continental Football League and borrowed its name from the baseball franchise that had moved to Los Angeles in 1957. The Dodgers hired the legendary Jackie Robinson, the first African-American to play Major League Baseball in the modern era, as general manager. Furlong was hopeful that if he could reclaim his kicking form with them that another opportunity would present itself to him with an NFL side. His brother Martin was on a visit to New York from Ireland and saw him playing on television.

One day at practice at Downing Stadium Eusebio and Pelé appeared. Benfica and Santos were in town to play an exhibition game and the pair of them were presented for a few publicity shots as they tried their hand at kicking an American football. "The first ball that Eusebio kicked, he kicked it from about 50 yards right through the posts. Pelé couldn't kick it for shit."

Furlong's Gaelic football took a back seat at this stage, though John 'Kerry' O'Donnell tried to fly him back to Ireland to play for New York in the National League final against Longford the day after he had played for the Dodgers against the Orlando Panthers at the Citrus Bowl in Florida. The logistics were too tight, however.

The Dodgers only lasted one season. The concept never took off as they struggled to attract crowds with their most regular home ground, Downing Stadium, way out on Randall's Island, a long way from Brooklyn. An opportunity came up to play for another CFL side, the newly formed Akron Vulcans in Ohio. Former Green Bay Packers quarter-back Tobin Rote was their general manager. Furlong signed for them but they too lacked stability and only lasted a few games before folding.

He also kept goal for Shamrocks, a team in the German-American Soccer League, around that time and sustained another debilitating injury to his right leg, just above the knee, while in action for them. Coupled with his mishap in Atlanta, it shaved a few yards off his kick. Not much, but enough to make a difference and erode his confidence. He had taken a two-year leave of absence from the Transit Authority to pursue an elite career in American football but with misfortune dogging him at every turn it was time to stick or twist. He couldn't live on fresh air.

"I decided when I was in Akron, I ain't going to make it," he says. "I had lost the length on my kicks." He resumed his old job and left the American football dream behind him. An opportunity that had promised so much had ultimately delivered little more than frustration. He wishes that he had sided with Boston rather than Atlanta but remains philosophical about the whole experience nonetheless.

"I could have had a big career but, I learned a long time ago, if you're wondering what could have been you'll crucify yourself."

"If I was Tom's coach," says Mickey Moynihan, "looking back I wouldn't have him as a kicker even, as good as he was. He would have been a wide receiver. I'm convinced that he would have been a wide receiver for a National Football League team here, without any problem, because he had the speed, which you had to have. He had the speed to do that."

Donie O'Sullivan agrees, adding: "The other thing is, if he had come through the college system he'd have walked through it. If he wasn't injured and if he had decided to go to college there in the '60s he'd have no doubt got a scholarship straight away for kicking."

Furlong's interest in the game didn't waver and he attended a number of Super Bowls in later years after the NFL and AFL merged. In 1969 himself and Moynihan were in the Orange Bowl in Miami when the New York Jets shocked the Baltimore Colts to win Super Bowl III, their only such success to date.

"We were coming out of the stadium afterwards," explains Moynihan, "and George Blanda of the Oakland Raiders, out of the blue he comes straight over to shake hands with Tommy Furlong. I'm just saying that he was known in the business. Tommy was known because Blanda wasn't a guy that would know everybody. He was a big-time quarter-back and field goal kicker."

Furlong says he has "nothing only bitter memories of Atlanta" and didn't maintain contact with anyone he rubbed shoulders with during his period down south, but some time later he happened to speak to another player who was on the books at around the same time as him. He told him a chilling story of the locker room banter that prevailed after he had left. The holder who had apparently fumbled the ball that caused Furlong to blow his knee out joked with his team mates about how he had left the thick Irishman sprawling on the turf. Furlong was never in any doubt that he did it on purpose. "They made a big laugh about it in camp," he adds.

In the very first game that the Atlanta Falcons played, an exhibition against the Philadelphia Eagles at Atlanta Stadium ahead of the 1966 season, the kicker they finally settled on, Wade Traynham, missed the ball completely from the kick off. Traynham had worked as a grave digger, funnily enough, and from there the Falcons found themselves in a hole that they struggled to get out of. In that NFL season the two clubs that dangled an elite football career in front of Furlong's nose only to swipe it away bombed spectacularly. The New York Giants finished bottom of the ladder in the Eastern Conference with the Falcons just one place above them.

Norb Hecker was fired early in his third season in charge having delivered just four victories in his 31 games. He was never hired as a head coach again.

CHAPTER 10

SLIDING DOORS

MARTIN FURLONG may have had a senior county title and a minor All-Ireland to his name having barely turned 18 but he was still a relative novice in the goalkeeping trade. In 1965 he remembers playing for Tullamore against Daingean, who opened the scoring with a point in the first minute. Furlong, in his innocence, gazed up at the ball as it sailed well over his head and through the posts. A Daingean forward came through and buried him in the net. A stunned Furlong started swinging. So did his opponent. The referee, Bunny Kavanagh from Kildare, spoke to them both when order was restored.

"Lads," he said, "that's not the way I play my football. To the line, the two of ye."

It was a hard lesson but it stood to him for the rest of his career. Once he was sure the ball was going over the bar or wide he always watched for an opportunist preying for a cheap shot. It was one of a few core principles that framed his goalkeeping philosophy. He always backed himself to get to the 21-yard line quickly if danger arose. He reasoned that if he had to go any further than that then there was something seriously amiss. Another essential was that while the ball or the man may get past you, both couldn't. Clean out everything in your path to stop that ball entering the net. If your defenders got taken out as well then that was just an unfortunate by-product.

"My philosophy would be that you'd have to go through him to get the ball," he says. "If that's what you had to do, that's what you had to do. Take all before you when you're going.

"Like the boxing parlance, keep your hands up, protect yourself at all times. If you're going for a ball you have to go to win it. You're not going hoping to get it. You've got to fucking win it."

Despite his heroics for the minor team in 1964, Furlong wasn't parachuted straight into the county senior team like Mickey and Tom had been before him. Instead, it was January 1966 before he made his National League debut, against Tipperary. The Battle of Templemore, as it was subsequently dubbed. Four players were sent off, two from either side. A row broke out in the second half. Some of the crowd came in on the field to participate. Furlong recognised one of them. He was a Tipp man living in America that had several spats with Mickey in Gaelic Park over the years. He was flash and was typically wearing a white suit while he tackled one of the Offaly players. Paddy McCormack and Furlong raced upfield and upended him.

"That was the dirtiest white suit that was around Tipperary for a while," says Furlong. "I'd say he regretted coming in."

His debut season was nothing to get excited about. Offaly played Kildare in the first round of the Leinster Championship and were beaten after a replay. A core of players remained from the early '60s, some of them past their best, some of them with plenty still to give. Others who came in in the meantime just weren't good enough and, on the whole, Offaly had been a dwindling force for a number of years. It would take time for the prospective senior players from the successful minor team of 1964 to develop.

There was progress though ultimate disappointment in 1967. The under-21 grade came into existence in 1964 and Offaly, naturally, fancied their chances in '67 after winning at minor level three years earlier. They crashed out to Longford, however, another timely reminder that while succeeding at minor provided a massive injection of confidence and a timely boost to the county's collective self esteem in a footballing sense, it offered no guarantees as they moved up through the grades.

The seniors made better progress, reaching the Leinster final with victories over Wicklow and Longford, who were National League champions the year before. Meath were waiting in the final. On a blustery day at Croke Park, Offaly trailed by 0-7 to 0-1 at half-time having played against the considerable breeze. It could have been worse but for the fact that Furlong twice denied clear cut goal chances for Meath. They pared it back to a point with 12 minutes to play but with Jack Quinn imperious at full-back for Meath they held on for victory with Mick Mellett kicking a late free for a turgid 0-8 to

0-6 result with Offaly left to rue late goal efforts missed when points might have been enough to save them.

"He brought off a brilliant save from myself," remembers Meath forward Mattie Kerrigan, who rates Furlong as one of the top three goalkeepers of all time, "because I sold a dummy to one of the defenders, who bought it, and I was going to let fly with it only he arrived on the toe of the boot. He played well that day, there could be no fault with him or the Offaly defence as well. We were probably the better team that day but found it hard to win.

"Martin Furlong was fearless. He certainly wouldn't flinch. You'd be guaranteed that if you were going for a ball in the goal mouth that he'd be coming for definite. He'd get the ball but he was well able to look after himself when he did come for a ball as well. An excellent reader of the game in my opinion, very brave and never flinched in coming for a ball. I would have rated him very highly after playing against him on many occasions. He was, for me, one of the best in our time, without a doubt."

With that defeat, three of the Furlong brothers had now played in Leinster finals and lost them all. Just as it was when Mickey lost out to Meath 13 years earlier, they went on to win the All-Ireland in 1967. But Offaly couldn't quibble too much. The team lacked quality and balance overall. The famed and feared full-back line of Paddy McCormack, Greg Hughes and John Egan was dismantled with McCormack at centre-back and Hughes at centre-forward in a bid to give the attack a bit more edge.

Ace marksman Tony McTague had graduated to the senior side by then but he couldn't be expected to carry the forward line on his own, particularly when his inter-county career was very much in its infancy. Offaly struggled for scoring forwards, as the meagre total of 0-6 would attest.

Meanwhile, over in America, Tom Furlong may have lost a little of his old magic but he was still capable of pulverising visiting inter-county teams from Ireland.

◆　◆　◆　◆

Tom was only 23 when his American football ambitions ran aground. What else was he to do but go back kicking a bit of football in Gaelic Park. In 1967 Galway beat Dublin by two points in the National League home final and were New York bound again. When Furlong had denied them a trans-Atlantic trip with his all action display at O'Connor Park on his final appearance for Offaly back home in 1964, Galway were on the cusp of greatness. They won the next three All-Ireland titles, as well as the National League at New York's expense in 1965, and looked poised to become the first side to win the four-in-a-row since Kerry in 1932 as they landed in New York.

Before the game Furlong met Micheál O'Hehir coming across the field and they exchanged pleasantries and chatted briefly about the game. Back in Ireland, his father wasn't well and he asked the voice of the GAA if he would mention him on air.

"You know the way it is Tommy," he said, "everybody wants to get their name mentioned."

In the first half Furlong rattled in a goal and O'Hehir shrieked: "That's a goal for New York by Tom Furlong and I bet that makes his father Tom very happy in Tullamore tonight!"

"I heard the old man was like a peacock," says Tom, "he heard his name on the radio."

New York led by that score at half-time but a Mattie McDonagh goal put Galway back in front in the second half before Furlong set up his side's second goal for Paddy Cummins and then added his second to seal a five-point first leg victory.

Galway looked set to wipe out that advantage in the second leg a week later when leading 0-7 to 0-0 approaching half-time before Furlong turned the tie on its head with another goal. After Galway had beaten Dublin in the home final, he saw a copy of the *Evening Herald* back home which had a picture of a crucial save Johnny Geraghty had made low at the feet of a Dublin player. Furlong made a mental note of it and dinked the ball over the Galway 'keeper as he advanced.

"Tommy was playing corner-forward on Enda Colleran, Team of the Century man," recalls Mickey Moynihan, centre-forward for New York that day. "The game was very close and Enda Colleran caught a terrific ball in the square over Tommy's head and Tommy kind of slipped and Enda comes out soloing out the field. Tommy gets up like a flash, out after him and as he tapped the ball on his toe, Tommy put his hand in from behind and pulled it back and turned around and blasted it into the net.

"That was the beginning of the end of Galway. We ended up getting a couple more goals afterwards but that was the start of it. That goal, in my mind anyway, was one of the finest goals I have seen. It just showed you the talent he had and the speed he had to come out."

New York won by five points for a decisive 10-point victory overall. It knocked the stuffing out of that great Galway team, who surrendered their long-held Connacht and All-Ireland titles when losing to Mayo a few weeks later. It would prove to be the pinnacle of Tom Furlong's football career and, indeed, the only major honour that he won at senior level was the only one that eluded his youngest brother. Indeed, his wife Yvonne still wears the medal around her neck on occasions.

Evidently, they had a quality side with the standard of player in New York well above and beyond what's there today. They may not have been a county team per sé, but they didn't lack motivation to prove that they could mix it against the top sides from back home.

"Well, that time nearly every one of the New York team had played for the county at home," says Furlong. "Kenny Finn was playing for New York. He had won an FAI Cup with Dundalk. He went on and he played professional soccer out here as well. There was a camaraderie too. Even against the Galway guys, we palled around with them after the game. The following Tuesday I played for Philadelphia against Galway. Micheál O'Hehir was announcing the commentary from the sideline. Then Galway went to Hartford and I was playing for Hartford."

There were trips back to Ireland for games regularly and the Cardinal Cushing Field Days were also something that New York players took seriously.

"That used to be a big day. We played Connacht in Gaelic Park once and the following Sunday then we played them in Boston and I remember it was roaring hot. Joe Corcoran never stopped running around, it was perpetual motion. I was playing full-forward on Noel Tierney that day and I think I scored a goal and 10 points."

While all counties were affected by emigration to varying degrees, losing key players of the quality of Peter Nolan, Paddy Casey and the two Furlong brothers to emigration slowed Offaly's ascension to the top of the footballing ladder. Certainly, scoring power like Tom's wouldn't have gone amiss back home in the '60s.

◆ ◆ ◆ ◆

Martin Furlong was never much of a betting man but as Offaly prepared to face Laois in the 1968 Leinster semi-final in Tullamore he just couldn't resist. They had beaten Louth comfortably in the first round and he was confident they could get back to another Leinster final and win it this time. He threw down £5, a week's wages for him. The lost by 0-11 to 0-6, the clean sheet being the only source of consolation. He never bet on a game he was playing in again.

The Furlongs' Leinster senior final duck may have finally been broken in 1969 but the year promised so much more than that. In the spring Offaly qualified for their first National League final, breezing past Donegal in the semi-final. The league final arrangement with New York wasn't maintained in 1968 but in '69 the home final winners would travel to Gaelic Park for a two-legged final proper. It raised the unique prospect of two brothers playing against each other in a National League final if Offaly could get over Kerry in the home final. That's always a big if, as Offaly learned extensively in 1969.

In the league final a player from both sides was dismissed within four minutes of the start by referee Mick Loftus, though if John Smith's sending off affected Offaly, Pat Griffin's certainly didn't deter Kerry, who led by 2-7 to 0-4 at the break. Mick O'Dwyer crowned a fine personal display in the second half with his second goal of the day as

Kerry ran out comfortable 12-point winners. Offaly were something of a rabble by the end of the game in which they only managed three points from play.

"The more I saw of Offaly," wrote John D Hickey in the following day's *Irish Independent*, "the more my wonder grew at how they came to reach the home final and in the end I settled for the explanation, groundless though it may be, that they must be better than they were because this was so startlingly barren an hour for them."

A few days later Willie Bryan was driving out of Tullamore when he picked up a hitch-hiker bound for Kilbeggan. Bryan said he'd drop him at the petrol station coming into Kilbeggan. It was owned by a fellow Walsh Island man, Peter Nolan. In the meantime they got to talking about the game the previous Sunday.

"How would they win?" the passenger exclaimed. "I was at a wedding there on Saturday and Willie Bryan and Martin Furlong fell out of the place."

"Oh," said Willie, who wasn't at any wedding that weekend, "would you know the lads well?"

"Oh I know them well, very well."

He didn't make him any wiser and when they got to the station Peter Nolan greeted him warmly as he pulled in. When he was driving away Willie looked in his rear view mirror to see his passenger quiz Peter as to who he was and then raise his hands to his head as the awful truth dawned on him.

"I used to meet that fella for years and he'd cross the street then," says Bryan. "You didn't abuse the situation but if you were seen in a pub everything was multiplied by 10. You didn't have a right to be there. Some of us got that name, some of it stuck but in the most part it was lies. A lot of it would have stemmed from the likes of that clown."

Time would prove them to be better than they were that Sunday but it was Kerry who jetted out to New York for the final six weeks later. For all their past glories, Kerry's confidence was a little fragile at the time having endured a barren few years by their standards since winning their last All-Ireland in 1962. Galway beat them in the finals of 1964 and '65 while Down maintained their hex over them in the '68 decider. Their previous appearance in the home league final had also brought defeat to Galway in 1965. They needed this league title.

In glorious June sunshine at Gaelic Park, the first leg of the final proved to be something of a shootout between Tom Furlong and O'Dwyer, who both finished with seven points each. Legendary Kerry midfielder Mick O'Connell suffered a back injury after a heavy challenge in the fifth minute and had to be withdrawn. "I was disappointed getting injured the first day because personally I thought what happened to me was not accidental," he says. "It was intentional. When I jumped for the ball somebody came under my legs which was playing the man as distinct from the ball but that's the way it goes. I'm not complaining now but that's what happened. They were a couple of exciting games."

There was little between the sides throughout in the first leg though Kerry looked to have stolen victory when O'Dwyer fisted a point with two minutes remaining to put them back in front. Back then, there was a hooter in Gaelic Park which sounded to signify half- and full-time. With time almost up Furlong moved towards the Kerry goal with possession.

"The ball came out to centrefield and Mickey Moynihan got it and he hit it across to me. I was out about 40 yards, out near the sideline now where 'Lefty' Devine used to have his box to do his broadcasting. This Kerry guy jumped on my back and he wouldn't get off me. Who was it only O'Dwyer. I got up anyway and (referee) Paul Kelly said to me, 'You'll have to score direct'. It was about 40 yards near the sideline on the right hand side. That was the toughest kick I ever had." He nailed it as the hooter sounded for a 0-12 each draw.

O'Connell wasn't expected to play in the second leg having been unable to train all week but by the Saturday he was feeling reasonably ok. With Kerry struggling, Jackie Lyne turned to him in the second half and asked him to come on. He gave a masterful display and kicked six points, including a late equaliser in similar fashion to Furlong seven days earlier to leave the sides deadlocked once again at full-time.

Heads were scratched with regard to what should happen next. New York wanted a replay the following Sunday. Kerry's flights home were booked for the following day. After a considerable delay, Kerry got their wish and an extra half hour was ordered. O'Connell picked up where he left off in what is considered to be one of his finest ever displays, adding another three points as Kerry skated away from New York to win by nine points with the help of goals by Derry Crowley and Brendan Lynch.

Donie O'Sullivan, wing-back for Kerry in those games, explains: "A lot of us had been through losing three All-Ireland finals and you'd think you'd never go again and it was great to come back. That was the first thing Kerry won in seven or eight years so it was a great thing. Playing in Gaelic Park, you had to be on the top of your game to beat them. At that stage I think Kerry really wanted to win something. If they didn't win that it was really the end of the road I suppose."

The day that Kerry won that rip-roaring league final at Gaelic Park, June 29, 1969, proved to be a landmark one in the relatively modest history of Offaly GAA up to then. In a Croke Park triple header, the minor footballers beat Louth, the senior hurlers shocked reigning All-Ireland champions Wexford and the senior footballers coasted to a 12-point victory over Westmeath. A Leinster double was on the cards when the footballers reached their provincial final with a win over Wexford though the hurlers failed narrowly against Kilkenny in their Leinster final, losing by two points.

The following Sunday Offaly would play Kildare in the Leinster football final. Their opponents were trained by Peter O'Reilly, a man with an impeccable coaching CV. He lifted the Sam Maguire Cup as Dublin captain in 1942 and three years later guided the minor hurling and football sides to All-Ireland glory. Two years after that he was in charge of the Tyrone minor side that pipped Mickey Furlong's Offaly in the All-Ireland semi-final before beating Mayo in the final. He masterminded a string of St Vincent's Dublin county titles in the '50s and then steered his native county to the All-Ireland in 1958. He came to Offaly in the summer of 1960 and turned them into winners as they claimed a first Leinster title and came desperately close to adding an All-Ireland that year and in 1961.

He eventually left in 1963 due to the travel involved and later was coaxed back into coaching by Kildare in 1967. "I hated leaving them (Offaly) because I had a wonderful relationship with both players and officials," he said ahead of the '69 Leinster final. "And I certainly never thought that one day I would be plotting their downfall."

Ultimately O'Reilly's time in Kildare didn't prove to be anywhere near as fruitful as his previous postings. Offaly were the emerging force in Leinster and would prove to be an insurmountable obstacle to Kildare in the coming years, starting with that Leinster final which they won by 3-7 to 1-8 with Mick O'Rourke, Pat Keenan and captain Pat Monaghan scoring the goals. It was just Offaly's third Leinster senior title, their first in eight years and also the first to feature a Furlong after Mickey, Tom and Martin had each played in losing finals prior to that.

Down were expected to come through Ulster and provide Offaly's opposition as they had in the two previous occasions they competed in the All-Ireland series but Cavan shocked them in the provincial final. The All-Ireland semi-final ended in a draw with Offaly fortunate to earn another day out after Cavan sub Micheál Greenan dropped a free short from the 14-yard line late on. Offaly led the replay from start to finish, eventually winning 3-8 to 1-10, to reach the All-Ireland final where, for the second time that year, Kerry would be their opponents in a national decider.

Naturally, Offaly were fired up after the trimming they had suffered earlier in the year. Late in the league final, with the result a foregone conclusion, an aeroplane flew over Croke Park which triggered an opportunity for a Kerry player to engage in trash talk. Pointing to the plane, he goaded his opponent: "There's Aer Lingus, off to New York, we're going there now. Ye fuckers will be going home to foot the turf."

It was just Offaly's second All-Ireland final appearance and, amazingly, they retained the same full-back line of Paddy McCormack, Greg Hughes and Johnny Egan as they had in 1961. O'Connell, Kerry's spiritual leader, was carrying an injury in the lead up to the game but when their supporters saw that he was fit to take the field an unmerciful roar went up.

Kerry were the overwhelming favourites coming into the game but, having lost three All-Ireland finals in the previous five years, they didn't assert themselves particularly well when playing with a stiff breeze in the first half. Having kicked nine wides, their lead at the break was a meagre three points and Offaly were well placed to make history. They had an opportunity to swing the game in their favour in the first minute of the second half only for Kerry goalkeeper Johnny Culloty to make a magnificent save to deny Seán Evans. As the game progressed DJ Crowley took over at midfield, Kerry adapted to the conditions, carried the ball smartly into the wind and dogged it out. Offaly couldn't find the scores and lost an error strewn final by 0-10 to 0-7 in the end.

"It was swinging this way and that way," says Donie O'Sullivan. "Johnny Culloty made a save that would have swung it the other way. If you get a break at the right time like that it makes a big difference."

Offaly were still a maturing team and the gulf in experience proved decisive in the end, particularly against the game's aristocrats. It was an All-Ireland final that was very winnable but they didn't have the tools with their attack, once again, lacking balance amid questionable team selection. But, apart from the full-back line, it was a young side with potential to improve. That defeat would be a critical lesson in their development.

"They knew how to win, they knew how to play hard and, I can guarantee you, Kerry didn't win all their All-Irelands by being nice. We were gobshites as regards to winning All-Irelands," says Furlong frankly.

They returned to Tullamore the following night to a raucous reception from thousands that touched Furlong and the players deeply. Even now, his voice quivers with emotion as he recalls it.

"It brought tears to my eyes that so many people turned out and we had no cup. It was very disheartening. Very disheartening. We talked about it afterwards and said, 'Fuck this, this is not going to happen again. We're not going to come back losers again'. I think most of us were gobsmacked that night.

"You're standing on the back of a lorry and all hell is breaking loose and people are cheering and waving and wishing you well. After you losing. That was the one thing. It was different in '64 – you came home with a cup. But in '69 you came home with nothing, your tail between your legs and still all that number of people turned out. Somewhere along the line, long before that, we were deemed the Faithful County but that sure as God proved it. No doubt about it, it put a bit of steel into us because it was enough to be disappointed for yourself but when you see the thousands of people out there and what it meant. You felt you let your county down. You let your supporters down."

Young Tom Furlong was in the crowd that evening having come home especially for the final. He strongly considered staying for good. He had been engaged a few years earlier but it fell through. In the meantime he had started seeing Yvonne Crowley, a bubbly young girl from Co Clare. They were set to get married but Tom figured if he tied the knot in America he'd never come home. He spoke to Yvonne and she was happy to come back to Tullamore with him. They had met in Gaelic Park, where many's a lasting union was made Sunday after Sunday. Firstly, though, he needed a job.

"I was still playing good football then. If I was ever going to make a move I had to make it that time or that was it."

He spoke to John Dowling, the Offaly county secretary, and told him he'd stay if the county board could fix him up with a job. They got him an interview with Volkswagen.

"It covered the southern part of Ireland. If a garage couldn't handle a problem they sent it on to somebody else, then they finally got to me and I had to go out and settle it. I was interviewed for the job. It seemed like it was a done deal."

Furlong had a prominent local Volkswagen dealer put in a word for him and he was confident the job was his. Then word came back that they didn't want to give it to "a yank".

"I said, 'For fuck's sake, I'm only five years out of the country'."

And that was effectively that. The New York team came back to Ireland to play Kerry in what was dubbed the "World Cup" a few weeks after the All-Ireland in Croke Park. The week before the game New York played Offaly in O'Connor Park with the Furlong brothers in opposition. Offaly won by a point and, strangely, Tom failed to raise a flag. The New York-Kerry game formed a double header with the Offaly-Mayo Grounds Tournament semi-final replay. For the second Sunday running the two Furlongs would play on the same field but, ultimately, never for the same team.

Offaly won by five points while New York were soundly beaten by Kerry, who they had run so close only a few months earlier in the National League final. That league final proved to be the last involving New York as the exiles' subsequent exposure to top class sides from Ireland became limited from then on.

Tom Furlong flew back with the New York team, resigned to spending the rest of his life in America. Not that it was a prison sentence or anything like it. He made a good life for himself there and him and Yvonne married in October of the following year at St John's Church on Kingsbridge Avenue in the Bronx, just off Broadway.

Still, it would have been intriguing to see how things would have developed if he'd stayed at home and played a few years for Offaly. With or without him though, the team was going places.

In 1970 he was playing for the Transit Authority against the Police Department when he dived for a loose ball just as an opposition player drew back to strike it. He followed through, kicking him on the head and knocking him out cold. Furlong was rushed to Colombia Presbyterian Hospital where it was discovered he had a blood clot on the brain.

"They told me that if I got hit again there it'd be goodbye so that was it," he says.

He was only 26 but Tom Furlong's football career was effectively finished.

◆　　◆　　◆　　◆

Offaly subsequently lost the Grounds Tournament final to Kerry after a replay, their third defeat to them in a national final that year, but 1969 wasn't all bad for Martin Furlong. A few years earlier, while working in Wakefield's, he had taken a shine to Katie Mahon, a Mount Bolus girl who worked further down the town in Timmy Smollen's bike shop. Wakefield's had their fruit and vegetables on display at the front of the shop and Martin would make it his business to root around at them when he figured Katie would be passing by. He'd give her a nod or a wink as he built himself up to asking her out. He took the long way around at first though.

Her sister, Bridie, worked across the road from him in Egan's. He told her he fancied Katie and wondered would she put in a word for him. She did but Katie refused, partly because she took a dim view of him appointing her sister as a makeshift Cupid.

"I didn't know who he was," she laughs now. "I said, no, I wasn't going to go out with him. Bridie said, 'Oh he works in Wakefields and he's really nice, you should go out with him'. And I was like, 'No, no, if he wants to ask me out he has to come and ask himself'.

"So he plucked up the courage. He was being real nice to me and he came into Tim Smollen's one day."

Their courtship took off from there. Martin later began working on the road for Donnelly's, a sausage company, and got a mortgage and a site to build on in Clonminch, just on the outskirts of Tullamore. He initially planned to build on half the site and sell the other half.

"I can't say I ever had a serious chat with my father," says Martin. "But I know one thing, when I had bought the site for the house, I had got planning permission for two houses on it. The one bit of advice that I ever took off him, I'd know for certain is, he said, 'If I was you, I'd put your house in the middle of the site'. And he said, 'You have the lane going up that way and you have the field the other side of you, that will never be sold'. That's what I did and I'm glad I did."

Himself and Katie were married on June 4, 1969. It was a glorious day which, it was felt, would be spoiled without a game of football. Someone nipped out to buy a ball and a full scale game ensued among the men in the front lawn of the County Arms Hotel in Birr. Still in their suits and with their shirts sticking to them, they laid waste to a host of flower beds while Katie et al waited for their husbands to return from playing football, something of an analogy for the years to come.

"Hottest day of the year," Martin recalls. "There were people melting in the County Arms that day. And we never looked back."

CHAPTER 11

THE FAITHFUL'S FIRST

LIKE many footballers, Martin Furlong's recollection of most of the big games he played in is hazy at best. No man pulled on the Offaly jersey more often than he did so perhaps it's understandable to a degree that some games get meshed together and others are completely forgotten. In a quirk of the mind, however, if you were to ask him about the car he was driving at a particular point in his life he'd most likely be able to quote the make, model and number plate for you. Quiz him about a famous save made in front of tens of thousands at Croke Park and it will most likely leave him scratching his head.

But ask him about the 1970 Leinster final defeat to Meath and he'll quote chapter and verse. For him and many of the Offaly players of that era it's the only scoreline that they can remember clearly. 2-22 to 5-12. It was a travesty of a defeat that threatened to break them. That it was and still is widely considered to be one of the greatest games ever played may be interpreted as more of a patronising nod to the Offaly players than a source of consolation.

Offaly had lost a two-game series in New York, who were minus Tom Furlong, in May of 1970 but reached the Leinster final after beating Westmeath and Longford after a replay. But this Leinster final would be different to any other game played before. A rule change came into effect that year whereby provincial finals and All-Ireland semi-finals and finals would be played over 80 minutes in both hurling and football, a practice that lasted until 1974, after which all championship games were then played to a 70-minute duration. So, in essence, this Leinster final would be 20 minutes longer than any game these players had ever played in their lives. Who coped best with that would go a long way towards determining the outcome.

Meath surged into an early lead, scoring the first five points without reply, but Offaly went on a scoring spree that appeared to be decisive as two goals from Murt Connor and one each from Seán

Cooney and Kieran Claffey sent them in with a seemingly unassailable 4-7 to 0-9 half-time lead. Team manager Alo Kelly insisted that they keep the pressure on in the early stages of the second half. "Get the first score of the second half," he said, "and we have these boys." Paddy Fenning duly obliged, kicking the first point after half-time to extend Offaly's lead to a whopping 11 points.

They didn't appear to be in any great danger when still leading by seven points after 55 minutes though a madcap couple of minutes saw that advantage wiped out. Offaly were making a switch between right corner-back Eugene Mulligan and left half-back Pat Monaghan. Amid the confusion Meath's left corner-forward Mickey Fay was left idle and scored two goals in the space of 30 seconds. Mick Mellett kicked over the equaliser.

Kelly had felt the momentum of the game shifting in Meath's favour. The selection process that governed the Offaly team remained very unseemly even at that time and he was blocked from making a substitution by the band of selectors.

"When I was manager I hadn't a say," he says. "I was manager of Offaly in '70 but I wasn't a selector. I wanted to make a change but they wouldn't let me."

After Mellett's equaliser, Kieran Claffey pointed to put Offaly back in front but Meath had all the impetus and pushed three points in front with time almost up. Willie Bryan punched a goal to draw Offaly level again.

"I know that when they got the goal," says Mattie Kerrigan of Meath, "Seán McCormack was in goals for us and Bertie Cunningham grabbed him by the back of the jersey and ran him out the field with the ball to kick it out and I happened to win the kickout and passed it on to Tony Brennan. He kicked a great point from the left hand side of the field."

Offaly would have one more chance to save themselves. Mulligan tore up the field and took a pass from Tony McTague, who anticipated a return ball. It never came.

"I kicked the last ball wide in that game and I should have given it to Tony McTague, who was running alongside me," says Mulligan ruefully. "We would have got out of there with a draw. I was captain of that team. The odd point in 55."

The final whistle sounded on the kickout.

"That is a game that I will bring to my grave," says Furlong. "Mattie Kerrigan scored points that day with his back turned to the goal and kicked them over his head, over his shoulder and over the bar. The two goals came from fuck arounds. Of games lost, and you can include All-Irelands in it, that's the biggest hurt. After the match was devastation. Devastation. How could you lose that match? As far as I'm concerned, in my lifetime of playing games, that was the hardest thing to swallow."

Despite the fact that Offaly had much the younger team, Furlong is in no doubt that they didn't handle the 20-minute increase in duration at all by comparison to Meath. Although they only lost by a point, they were comfortably outscored by Meath, who registered 2-13 to Offaly's 1-5 in the second half.

"I'll tell you why he's right," offers Kerrigan. "We had a new trainer in that period, Micheál Campbell, and Micheál was one of the new Gormanston coaches. They were into the fitness thing in a big way and we did a huge amount of training that year. So I would agree with Martin and say that we were fitter in that game.

"Brendan Hayden refereed it and I actually was talking to Brendan last year down in Carlow and he was telling me that Willie Bryan got on to him. 'Bejayus,' he says, 'Brendan, are you going to give me a free at all today?' And Brendan says to him, 'I will, as soon as you get fouled!' There wasn't a whole lot of cynical fouling in it but it was a great game of football, a very entertaining game. When we were back in the dressing room, you still wondered had you won the match.

"In 1970, Offaly were certainly on the cusp. We would have known that this was a team that was going to win something in the next few years."

He was right. Their darkest hour came before dawn.

◆　◆　◆　◆

Paddy McCormack didn't play in the 1970 Leinster final having been sidelined with a ruptured Achilles tendon for the year. His leadership certainly wouldn't have gone amiss as Meath eroded Offaly's advantage in that second half. Johnny Egan played corner-back that day but the great old full-back line that had served the county for a decade was breaking up. Egan and Greg Hughes never started another championship game for Offaly after 1970 and as the championship approached in '71 McCormack had auditioned extensively at full-back.

McCormack's footballing education as a youngster was cutting edge. He grew up right beside Jack Casey's old forge in Croghan. Jack's sons Mick and Paddy later took over the running of it before Paddy moved to Dublin to work for Guinness and then emigrated to New York not long after Mickey Furlong. The young McCormack looked up to the giant-like Casey brothers. They may have been the best footballers in Offaly but they were more than that. By being selected regularly on Leinster teams the Caseys carried a rare prestige in the county.

"Sure that's what started me off really," says McCormack. "Back in them days there was no such thing as cars, it was all bikes. We used to drop home the turf, myself and Paddy Casey, with an ass and cart, and we'd bring a football with us and he used to put me in the goals and he'd be kicking them in to me. I was only a nipper, six or seven. We used to always play in Casey's in front of the forge, Flynn's Field, about 20 or 30 lads there every night playing football and I followed the balls for them."

By the time McCormack got to play for Offaly, Mick Casey was heading for the veteran stage of his career though still hanging on in the hope of making the breakthrough after years of near misses. In the first round of the 1960 Leinster Championship, Offaly were struggling against Carlow. McCormack and Casey were on the bench. McCormack was best known as a forward at the time but when corner-back Phil O'Reilly got injured he was dispatched in his place alongside

Hughes and Egan. That was the day that the legendary full-back line was first formed.

Casey was introduced as a sub, Offaly got out with a three-point win and the blacksmith was never left on the bench for the rest of his career. He got a couple of Leinsters but didn't win an All-Ireland medal, a fate that looked like it may befall McCormack too, particularly after sitting out 1970.

He was an uncompromising footballer to say the least and the nickname 'The Ironman from Rhode' was coined with him in mind.

"It got me more belts," he says. "The Iron Man? I was no more iron than anyone else. It's just we were hard. Mick Casey was the iron man really. He was the blacksmith from Rhode. We were tough nuts. We didn't let anything pass if we could at all.

"I was there for a long time and I was there in the tough times. When I was a young lad and we were going to play Kerry in the '50s, '59 or that, by Jaysus you got a belt going for it, you got a belt when you got it, you got a belt when you were kicking it. That was the game at that time."

In 1986 McCormack took a trip to New York and, as usual, was staying with Paddy Casey. Casey gave him instructions on what bus he should take from the airport to his home but when he boarded McCormack was informed that the exact fare was required. Having only stepped off the plane, he didn't have any change on him though the bus driver was Irish and asked him where he was from.

"Says I, 'Offaly'. And he says, 'What part of Offaly?' 'Rhode'. He says, 'Did you ever hear of the Iron Man from Rhode?' Says I, 'I did'. Lord Jaysus, it's a small world. Says I, 'Was it Mick Casey?' 'No, it was Paddy McCormack'. Says I, 'You're talking to him'. He stopped the bus, gave me a whole heap of tickets for the rest of the week. Three thousand miles away. Unbelievable, isn't it?"

While he was certainly unflinching, the nickname overshadows his footballing ability to a degree. Because McCormack could play.

"Paddy was more threatening," says Mattie Kerrigan. "He would be talking on the field of play. He'd be reminding lads that if they came in near him that he'd put them back out again but I played on him on umpteen occasions and he'd certainly foul you alright but I don't remember him doing anything untoward. I suppose if he got a cowardly lad he might run him out of the place alright. He was a good footballer, that's what he was. A good reader of the game."

Over the years, Offaly had fiddled with McCormack in different positions but he was a corner-back first and foremost. Adapting to full-back at 32 years of age in 1971 was a big ask. Playing in front of Furlong, who was something of an auxiliary full-back himself, added an extra layer of comfort and insulation though as McCormack found his feet on the edge of the square.

"Martin wouldn't draw back anyway and that is the truth," says McCormack. "You know there's safety behind you all the time. I never liked full-back. Corner-back was a grand position to play, in my book."

Bizarre as it might seem given the premium placed on kickouts in today's game, back then, goalkeepers generally didn't take them. Indeed their only duty surrounding restarts was to, almost patronisingly, place the ball for the full-back to bomb it down the field as far as he could, which in Offaly's case was McCormack.

By then, the Rhode bulwark's leadership skills had seen him absorbed into the management team. Fr Tom Gilhooley, the Tullamore-based curate who was in charge of the successful minor team of 1964, was appointed as manager with Alo Kelly his right hand man. McCormack and Seán Brereton were the additional selectors and Tom Darcy was the physical trainer. At last, after years of complicated, unwieldy and incompetent managerial set ups, Offaly had a more streamlined management team that would dovetail nicely together as it proved.

"Now, Fr Gilhooley was a great man," says Willie Bryan, "but Kelly was the brains." It's an opinion that is almost universally held among the Offaly footballers of that era. But Gilhooley carried a strong presence in the dressing room, where he gave stirring orations, and fostered a feel good factor around the camp. Critically, he had a knack for keeping the wives and girlfriends onside.

"Women today wouldn't put up with the shit that women put up with that time," says Furlong. "Out training and drinking and that. It was accepted then more. By most women. I won't say them all, but by most."

"Alo did, we'll say, the football skills and the match but Gilhooley would be in the middle of the field roaring at you," says Mick O'Rourke. "He had another great habit as well. If you were gone back a little bit in training or something, he'd go down to you and he'd say, 'Take a walk', and he'd chat you to see if there was anything bothering you. He was brilliant that way, a brilliant man-manager."

Offaly played Longford in the first round of the Leinster Championship in 1971 and won comfortably. Paddy Fenning looked to have nailed down a spot at wing-forward and Oliver McGlinchey, father of his girlfriend, now wife, Kathryn, had invited him to go on holiday to Spain well in advance. It turned out that the trip clashed with the Leinster semi-final against Laois. He went to Spain, and paid a heavy price when he returned after Offaly's eight-point victory. At his first training session back one team mate "signed his autograph with his cogs" down his leg. He failed to win his starting place back for the rest of the year.

"Fr Gilhooley, first of all, ignored me for a whole month because I let the boys down," Fenning recalls. "Going to Spain in 1971 was like going to Mars. These fellas, while they did trips to America and all that, I was a little bit of an upstart going off and arriving back. And I had to take an awful lot of shite in there. Imagine going over to Edenderry, that's where we trained, and me with my townie brown legs trying to play in and out with these fellas."

Offaly only had three Leinster titles to their name at senior level and each of them had come with a struggle. But, steeled by the lessons of the previous couple of years, Offaly were now reaching a level of maturity, backed up by a more harmonious set up, and they cruised through the province in 1971. They crushed Kildare the Leinster final. Approaching half-time they were leading by 1-10 to 0-0 when O'Rourke conceded a free which allowed Kildare to get off the mark just before they headed for the dressing room. McCormack read the riot act at half-time and lit on him.

"What the fuck were you thinking of? We could have had these fuckers with nothing on the scoreboard!"

Offaly met Kildare in numerous Leinster finals in that era which only served to heat up the rivalry between the bordering counties further. A few Offaly players were based in Dublin at the time and would stop off in places like Prosperous and Clane on their way back from training in Edenderry for a jar or two. The locals would get to chatting them and, being Kildare people, were eternally optimistic about their team's prospects and weren't shy about putting a wager on it. The bets would be modest enough to start out with but they'd roll on week on week as Offaly kept winning. By the end of it, the Offaly players would have the price of a nice holiday in Kerry.

In the All-Ireland semi-final Cork were beaten by five points with McTague striking 0-9 against his county of birth. "I'm lucky," Fr Gilhooley told reporters after the game. "I've got a bunch of lads who would do anything I ask and I've got a million people praying for us." He then visited three hospitals before reaching the team hotel for the post-match meal.

"They had us written off that time and we beat them," says Bryan. "I do particularly remember the semi-final and it was hardly worth our while turning up. I think we beat them reasonably easy. There was a cockiness in Cork; you didn't have that in Kerry. Kerry treated you with great respect."

Galway would be their final opponents, a team that Offaly enjoyed a good record against at that time. They certainly weren't anywhere near as formidable as when they had the all conquering side of the mid-'60s. On all known form it ought to have been as straightforward a victory as Offaly had been enjoying throughout their run to September but finals rarely come that easy, especially to a county desperate to make a breakthrough.

While Offaly's followers were hugely supportive of the team after they had come home beaten in finals before, there was a different feel to this decider for the players, which brought its own pressure. They were the strong favourites and having contested a couple of senior finals and won a minor title in the '60s before losing an epic to Meath in '70, the only logical progression was for Offaly to finally claim the Sam Maguire Cup. If they lost in '71, there would be no scope for filing it away as another valuable lesson learned and looking to next year. This final just had to be won.

Whatever Offaly's shortcomings, fitness wasn't one of them, as it may have been in 1970 when Meath pipped them in their first 80-minute game. The physical trainer, Tom Darcy, had trained in Strawberry Hill in London and adapted them to the longer contests.

"I remember Tom Darcy told us after a very, very hard session, 'Now, you're doing the same training as Arsenal when they won the double'," says Paddy Fenning. "You feel good when you hear something like that."

However, if the charge of being a fanatical trainer was levelled at Martin Furlong it would immediately have been thrown out on the grounds of flimsy evidence. On the dark winter nights when Darcy subjected them to seemingly never-ending laps, they'd find their way around the field with the help of car lights shining at one end. Bryan wasn't too keen on training either and one night in Ballycommon when he reached relative darkness at the opposite end, he slipped in behind a tree figuring Darcy wouldn't miss him if he took a break for a lap or two. Furlong was already there, sitting at the butt of the tree.

"If I was to try and pick something you could say bad about him, I couldn't," says Bryan. "But he hated training. There was some great lads to train and we were definitely two that, well we did our share, there's no doubt, but we certainly could have done an awful lot more."

Offaly was humming with expectation as the game approached but Martin Furlong could barely get out of bed as the most momentous day of his footballing life approached. He was struck down by a dose of the flu and a ripple of panic spread throughout the team and management. An All-Ireland final was no testing ground for a rookie goalkeeper. Mercifully, by the weekend he was improved sufficiently and would start in goal.

By then, Furlong had a long established habit of taking a swig of brandy in the dressing room before a game. He'd take it out onto the field with him and maybe avail of the odd sip during the game too. He had always suffered with nervousness and sleep would never come easy on the week of a big game. He'd yawn incessantly in the dressing room before a game and was constantly in and out of the toilet, usually producing little more than a dribble.

The brandy gave him a bit of "false courage", as he calls it now. It became a ritual among him and a few of his team mates to take a drop in the corner of the dressing room, huddling around the bottle wrapped up in a towel so as to douse Fr Gilhooley's suspicions.

"It was only years after that we discovered Gilhooley knew the whole time," says O'Rourke. "He reckoned it was doing no harm."

All-Ireland final day, September 26, 1971, was not conducive to good football with high wind and driving rain. Offaly had no experience of winning All-Ireland finals and Galway had very little themselves, with only a few of the three-in-a-row side still on board. With so much at stake, it all added up to a desperately poor spectacle played to a low standard throughout. Gaelic football was much more of a kicking game back then with aerial duels taking place all over the field as the ball was launched long and often. Even at that, gone was the fluency that marked Offaly's play in their march to the final, particularly in the early stages.

Following their semi-final win over Down, Galway lost their free-taker, Joe McLoughlin, to a knee injury. In the final they had a range of players on place-kicking duty, none of them to any great degree of success. Early on Liam Sammon drove what should have been a routine close range free in front of the posts in around crossbar height. Furlong batted it out and was fouled as he went to retrieve possession in the goal mouth scramble. Amid all the excitement, he drew a punch on Galway corner-forward Jimmy Duggan, leaving him sprawling. Referee Paul Kelly of Dublin awarded the free out for the initial foul on Furlong and took no further action against the Offaly goalkeeper. He was fortunate not to get the line and puts his over the top reaction down to early nervousness.

"I'd say that was a lot to do with it. Jimmy Duggan was one of the finest footballers that ever laced a boot. An exceptionally clean player. You ask me why I did it? I don't know. To this day I don't know. It's just put down as a mystery of religion."

There was unmerciful skelping going on in various parts of the field, not least in the Offaly full-back line. Kelly called over Bryan, the Offaly captain and midfielder, and asked him to have a word with McCormack and Co before he was forced to send one of them off.

"Willie was the captain but McCormack was the old stager," says Furlong. "Willie, in fairness to him, wouldn't be pushing himself. He wouldn't be saying, 'I'm the man, I'm the captain of this team and this is what we're going doing...' and that sort of shit. He'd have his few words to say but McCormack was the leader. He was the guy you looked up to."

It was in that context that Bryan faced into his full-back line asking them to tone it down a little.

"O'Rourke and McCormack and Ryan, they were mowing all round them," he says. "So I toddle in. I was only 23 or 24. Imagine going into McCormack... But anyway, I was seen to go in, 'By Jesus, take it easy lads...' or words to that effect. 'Get out to fuck,' says McCormack. 'If you were catching it out there we wouldn't have it in here!'"

"That was the sort the team was," McCormack maintains. "It was a big family. No one got insulted. It was only for the game. One day Mick Ryan got an unmerciful rap on the back and he came to me, 'Paddy, me back is sore'. 'If it is, Mick, fuck out and let in somebody else'. It was better like that. You know what goes on on a football field."

Galway centre-back TJ Gilmore doesn't remember anything out of the ordinary in the physical stakes, saying, "It was more part of the game at the time. Maybe there were some heavy tackles went in at the other end of the field from where I was and there were a few individuals on that Offaly team that had a reputation for being physical and maybe over robust. There was a lot of teams around with players like that but I certainly wouldn't be condemning their tactics or anything.

"The game was there to be won and whatever it took to win it, that's football. Nobody asks questions afterwards. I wouldn't say it was a deciding factor that day. I'd be a player myself that would like to play it physically and take the hits and give them and get on with the game."

In the 18th minute of the match, another Sammon free dropped short and appeared to be sailing harmlessly into Furlong's hands. But he spilled it and as another scramble ensued McCormack's boot made contact with Furlong's head and left him flat, face down, on the ground. It broke to Séamus Leydon, who booted the loose ball to the net for the game's opening goal. Furlong received treatment but, at this remove years later, is in no doubt that he was concussed. "I was in cuckoo land. I couldn't see any further than midfield before half-time."

Offaly were rattled collectively too. McTague had amassed a personal tally of 1-29 over the course of the summer but drove a routine free wide from in front of the posts shortly afterwards. Furlong, despite his ailment, made a great diving save from Duggan at a stage when Offaly were treading water. They got to the dressing room at half-time trailing by five points. Any more than that and there mightn't have been a way back for them. Fr Gilhooley offered his usual stirring few words at the break and then McCormack asked him to leave the dressing room before taking centre stage. Given that his head was spinning from McCormack's stray boot, Furlong's recollection of the scene is no more than hazy, but he can hum the tune.

"He didn't want Fr Gilhooley to hear the few fucks that he was going to let fly out of him. I think he told us we were playing 'like fucking oul' ones'. Like oul' ones. And he read the riot act anyway and he said if we didn't get the finger out of our ass and go out and play like men that we were going to lose this All-Ireland too and that, in his book, was not kosher anyway."

The rain fell in torrents throughout the second half, forcing spectators to scurry back from the front rows of the stands for cover. Early on, Offaly made a key switch with John Smith coming on for Kieran Claffey, slotting in at centre-back as Nicholas Clavin moved to midfield alongside Bryan. By the 14th minute of the half they were level.

Leydon pushed Galway back in front with a free but Clavin equalised once more. Offaly took a decisive lead through Murt Connor at the midway stage of the half after he fielded a Seán Evans centre and fired it to the net and though Galway quickly responded with Leydon's second goal of the day, the momentum of the game was moving in Offaly's direction. Evans kicked a point and McTague floated over a 45 to give them a two-point lead with 13 minutes remaining.

The closing stages were low on quality but the entertainment value and level of drama wasn't diminished for that. Galway laid siege to the Offaly goal but couldn't work a score. Frank Canavan broke through at one stage and was met by McCormack's elbow into the cheek.

"I hit him a shocking belt that day," McCormack admits. "I was sorry after but sure we won the All-Ireland. All over that rap I lost an All Star that year."

Leydon missed the resultant free, one of a few that went awry for Galway in the closing stages. "We really went into that All-Ireland final with no recognised free-taker on the team and it cost us dearly because we missed quite a lot of scoreable frees," says Gilmore. "When I look on the Offaly side, Tony McTague was kicking 45s over and we'd been missing them from much closer. You can't get across the finish line by missing them sort of chances. On the day, if we had taken our chances the result could have been different but on balance, throughout the year, Offaly would have been slightly the better team overall from one to 15."

With a couple of minutes left Kevin Kilmurray kicked another point for Offaly. It was an insurance score and he knew it as he embraced his team mates close by. They held out for a 1-14 to 2-8 victory. The downpour became an irrelevance as Offaly people flooded the field.

Among them was young Tom Furlong, home from America for the game. It was too much of a stretch for Mickey, who had an ever expanding family in New Jersey at the time. Tom lost his wallet amid the bedlam as he made his way down to the Canal End goal to find his brother where he embraced him having fought off a few supporters for the privilege.

Someone had given Tom a t-shirt with "Offaly, All-Ireland Champions 1971" written on it before the game. He had cast off the drenched shirt he was wearing over it by the time he reached the team banquet in the South County Hotel later that evening. He was sitting at the top table as president of the Offaly Association in New York while all around him were suited and booted. "But it was a big hit," says Tom of his attire, "a lot of people got their photographs taken with me wearing the t-shirt."

Tullamore was heaving the following night but it was all lost on Martin Furlong. Having been driven to tears by the reception when they returned home beaten in 1969, now he was in no fit state to take any of it in. His head was frazzled from the moment he shipped the blow the day before and he had no recollection of much of the game, Willie Bryan lifting the cup, his brother's embrace or any of the post-match celebrations. The team doctor, Brendan White, could tell he was rattled and took him home early from the Central Ballroom.

By Tuesday he was back on his feet and looking to make up for lost time. The cup would be going to Walsh Island, home of the captain. "Walsh Island put on a woeful spread," says Bryan, "probably one of the biggest things that ever happened in Walsh Island. They had a big marquee and it was packed and the heavens opened, a horrible night. Martin and Kieran Claffey stayed in our house. Poor oul' Claff, he had a great way about him, a lovely fella. But he woke up and he didn't know in the name of Jaysus where he was.

"My mother always had the pan on anyway and Kieran was as sick as a dog. Of course the last thing Kieran wanted now was a fry. By Jaysus, they weren't leaving until they were fed anyway. I know

Martin held it down alright but on the way back in, Claffey had to stop and he let the whole thing out. You could have put it back on the plate."

In May of the previous year Martin and Katie celebrated the arrival of their first child, Joan, and Katie was heavily pregnant again. She went into labour the Friday after the All-Ireland. As was customary back then, Martin dropped her to the maternity ward in Tullamore General Hospital and headed off about his business, most of which involved celebrating with the week that was in it. Word reached him later in the day that his first son, Ken, had been born.

As if the festivities didn't need another dimension, Tom, just back up from the Listowel Races, landed into Hayes' Hotel where the champagne was flowing to be told that he too was a father. His wife Yvonne wasn't due for another three weeks but had gone into labour the night before. The Furlong house didn't have a phone and, in any event, that was the last place to find him that week.

Tom put a call through to the Union Hospital on Fordham Road. His friend Joe Wrafter had told him Yvonne had given birth to a girl and when he eventually got her on the line, he exclaimed, "A girl!" "What?" she said, "a boy!" "Oh, there's two of them?" The line went dead and Tom repaired to the bar to celebrate the birth of twins. In reality, Wrafter was misinformed, Yvonne hadn't had a girl or even twins, just a baby boy.

The nurses in Tullamore General had suggested to Katie that she should call her baby Sam for obvious reasons. She was having none of it. Neither was Yvonne. Tom sneaked onto a flight back to New York and landed in the hospital with Wrafter, insisting his son be called Sam Maguire Furlong. He needn't have bothered. In America, the child's name had to be registered very soon after the birth. "Call him after his father and his grandfather," Yvonne had already told the nurse. Tommy it was.

For all the joy and emotion, that All-Ireland week wasn't without its poignant moments either. A number of years earlier, old Tom Furlong had staved off prostate cancer and came back strongly from it too. But now the cancer had returned, in his stomach. He was ill for quite some time and before one of the games that year a journalist quizzed Martin as to whether he would play if his father passed away. He thought the question insensitive but answered it nonetheless. He'd have played because he was in no doubt that that's what his father would have wanted.

He was in no position to attend the All-Ireland final and watched it from his hospital bed. Martin and Willie Bryan brought the cup in to him on the Tuesday morning after the game.

"We had a bottle of brandy, we put a drop into the cup and he took a little sip out of it," Martin recalls, filled with emotion. "A token sip out of it. He was very weak at the time. It meant a lot to him."

"I know my father got a great kick out of it," says Tom, "that he got his hands on the cup anyway."

By the following May he hadn't much time left and was allowed home. He was in considerable pain and it was unbearable for the family to watch. Near the end, he looked to Margaret, grabbed her by the wrist and called out to her.

"It was amazing," says Martin. "It was like he knew. He'd grab her arm, and you'd want to see the strength in that man, he buried his hand into her."

He drifted into unconsciousness there and then and died the following day.

CHAPTER 12

CROWNING GLORY

THE All Star scheme was rolled out for the first time following the 1971 championship and Offaly had four representatives, Eugene Mulligan, Nicholas Clavin, Willie Bryan and Tony McTague, a tally that subsequent history would reflect as a low one for All-Ireland champions. Mulligan, though, was the only player nominated for the right half-back position such was the quality of his performances throughout the campaign. He was also named as the Texaco Footballer of the Year. Furlong was pipped to the goalkeeping position by Galway's PJ Smyth, his error resulting in the first goal in the All-Ireland final most likely costing him.

Writing in his *Sunday Independent* column several years ago, Colm O'Rourke recalled how he and a bunch of footballers sat down to pick an All Star line-up of a different variety – the dirtiest team of all time – while on a session one night. He claimed that the concept had to be abandoned after five of the first six positions were filled by Offaly players of the '70s. Granted, O'Rourke was writing in a tongue-in-cheek fashion but in its own way his tale reflected the perception of that Offaly team. While they were no shrinking violets, the hard man image has tended to overshadow their footballing ability to a degree.

That impression begins, though certainly doesn't end, with Furlong in goal. He makes no apologies for how he or his teammates played the game.

"Do you think Kerry won all their All-Irelands by being nice guys? Any team that ever won an All-Ireland had to be hard. We just did what other teams had done to us. We learned. Nice guys don't win. I honestly saw nothing only the ball. And whatever was in front of me, I took with it."

He cites Bernard Brogan's opening goal in the 2013 All-Ireland final, when the Dublin forward flicked Paul Flynn's long delivery to the net as Mayo goalkeeper Rob Hennelly advanced off his line, as something anathema to him.

"My idea of that is either go and take the whole lot in front of you or stay, and he did neither. Now, I don't consider myself a dirty player. I was only sent off once in my life when I was only a kid. Other people might think differently but it was hard times. If I didn't make my mark I would have paid the price."

Sometimes his teammates paid the price. In a league game down in Kerry once, John Smith was playing in the full-back line and when a ball went over the top at one stage in the game he raced back towards the Offaly goal to gather possession along with an opposition forward. Furlong flew off his line and jumped to collect the ball with his knees in the air, following straight through into Smith's chest.

"He's lying on the ground with two broken ribs and he grey in the face. I remember him saying, 'You rotten fucker, you rotten fucker!' And he got carted off."

If his own teammates were wary of him, then he certainly inflicted a fear factor in many opposing forwards.

"I'd say there was one or two of the Kildare lads that were a bit afraid of him alright," smiles Eugene Mulligan. "I won't mention names."

Those that played against Offaly in that era don't seem to quibble too much with their approach.

"I'd say Offaly had a reputation that Meath had as well, which was of being a tough team that could play football," says Mattie Kerrigan. "I played against them on umpteen occasions and I could safely say, looking back over it, I can't remember something that was done on the field that you would complain about. They were tough.

"They were hard men and they played it hard, they played it tough but they were good footballers and I think that's a thing that Meath in the '80s were as well. They were tough lads but they could play football. I think that's why Meath fellas have a huge respect for Offaly players."

"They were hard and fair," adds Donie O'Sullivan. "They were tough. I think if anybody stood shoulder to shoulder I wouldn't crib with them anyhow. What I found afterwards is that if they would give it they would certainly take it as well and they wouldn't complain. That's my truthful summation. I had great respect for Offaly."

Offaly resumed competitive action after winning the All-Ireland with a string of victories, including a useful eight-point win over Kerry, in the National League that was only halted when they drew with Mayo in the semi-final. They lost the replay but no one was too fussed. Having won an All-Ireland which they were setting out to defend, going bull-headed for a league title was never going to be a priority.

GAA history has shown that there are few rookie champions that go on to retain the All-Ireland. Even the great Dublin and Kerry teams that came after Offaly had to regroup after winning their first titles together before putting All-Irelands back to back thereafter. In Offaly, it was particularly challenging for players to refocus in light of becoming the first group of players from the county to win an All-Ireland. The whole of Offaly went crazy on the back of it.

"It's heavy oul' going but, again, you were young and it was a novelty," says Furlong of the schedule he and his teammates endured throughout the winter. It's commonly said that winning an All-Ireland is a life-changing event but he just shrugs at the notion. "I don't think it does, I don't think it should. What are you going to change? Unless you go around and get a swelled head or something."

Offaly's impressive league form in 1971/72 suggests that the players struck the right balance between the festivities and football. Things were different then in that the league kicked in a few weeks after the All-Ireland final whereas now players largely switch off from football for three months until the New Year.

"You were All-Ireland champions then. You were a sitting duck. People wanted to take you down. You had to be on your game. They'd give you a guard of honour going out on the pitch and then try and kick the shite out of you."

Again, Offaly encountered little difficulty in Leinster. Meath may have broken their hearts in the Leinster final of two years earlier but Offaly had bloomed since then. They cruised into the provincial decider with nine points to spare over them and for the third time in four years Kildare were their final opponents. They only got two points closer than Meath did. The tricoloured hooped jersey was becoming a symbol of something unyielding and relentless. While Offaly were making roadkill of most opposition, they had a psychological hex on many teams when it came to the crunch in tighter encounters too. As Willie Bryan puts it, even if they were behind late on, they still knew they were going to win. And the opposition invariably knew it too.

"We had that on teams," says Bryan. "You never accepted defeat. Teams often played into your hands thinking, 'Jaysus, you'll never have these hoors beaten'. Meath were great for that. They'd never let go. But we had that in Offaly. Unfortunately, we've lost it. Certainly back then we were probably thick enough not to realise when we were beaten. We won an awful lot of matches that we shouldn't have won."

In the All-Ireland semi-final that year Offaly faced something of an unknown quantity in Donegal, who had won their first Ulster title under the stewardship of player-manager Brian McEniff.

"Roscommon had played Kerry the week before," McEniff recalls, "and suffered an awful beating. The late John D Hickey said in the paper during the week that they'd have to close the door of Croke Park to keep the crowd in, such was the beating we were going to get, which greatly peeved me.

"But I suppose I was a young, enthusiastic manager at the time. I knew that we had good footballers. We measured up to Offaly that day. Martin Carney scored a good goal and to this day I still don't know why it was disallowed but had we got that we would have been up seven points at half-time which would have been a sizeable lead. We were exceptionally fit, physically fit, but in the heel of the hunt they had that experience.

"They were a tough team but they were a good team. They were tight boys but they were good footballers. Furlong in goals, he was a great one. He was a huge shotstopper and he was brave to a degree where it was dangerous."

Offaly beat Donegal by four points in the end to set up the type of challenge the team was desperate for: Kerry in an All-Ireland final.

Three years earlier they didn't have the know-how, experience and all-round ability required to take down the game's market leaders. Now they were sure they had all those qualities in abundance. The final the previous year against Galway was an underwhelming affair in which Offaly stumbled to victory in the end. Performing against and beating Kerry in a final would remove any asterisk placed beside their breakthrough success of 1971.

"Right enough, we did just fall over the line in '71 and we nearly handed it to them but, yeah, '72 was a different ball game," says Bryan. "The monkey was off our back and you played then with a bit of freedom. You felt you could express yourself."

In the final Offaly were never led at any stage and took a two-point advantage to the dressing room at half-time. In the second half they were seemingly well on the way to retaining their title when Seán Cooney goaled to put them five points up, not long after Furlong had brilliantly denied Dan Kavanagh at the other end. "I went out and Dan Kavanagh got in behind me and Martin came and took him, ball and all out of it," says Paddy McCormack. "That's what you want." But, straight after Cooney's strike, Brendan Lynch gave Furlong no chance, rifling the ball into the top corner of his net from some 20 yards.

Lynch kicked a point with 13 minutes remaining to draw Kerry level. A point from Kevin Kilmurray and a free by McTague, who had miscued a few earlier efforts, nudged Offaly ahead once more but Lynch was on hand to halve the deficit before Paudie Lynch placed Mick O'Dwyer to kick the equaliser with three minutes remaining. It finished level and the replay would be held three weeks later.

"If anything, I'd say we were lucky enough to draw it, maybe," admits Kerry's Donie O'Sullivan. "That's what I can recall of it."

The general consensus was that Offaly, having bossed much of the game and failed to get the result, had missed their chance. Kerry, after all, hadn't lost a replay since Cork beat them in the 1956 Munster final. It was five years before that again since they had lost a replay at Croke Park.

Tom Furlong dug deep in his pockets. He had been back to Ireland in April of that year when his father's health was deteriorating badly. Within a couple of months he was home to bury him and then again for the All-Ireland final. A fourth trip to Ireland in the space of six months was more than he could afford. One of his regular watering holes in New York at the time was a bar called the Lakes of Sligo. The owner, Peter McAleer, heard of his predicament and came to him one evening. "Tommy, you'd want to get home and see that game," he said, as he threw him a couple of hundred dollars.

Tom was still only 28, young enough to be part of that Offaly team if his life had veered on a different path. He wasn't ravaged with thoughts of what might have been, however. "No, that time I had passed on. I didn't have any regrets. I just wanted to make sure Martin played well and, of course, he was a cool man so I didn't have to worry about him."

Offaly, shooting into the Hill 16 goal in the first half of the replay, blew Kerry away in the opening 10 minutes and had five points on the board before their opponents, who were playing with the wind at their backs, had even registered a wide, never mind a score. Kerry looked to Mick O'Connell. He was 35 now but if anyone was going to drag them out of this hole it was him. And he did.

A five-point deficit when playing with wind advantage in an All-Ireland final was no small handicap but he almost single handedly hauled Kerry back into the game. Paudie Lynch moved from wing to centre-back for Kerry and O'Connell started getting his hands on the ball around the middle. He put on an exhibition of place-kicking and by half-time had four points from distance and the sides were level at 0-8 each. By then, Offaly had lost Seán Cooney and reigning Footballer of the Year Mulligan to injury, severely depleting their options in terms of making game-changing substitutions in the second half at a time when a maximum of three replacements were permitted.

However, any conversation about the second half of that game can only begin and end with Willie Bryan. The classy Walsh Island midfielder personified how the Offaly team had developed and matured since Kerry had beaten them in 1969.

"I suppose in '69 I was terrified but after that it didn't really bother me," says Bryan of his tussles with O'Connell. "I had a job to do. You'd be better off if you were playing on a lesser man but he was an easy man to play on. He went for the ball and I used to go for the ball and there was no pushing or knocking so it was kind of catcher's game that time. It was enjoyable playing on him. If you did 50-50 with him you'd be doing alright.

"He would be very fair. I think overall I did quite well on him. We clashed a few times in other matches, Railway Cup and the likes, and overall we probably came out even enough. Now, I was a good bit younger than him."

Kerry maintained the momentum they had built in the latter part of the first half after the restart and Mick O'Dwyer put them two points up before the game's turning point arrived. Paddy Fenning gathered possession around 50 yards out from the Kerry goal, veering towards the sideline. He lobbed a speculative point effort that appeared to be dropping short into a thicket of bodies around the Kerry goalmouth. The ball took a wicked bounce off the turf and flew past Kerry goalkeeper Eamonn Fitzgerald, into the top of his net. Offaly were a point in front.

"I keep telling Séamus Darby that, 'Sure anyone can score a goal from 13 yards, I scored mine 10 years before from 50'," smiles Fenning. "It could be 70 when I have a few drinks."

It was Bryan's cue to come into his own. He followed up the goal with a point, the first of eight that Offaly would score in a glorious 12-minute spell as he emerged as something of a shield preventing the ball from exiting Kerry's half.

"He gave an exhibition of football," says Furlong, "particularly in the second half. He just owned the ball. I'd say if Willie had gone into the stand for a piss the ball would have turned up in there. It was one of those tremendous days but he made it look so simple. Willie just had a tremendous knack of when he'd come down with the ball, taking one step back and he seemed to have the whole parish to himself. It's not something you see too often. Most fellas come down and they'd run straight into trouble."

"I had a lot of luck too the way the thing fell into place," Bryan says modestly, before checking. "Well, I suppose, you make your own luck but a lot of things fell into place for me that day.

"I don't have a great memory of matches but I do know that there would have been matches that I probably dominated for longer but I suppose I came good at the right time in that match and the fact that it happened in a final against Kerry and against O'Connell too, the whole thing builds up to make a good story.

"I did pick one out of his hands that he had caught and that always gives you a big lift. He had his hands on it and I lifted it from him. When things start happening for you on days like that it's like you're out on the field on your own. And then the whole team was playing so well. You'd have another day when the fucking thing would hit you on top of the head and you'd be a yard wrong here or there whereas that day you had the yard right."

As the deficit yawned for Kerry, they tried to burrow through for goals but to no avail. Paddy McCormack, at 33, played one of his best games for the county and Furlong franked his status as the game's premier goalkeeper ever further. McTague, now the team captain, kicked 10 points. But then it was one of the those days when everyone played well as the team clicked.

It's an often forgotten fact that Séamus Darby played at corner-forward for Offaly that day. He bent over a wonderful point off his left foot near the end. That score was only an ornament at that stage but, of course, that same shooting action would thwart Kerry to a much greater degree a decade later.

When the final whistle sounded Offaly were ahead by 1-19 to 0-13. It was and is Kerry's biggest defeat in an All-Ireland final. It proved to be O'Dwyer and O'Connell's last championship games at Croke Park and effectively marked the end of an era before the former instigated the most glorious one of all.

The doubts about the validity of Offaly's success in 1971 were swept away with that performance, possibly the best served up by any team that ever left the county, and ensured their legacy as a truly great side.

"They were fresher," admits Donie O'Sullivan. "They were younger, they had more confidence as well. They had been around for a good while, they had an extra few years of experience and I think they had an extra few players as well."

By now, Mickey Furlong was a bus driver in New York. He abandoned his run that day to stop into a theatre on Fordham Road that was showing the game, parking the bus outside. He celebrated as heartily as anyone back in Tullamore.

"It's not that it would mean more," says Martin in terms of differentiating between the successes of '71 and '72. "It's very hard to say it's more or less or whatever. To win your first anything is hard to beat but the fact that it was Kerry that we had beaten in an All-Ireland final replay, and beaten them well, I mean there's not much more you can ask for. People said, 'You didn't beat Kerry' so that's the true mark of a good team. You beat Kerry. It stamped you."

CHAPTER 13

SEVEN MILLION DOLLARS

TOM FURLONG was ambitious as a footballer but, when his American football dream died, he channelled that into his work instead. He resumed his job with MaBSTOA and was always on the lookout for ways to better himself. Initially, it was through more mundane activities such as undergoing a fireman's training course, for example. That meant that he and a colleague were the only ones in the Transit Authority with a licence to operate sprinkler systems, allowing him to oversee maintenance at various bus garages.

He became a shop steward in the plant and equipment section of the Transport Workers Union and filled the role for three years before being elected vice-chairman. After a year he became the chairman, with around 900 workers falling under his remit.

"The Irish guys pushed me forward because there were a lot of Italians in charge at that time, they were kind of doing the Irish men out of it," he explains. "The Irish men didn't get a look in and they took all the overtime and at the end of the year it all added up when it came to the hours. So I went in and when I became vice-chairman then I got a say in what was done but it didn't suit the Irish guys because I said I wanted everything fair and square. I posted an overtime sheet on the bulletin board. The man who worked the least hours got to work the overtime.

"The Irish guys didn't want that, they wanted Irish guys to get all the overtime. But I brought them out of that and they were happy enough to see it squared away. As chairman I had a vice-chairman and I had a recording secretary underneath me. And I had shop stewards underneath me. They reported directly to me. I had my own office and telephone extensions and all the rest of it."

In 1966, early on in Furlong's union involvement, the TWU called a strike which lasted for 12 days and saw public transport in the city grind to a halt from 8.02am on New Year's Day, affecting millions of commuters. It made for a testing start to John Lindsay's tenure as Mayor of New York having just succeeded Robert Wagner.

The strike was led by Kerry man Mike Quill, the long-time president of the TWU. The union rowed back on some of its initial demands but the Transit Authority obtained a judge's order for Quill's arrest along with eight other union leaders. He was in ill health at the time and declared that "the judge can drop dead in his black robes. I don't care if I rot in jail. I will not call off the strike".

Eventually a settlement was reached on January 13 with workers getting a wage increase from $3.18 to $4.14 an hour, which was the biggest coup. They also got additional holiday pay and increased pension benefits among other things. A couple of days after giving a rousing victorious speech to the strikers, Quill passed away.

The strike strengthened the TWU's position when future contracts were being negotiated, talks that Furlong had a key role in as he swiftly made his way through the ranks.

"They would have their experts and we would have our experts and their experts would come up with figures that would show that the Transit Authority was broke and couldn't afford to give us any money and we would come up with figures to show that they had plenty of money to give to us. It's amazing how these people could get the same figures to arrive at different conclusions.

"We got a lot of support and we got a lot of things in the contract that we fought for. My job was strengthened because I was a strong union leader and I had the support of my men. The bosses, believe it or not, their contract was similar to ours but they didn't go on strike. We went on strike for it. So they reaped the benefits of the strike. They went on the pension scheme with the percentage increase and they were making more money than us so their percentage raise was greater than ours. So the gap between top and bottom was getting bigger and bigger."

◆　◆　◆　◆

Among the many workers who benefited from the TWU driving a hard bargain with the Transit Authority was Mickey Furlong.

Years working as a bartender and beer salesman didn't lend itself to him leading the most appropriate lifestyle given that he had a wife and ever expanding family to care for. They moved way out to Hazlet in New Jersey and, to Tom's surprise and that of Paddy Naughton, a Tullamore man who had a prominent position in the Transit Authority, he picked up a job with MaBSTOA as a bus driver.

"I was passing through the personnel department and I look around and who's there only Mickey," Tom recalls. "I says, 'Jesus Christ, what are you doing here?' He said, 'I'm applying for a job'. 'It's the first I heard of it'. He said, 'Paddy Naughton said to me, "You're the last guy I expect to see here"', because he didn't figure Mickey would last as a bus driver. He got himself straightened out later on. Mickey liked to party."

He drove a bus in New York for more than 20 years afterwards, albeit it required a lengthy daily commute from his home in Hazlet, and eventually brought much greater structure to his life. It took time, though, and it was only after the birth of his seventh child Eileen, a pleasant afterthought, in 1976 that he finally resolved to rein himself in. He came through it with resounding success and never touched the drink again.

"That was a gift from God," says his wife May of Eileen's birth. "The rest of the kids were grown up and along comes Eileen and he got those years with her."

His elder children particularly endured some difficult times during their upbringing but not to the extent that their relationship with him was fractured beyond repair, or anything like it. He may have had his dubious periods but it didn't dilute his innate likeability and over time he mended fences. Mickey Furlong tended to excel at most things once he put his mind to it; fatherhood was no different.

"He was a great father," says Michelle, his eldest daughter. "Out in Bethany Road in Hazlet we had the big back yard and he wanted all of his kids into sport and everything. Even as girls, we were very athletic. We'd have the big back yard and all the kids there.

"As far as the Gaelic stuff and going to New York goes, that was too far away from us. If we were maybe in New York that would have been different but we were in New Jersey and people didn't hear about that."

"We were a great family but we had our own struggles," admits Mary, his second daughter. "We talked and he had regrets."

In time, his marriage blossomed, almost beyond recognition, too.

"When he'd be talking to his friends he'd say, 'I got seven million dollars, and the old hen herself is worth two!'" May smiles. "That was his famous saying. We used to sit there for hours, the two of us. At the end we had great years."

In 1972 Tom took a trip to California for a few days and, while there, was involved in a car accident. A doctor checked him out and assured him that he was fine. He flew back to New York and resumed work a few days later but while sitting at his desk began to feel ill. He collapsed and an ambulance was called. Mickey was nearby while on a break from his shift and a colleague told him his brother had suffered what appeared to be a heart attack. It turned out to a be pulmonary embolism and he was lucky to survive. The flight from California to New York had brought about deep vein thrombosis in his leg following the accident.

"I had an out of body experience while I was in hospital," he says. "I was looking down on my body and the two doctors were examining me. They decided it wasn't a heart attack and the guy says, 'It must be thrombosis' and they said, 'We better see what it is, in the next two minutes we'll know one way or another'. I'm up in the corner of the room looking down on them, that's God honest truth, and I saw Mickey in the corner of the room. It took me about three or four years before I asked Mickey was he in the room that day and he says, 'Yeah, I was'."

Despite suffering injuries which brought his playing career to a premature end and a near death experience now behind him, Furlong began to get itchy feet once again. He had trained the Offaly team for a couple of years but when it was announced that New York would be going on another world tour in 1975 he wanted in.

Despite the warning he received from medics a couple of years before, he resumed playing well in advance of the tour so as to justify his spot. A broken elbow had cost him a place on the 1964 tour and, realistically, there weren't going to be any more chances to see the world on this scale thereafter. The National Hurling League final of 1970 effectively brought the curtain down on New York competing against teams from home in a meaningful way. Referee Clem Foley was coming off the field in Gaelic Park after Cork had beaten New York over two legs to take the title and had his jaw smashed. New York were banned for two years but were effectively marginalised for a decade.

The world tour would see them take on Irish selections in various outposts rather than elite opposition from back home. It was just as well too as standards were slipping in New York. The club teams were becoming more and more about whisking star players out from home for a weekend to pack the side. The New York team that went on tour was well short of the standard they set for themselves when going hip to hip with the likes of Galway, Kerry and Dublin in '60s. Tom Furlong was proof of that himself, by his own admission a shadow of the player who had lit up Gaelic Park in his prime, but then football was almost incidental to the trip in any event.

It may have been a world tour in name, stretching over six weeks, but it was mainly concentrated in Australia and New Zealand.

"We went from New York to Honolulu. We stayed there for six days getting ready for the Australians! When we got to Australia we were there for two weeks. Mainly in Melbourne and Sydney and then we went to Canberra. We played the New South Wales team twice. Fairly dirty games. They were out for scalps and we thought it was just an exhibition game.

"We got two broken arms and one broken leg in the first game. That screwed them up for the rest of the trip. Then we left there and we went to New Zealand for two weeks. There was a guy there Mike

Dillon, he was a Leitrim guy. He owned the big sawmills and he brought out these Maori to give an exhibition of wood-chopping and all that."

It was in New Zealand that he played his final game of football, back where he had started, in goal. Another goalkeeper had struggled in one of the games in Australia and Furlong was asked to man the nets.

The last stop was in Las Vegas on the way back to New York and Furlong was skint. He borrowed a few dollars and won enough playing black jack to see him home, arriving back at JFK Airport with a quarter in his pocket. He gave his boots, the same pair that he had worn on his best days with New York, to Yvonne to stow away for good this time.

At work he made a bid to get on the executive board of the TWU but, despite polling well, came up short. "I had all kinds of odds going against me but I got over 600 votes though it wasn't enough. I stayed on as chairman of plant and equipment for another six years."

That too became a drag over time and he eventually quit and moved into a less taxing role. "It was getting too much," he admits. "I was drinking too much."

Like Mickey, Tom had his troubles with alcohol and grappled for years to get on top of it. For long periods he did, quite successfully, going dry for 10 years at one stage. His personality was different to Mickey's though and he was more laid back, not quite the life and soul of the party but he had an entertaining streak in him all the same. Mickey Moynihan's brothers owned the popular Red Mill club in the Bronx and when the band he had booked was 45 minutes late one night, Furlong stood in and treated the large crowd to a selection of his favourite Johnny Cash and Buddy Holly numbers.

"He could entertain you, if you needed a song he was quite capable of dishing out a few songs to you," says Moynihan. "He could entertain us as well as play football. I was with Tommy Furlong many, many times now and I never saw Tommy Furlong out of control. Did he take a drink? Absolutely. Did I? Did Willie Nolan? Brendan O'Donnell?

Absolutely. Brendan would hang out with you for two days and you wouldn't hear a word from him and you wouldn't think he had a beer. Tommy was that type of a guy. Tommy would hang out with you all night but did I ever see him that he looked like he was under the weather? No, the answer is no, but he certainly did like a beer and that's not telling tales, let's put it like that."

Tom's years as chairman of plant and equipment in the TWU left him in a strong enough position that he could effectively cherry pick whatever job he wanted when he quit the role. He took on the midnight shift, which ran from 11.30pm to 7.20am. It involved him effectively being on call to deal with whatever problems might arise with the buses overnight. Not too taxing a role then.

Naturally, he'd be most busy during the winter while in the summer he might squeeze in a couple of hours' sleep during the shift. Once finished, he'd head for Nanuet Cemetery to dig graves, albeit with a digger. He might do that until four o'clock and then do a spot of cleaning in a few banks at five.

The plan was to fill his boots as best he could as he worked towards retiring from MaBSTOA at 50 in order to make the most of his benefits, as had been thrashed out in the trade union talks all those years before. Yvonne had a flair for hospitality and he figured she'd make a bar run like clockwork. Buying their own business was something he built towards as he worked around the clock. It was quite the workload but his willingness to embrace it was framed by the environment he had grown up in, created by his selfless parents Tom and Margaret.

CHAPTER 14

DISCARDED

THE backs of the Offaly players were raw with slaps following their successes in 1971 and '72. Virtually all of them came from humble backgrounds and the hero status bestowed on them was somewhat bewildering to them. They had their All Star tours to America and saw parts of the world they never dreamed of, all through football. Seven Offaly players won All Stars in 1972 including a first for Martin Furlong, while Willie Bryan was named as Texaco Footballer of the Year as a matter of course.

However, before 1972 was out, one of the team's central pillars had fallen. That November Offaly played Donegal in the final of the Grounds Tournament at Croke Park. They were wrapping up a comprehensive 16-point victory late on when Donegal wing-back and player-manager Brian McEniff sallied up the field with the ball.

"I was travelling deep into Offaly territory," explains McEniff. "We were being well enough beat. Paddy McCormack came out to get a piece of me and the late Séamus Bonner drew back his hand. He had his back to McCormack but he could see that McCormack was coming from behind him and he just threw back his open hand and whatever way he caught McCormack's eye..."

McCormack's version of events is somewhat different though they are in agreement on one issue at least: the blow was purely accidental, however it occurred.

"A lad went to punch the ball or something," says McCormack. "I think it was one of my own men that did it anyway, I'm not really sure. I don't think it was him, poor oul' divil, he's dead and gone now, Séamus Bonner.

"I got my nose broke and I lost the sight of my eye the same day. What did I do? I went back into the goals and let Furlong out full-back. The match was nearly over. And the blood flying everywhere.

"I was concussed naturally enough after the game and I had to go to the eye and ear and I had to lie on my back for two weeks to save the eye, not the sight, to save the eye. It was haemorrhaging in at the back. The back of the eye all ruptured. I have about 20 percent sight in that eye, that's about it, if I have it. You wouldn't want to be depending on it now to tell you the truth."

McCormack made a stab at a comeback a couple of years later but it was fruitless; he'd played his last game for Offaly. Given that the team had finally found its way and he was at the veteran stage anyway, his influence wouldn't have been missed to the same degree as if it had happened a couple of years earlier. There wasn't exactly a huge leadership deficit at that stage in the team's development but it was still very much unexpected that he would bow out so abruptly.

Offaly made decent progress through the National League in his absence and wound up in the final where they would face Kerry once again. The team was just back from the All Star tour to San Francisco and served up a flat performance. Two goals from Brendan Lynch saw Kerry to a 2-12 to 0-14 win with Tony McTague's marksmanship unerring as he accounted for all but two points of Offaly's total. A National League title would have completed the collection for that Offaly team but there was no great outcry following the result either.

However, when they struggled past Louth in the opening round of the Leinster Championship, some eyebrows were raised. Ahead of the semi-final against Kildare, an article appeared in the *Irish Independent* claiming that Offaly's preparations for the Kerry and Louth games had been undermined by poor attendance at training and that it had shown no sign of improvement in the meantime.

The team was rejigged for the Kildare game and Fr Gilhooley went on the defensive, rubbishing reports of a decline in training numbers. "Nothing could be further from the truth," he said. "We had a full muster of 22 players for the past couple of weeks and that does not suggest a decline."

He insisted that while numbers may have fallen, they were for genuine reasons with players injured and others released to play for their clubs in tournament games. "Nobody checked with me about training attendances by the players," he added. "Had they done so it might have scotched these rumours. The old spirit is now back and the players are prepared to give of their best."

Regardless of the truth of the initial reports, stories such as this weren't surfacing in the previous couple of years and the episode didn't exactly send out positive vibes from the All-Ireland champions' camp. Other issues had been simmering over the years too, despite the team's success, and were threatening to compromise the players' focus.

"I remember coming out after a meal after a Leinster final and I'll never forget it," says Seán Lowry. "Nuala (his wife) was with me and there was only about five wives at the meal afterwards and we got a bill going out for a meal for the wives. It took our eye off the ball. There was issues like that going on and it was very disruptive at the time."

Offaly improved dramatically without reaching their best and strangled Kildare in the second half to record a six-point victory. Meath were the opposition in the final, the first time the counties had met over 80 minutes since the famous game of three years earlier. Offaly cruised to an even more comprehensive victory than what they had enjoyed over them in the previous year's provincial semi-final, this time finishing with 12 points to spare.

Meath trainer Micheál Campbell told reporters after the game that there "isn't a team in Ireland could have lived with Offaly in that second half". The Offaly supporters chanted "we are the greatest" as they chaired the players off the field afterwards. Another All-Ireland was within touching distance with their third successive Leinster title stowed away, the first team to achieve that feat since 1938. A young Cork team had beaten Kerry in Munster and Galway would be Offaly's semi-final opponents.

Offaly enjoyed an excellent record against Galway and were hot favourites to advance to a third final in-a-row. Back then, it was customary for Gaelic games correspondents to visit the competing counties and get the views of supporters on the week of big games. Those whose views were recorded on the week of the Galway game could see nothing only an easy victory as they eyed up a final against

Cork. While opinions from giddy supporters should never be taken too much heed of, there was similar guff spouted by former players who ought to have known better. Still, as long as it didn't seep through to the players there shouldn't have been too much to worry about. But many believe it did.

"When the ball was thrown in every Offaly forward was clocked," insists Paddy Fenning. "Johnny Cooney got fierce treatment. I got hit when the ball was thrown in. I was corner-forward and I lost it for a couple of minutes."

Complaints from that Offaly team about an overly physical approach from their opponents would have carried a hollow ring. At their best that Offaly team had no qualms about mixing it physically if that was the path a game veered in. That they struggled to match Galway in that department spoke of complacency.

"We were more up for it," claims Galway centre-back TJ Gilmore, "it was a score we had to settle from two years previous. The team was more mature."

There didn't seem to be any great cause for concern at half-time with the sides level at seven points each. Offaly had overpowered both Kildare and Meath in the second half and were optimistic they could do so again, despite the fact that they were struggling to come to terms with the pitch of the game in various sectors.

Galway scored the first four points of the second half but McTague hit back with a goal and Seán Evans kicked a point to draw the teams level. Crisis over it seemed, but no. Galway flashed over the next four points. Evans hit back with Offaly's second goal with six minutes remaining. They spurned numerous chances to draw level before John Coughlan kicked the clinching point for Galway. The three-in-a-row dream was over. It was only a two-point defeat in the end but it flattered the champions.

"It was probably a case of Offaly were there for the taking, they were after winning two All-Irelands in the two previous years so they were probably sitting ducks to a point," says Gilmore. "We went out and we threw everything we had into the game and probably did catch them unawares. Offaly had it all to lose, they were title holders. It's one of those things that happens nearly every year where teams are sitting ducks and they're caught on the hop at some stage."

Winning the first All-Ireland in 1971 gave the team huge belief but given that they were perceived as unconvincing champions that year, they still retained an edge as they set about defending the title in '72. That edge was blunted once they successfully achieved that, Furlong believes.

"Winning the second one probably gave us too much confidence," he maintains. "That's why we lost against Galway in 1973. We were definitely overconfident. I have no doubt about that. I think we had our eyes on Cork, they came through in the other semi-final. We figured we could beat Galway. It was definitely a mistake on our part.

"Galway, of course, came with a gameplan to hassle and harry our forwards especially and they got inside their heads. I know there was a lot of shirt-tugging going on. We were getting fouled, niggly fouls sort of style, and we didn't like it. Instead of getting stuck in we probably got knocked off our game."

In the following day's *Irish Times*, Paddy Downey wrote, "I think it is appropriate to pay tribute to the defeated, who, over the past two seasons, were acknowledged by all as one of the greatest teams of modern times – some would say of the century."

With the exceptional Down and Galway sides that came before them in the '60s and the Dublin and Kerry teams that revolutionised the game afterwards, that Offaly side perhaps struggles to command the same gravitas by comparison when the great teams in football history are discussed. They were front line All-Ireland contenders for several years and, on reflection, could have achieved more.

"I've often said that with a little bit of luck we could have won in '69, '70, '71, '72 and '73," says Furlong. "We could have won five-in-a-row."

"I would say that the Offaly '72 team, for me anyhow, was one of the best teams that I came across in my footballing career," insists Mattie Kerrigan. "I'd put them up with the very best that I've seen.

Dublin might have lived a little bit longer but I think Offaly should have won a bit more in that period.

"If they won they didn't do any gloating. If they lost they'd shake your hand, take it on the chin and walk on. I never heard any of that other rubbish out of them. It was different now with Kildare and Louth and these lads, they'd be forever whinging about something or other. There's huge respect out there for Offaly football.

"Furlong epitomised Offaly football. He went about it calmly and ferociously, if you like, at times. But, when the game was over, that was it. We'd meet in Barry's Hotel afterwards and you could have a drink with them. They were great sportsmen and they'd be one of my favourite teams in the years that I played. I never heard an Offaly man gloating when the game was over."

The Offaly players didn't spare each other while on club duty. Furlong was playing full-forward for the Tullamore senior hurlers against St Mary's on Mick O'Rourke, one of his closest friends, once and they wore timber off each other for the hour. As Furlong waved yet another broken stick in the air and called for a replacement, a Tullamore mentor told him, "Martin, that's the last hurl we have. If you break that you may come out."

Furlong closed out 1973 by claiming his second senior football title with Tullamore, a decade after they had won their last, ending the longest drought in the club's history. He largely played out the field for the club and was centre-forward when they claimed the championship that year.

"He wasn't a classic forward but he made an awful lot of running," says Pat Heffernan, a clubmate. "You could have two or three young players around him and he'd be looking after them and there would be no one messing. Anyone who messed with a young fella, Martin would do-bar them, no question. He'd break ball, he had a great head. When Martin Furlong was playing centre half-forward, the opposition weren't blackguarding any forward."

Earlier that year Furlong had spent a few weeks in America with the Offaly team on an All Star tour and stayed on a little longer, doing some bar work for Mickey Moynihan in New York. He toyed with the idea of staying on and moving the family out but thought better of it.

He was turning his hand to various jobs back home at the time. He worked as a salesman for Jackie Finlay and helped him run the Harp Ballroom in town. He had something of a flair for showbiz, too. When Dana was heading to the Eurovision Song Contest in 1970 Furlong, fancying her chances of success in Amsterdam, wanted to book her there and then but was overruled. They got her when she came home, but at a greater cost.

He later started work as a rate collector with Offaly County Council, a post he would remain in for several years. It was a thankless job to a degree.

"Who the hell wants to see you coming? I have to say though, in general, most people were very good. With the rate collectors, most of my area was rural so I was dealing with farmers and that, shopkeepers. For the most part they were all very, very good. The rate collecting was fine and then they changed it around so you were a revenue collector. You were collecting rents in houses and water rates and anything that was going at that time. So it became a different kettle of fish then altogether. I was at that for 17 or 18 years."

Given that he covered the countryside, his work with the Council didn't demand a 40-hour week and he certainly wasn't paid on those terms either. So, to supplement his income, he did a bit of bar work. Over the years he pulled pints in Wrafter's and the Offaly Inn on Harbour Street in Tullamore, The Thatch in Rahan and Kelly's Roadhouse in Mucklagh. He was supposed to do a few weeks in the Cherry Tree in Birr and ended up staying three years, relocating his family in the process, before returning to work in the Manor Lounge in Tullamore.

His summers weren't being filled with big championship days in Croke Park any more either. In 1974, Offaly were pitted against a lowly rated Dublin side in the Leinster quarter-final. Kevin Heffernan was in his first year as manager, bidding to revive the team's flagging fortunes with Dublin having dipped alarmingly since winning their last Leinster title in 1965. Furlong was captain of Offaly given that Tullamore were county champions.

In their best years Offaly didn't have to worry about Dublin. The counties hadn't met in the Leinster Championship since the 1962 final, when Tom Furlong played in his only senior provincial decider. While Offaly were enjoying lengthy runs in Leinster and beyond, Dublin were often no more than a footnote in the story of the championship, invariably sent packing at an early stage. Two weeks after winning the All-Ireland in 1972, Offaly received a guard of honour from the Dubs before a league game at Croke Park and strolled to a 13-point victory.

Furlong had been a regular on the Leinster Railway Cup team for years by then and captained the side which won the competition for the first time in 12 years in '74. Often, his understudy was Dublin netminder Paddy Cullen.

"I was on the Leinster team a few times when they were backboned by Offaly," says Cullen. "I remember going down to Cork and we used to play in the old Mardyke. I was on the train and you'd be looking at these fellas with All-Ireland medals and saying, 'Holy Jesus'.

"Martin Furlong was brilliant. I was raw. We hadn't been anywhere, we hadn't done anything, I hadn't won anything so you were glad to be hanging around. I never got on though.

"He was kind of an awkward goalkeeper but effective, I'll put it that way. He was a great man for using legs and arms. He was all gangly and he spread himself well but that's what goalkeepers do. He was unusual and he always had his tongue sticking out as well."

Heffernan was looking for a spark to ignite the Dublin team. They hadn't been impressive against Wexford in the opening round and weren't given much hope of toppling Offaly, bidding for a fourth Leinster title in succession. He recalled 29-year-old Jimmy Keaveney to the squad ahead of the game and put him straight into the full-forward line. The player to lose out as a result was Bernard Brogan.

"I was asked to play for Dublin and I turned it down," Brogan recalls, reflecting the apathy towards the team at the time. "I said I wouldn't, and Heffernan came out and asked me a second time and I started training in October and we went on and we got to the final of the Division Two League, we were beaten in that and then we played against Wexford in the first round."

Just like the Galway game the year before, Offaly were dragged into a battle that they hadn't reckoned on. The game was tight throughout and Brogan was introduced at midfield to telling effect in the second half.

"I made a big impact on the game and I twisted my knee maybe with five minutes to go. We'd used all our subs, I went into the corner, I played out the game. I had an operation two weeks later and didn't play for nine months."

He was loitering up front in the last minute with the sides level when Seán Lowry was blocked down by Brian Mullins and the ball was worked to Leslie Deegan, who kicked the winning point to condemn Offaly to their earliest championship exit since 1966. The innocence of youth in Brogan's attitude towards playing Offaly largely summed up why Dublin were going places while Offaly were stalling. Heffernan was ushering in a new regime with new players who weren't scarred by previous failures.

"Personally, I wasn't afraid of them. I wasn't playing county football the year before, it was all new to me. I thought I was as good as anyone else out there."

For years before that Offaly had been making roadkill of aspiring teams like Dublin in Leinster. If they didn't pummel the opposition in their best years they were happy to grind out a win through their reputation as much as anything else, but suddenly that wasn't happening any more. The team had become stale. And by losing to Dublin they helped create a monster. Heffo's Army packed the Hill throughout that summer as Dublin grew into one of the most formidable and celebrated teams in GAA history.

"The momentum and the support of the team began to change after beating Offaly," says Brogan. "In the first round there was nobody at the match. When I say nobody, there was no one in Croke Park. After we beat Offaly there was a crowd on the Hill, the flags were coming back, there was great momentum. The momentum of beating Offaly carried us on."

Dublin won the All-Ireland that year and ruled Leinster mercilessly for the rest of the decade. In 1975 Offaly even lost to Kildare for the first time in years. Tony McTague was only 29 but quit afterwards in frustration at county board penny pinching. Tensions had been simmering for years over issues like players' wives being refused entry to post-match meals.

Fr Gilhooley departed as manager and McCormack took over for the following year. In theory it seemed like a sound move but it didn't work out. More players began to follow McTague's path in frustration at the county board. A story has been told of how one player asked McCormack to vary the training during the year. He told him that they could run around the field in the opposite direction.

"Somebody approached me to see would I take it," he says. "It was a foolish thing to do really, when you think about it. Sure who were you managing only the lads you were playing with? Then there were some of the lads retiring and there was a bit of a fallout then and a lot of the lads didn't bother playing. We were after getting to a few league finals as well and that's where the money was all generated and, if you think about it, if you were to put it all down for expenses for the year, at the time, two or three hundred would have covered the whole bloody lot. Anyway, it didn't materialise and the boys threw in the towel a bit. They were probably fed up of the bloody football too but there was good lads retired too early in my opinion."

Having been the players that made the glorious breakthrough, they retained hero status in the county, but the glow was certainly fading.

"You were in the limelight and you would get fairly sick of attention," says Willie Bryan. "You didn't have a lot of time to yourself. You were in for a pint and some fella stuck in your head. You would get sick of that. And then of course it's gone. Maybe for a while you'd like a bit of it again but you wouldn't like to go back to where it was. There's no doubt the attention is great, but you soon get sick of it.

"If you were in having a drink and you could be in a corner with a couple of guys and there'd be always some slob that will stick his nose in and he'd ruin the whole night on everyone, would crawl over people to get at you or someone else, it mightn't be just yourself. I think anyone that's in the game will tell you that – they want their life back."

McCormack stood down and Offaly pulled his replacement right out of left field. The county board chairman at the time, Fr Seán Heaney, had noticed the work of a young coach with a star-studded UCD team in Dublin. They had dominated the Sigerson Cup and won an All-Ireland club title. Eugene McGee offered something different and Fr Heaney got a glowing reference on him from Kevin Kilmurray, who had played under him in Belfield.

"I remember Fr Heaney was the main man in bringing in McGee," says Eugene Mulligan. "He was right – we had to get away from where we were and get in somebody that was totally different and had fresh ideas."

McGee spoke of wanting to build a team over the next three years and didn't see the point in retaining players who he felt weren't going to be there at the end of the cycle. Several big names were cut adrift, among them Bryan and Furlong.

At the time, McGee was forging a career as a prominent journalist. Indeed, a few years earlier he conducted a serialised interview with McCormack where he coined the phrase 'The Ironman from Rhode'. A few months before accepting the job he wrote a piece in the *Sunday Press* that effectively amounted to an obituary to the great Offaly team of '71/'72 after they had lost a league relegation play-off to Mayo. Nobody was in a position to argue with its content.

"Even if I say so myself, it was a very good article," claims McGee. "I was at the match in Roscommon and it was just so sad to see the end of an era.

"The whole thing was a transition between the '71/'72 team and a new team. There was no major problems. I don't think anybody ever fell out permanently about it or anything like that. I think they began to see that there's going to be a new Offaly team and it's going to take two or three years at least and they wouldn't be around anyway.

"I think Martin probably fell into that category where I couldn't go with a whole old team because it was five years after they won the All-Ireland and it wasn't a realistic proposition."

"McGee was good," Bryan admits. "He took a lot of hard decisions and dropped a lot of us but he was right. I suppose in a way we were probably a little bit cocky. We were probably tired, of course, as well. There was a different regime. Things were starting to hot up. The whole thing was getting more professional."

Mick O'Rourke was also surplus to requirements but he recalls Furlong's axing causing a particularly big stir.

"I remember coming through Daingean one evening and I went into McCann's pub and the whole talk was of Martin after being dropped. And Mick Casey was there. He says, 'I know you can't go on forever but why would you drop a man when you don't have a replacement?' And I never forgot those few words because they didn't have an outstanding goalkeeper at the time."

Furlong was cross over it at first but didn't tie himself up in knots for too long either. Looking back, he admits that McGee's decision was informed by the inertia that had infected his approach to football.

"You had no pressure on you," he says. "In hindsight the man was probably right. I probably wasn't training like I should have been. I'd say I had got complacent about the position. I probably wasn't playing well enough either. When you're not training right and not doing the right thing, and I was working in the bar so I was drinking more than I should have been.

"I suppose it didn't sit too well at the start. After a while, it didn't really matter."

He had his two All-Irelands and four Leinsters, an All Star and a Railway Cup; he closed the book on that part of his life.

MY BALL: Kerry's Dan Kavanagh fails to get to grips with Martin Furlong during the 1972 All-Ireland final replay.

CAPITAL GAINS: The Offaly team pictured in Washington in 1970. With them is Tom Furlong, who was unable to play for New York against Offaly on the tour having been forced into early retirement.

MENTOR: Séamus Morris was one of the biggest influences on Martin's life. Here he is pictured with Martin's son Ken on his Confirmation day.

COME IN FOR YOUR TEA: Margaret always kept a watchful eye on John. Quite literally in this case as she peers out at him from Tom and Yvonne's house in New York.

IN CONTROL: Martin Furlong takes the ball away from his goal as Kerry's Tom Spillane and Eoin 'Bomber' Liston give chase in the 1982 All-Ireland Final. Below, left to right: the Offaly squad that day; Martin saves Mikey Sheehy's penalty to break Kerry hearts; Martin the hero; collecting Sam.

RECOGNITION: Noel Skehan, Martin Furlong, Ronnie Delany, Ollie Campbell and Barry McGuigan at the 1982 Texaco Sportstar Awards.

THREE'S COMPANY: Tom, Margaret and John Furlong pictured in Arlington Cemetery, Washington in 1982.

DEAR JOHN: John Furlong with his nephew Tommy, Tom's son, in 1982.

HERO: A young Ken Furlong, Martin's eldest son, pictured with Matt Connor in O'Connor Park in 1983.

GOOD SIGNS: Mickey and Tom Furlong with Gabriel Hayden outside Furlong's Bar in East Durham.

END OF AN ERA: Martin Furlong pictured following the final game of his career, a defeat to Gracefield in Daingean in the 1985 Offaly Senior Football Championship. He's joined by then Offaly manager John Courtney (left) and Gracefield's Pat Fitzgerald, a long-time Offaly teammate.

BACK TOGETHER: Martin and Mickey Furlong (right) outside the dressing rooms in Gaelic Park in 1985.

BROTHERS IN ARMS: Tom Furlong was guest of honour at the 1989 Offaly Association, New York Dinner Dance.

MEMORIES: The Furlong brothers, pictured when Martin was guest of honour in 1996.

THE FAMILY FURLONG

ALL TOGETHER NOW: Various strands of the Furlong family pictured outside Tom's bar at a gathering a number of months after Mickey's death in 2002.

WEDDING BELLE: Tom and Yvonne with their son Tommy and his wife Caron on their wedding day in April 2006.

AISLE BE BACK: Following Mickey's passing, Martin stepped in to give his daughter Mary away on her wedding day some months later.

CLAN: Martin's family pictured at the wedding of his son Tom in December 2012. Back, l-r: Tom Minnock, Joan, Mark, Katie, Tom, Doreen, Martin, Ken and Paula Furlong. Front, l-r: Tom Furlong, Joe Minnock, Liadh and John Furlong, Ruth and Katie Minnock, Niall Furlong, Abbie Minnock.

MICKEY'S SEVEN MILLION DOLLARS: Eileen, Aggie, Mary, Johnny, Michael, Thomas (Toby) and Michelle.

OLD FAITHFUL: Cutting the tape to enter the Furlong Bar in 1998.

FOOTSTEPS: Three generations of Furlongs, Martin, Tom and Ken at Tullamore GAA Club's 125th anniversary Mass in May 2013.

NET MINDER: Young John Furlong hints at maintaining the goalkeeping legacy here.

25 YEARS ON: Martin Furlong waves to the crowd before the 2007 All-Ireland Final between Kerry and Cork at Croke Park.

PUPPY LOVE: If Martin isn't with Katie he's generally with his much-loved companion, Hughie. Here he is with them both at their home in Nanuet.

CHAPTER 15

FLUSHING THE JACKS

THE reservoir of inter-county standard goalkeepers in Offaly didn't run deep once Martin Furlong was considered surplus to requirements. Eugene McGee found that out the hard way in his first championship season in 1977.

"Martin got rid of a good few now in his day," says Willie Bryan. "Fellas got wore out, they were subs for so long. There was no one coming near him. Even a brother of mine was sub goalie for a while, Pat. Pat said, 'Unless I shoot this fella...' He wasn't going to get a match and he wasn't prepared to hang about."

Offaly set out in the 1977 Leinster Championship with Joe Murphy from Gracefield in goal. He kept a clean sheet in the opening game as Offaly coasted to a 12-point victory over Wicklow to set up a Leinster quarter-final meeting with Wexford. However, three goals went in in the first half and substitute 'keeper Mick Dunne was sent in. Wexford won by 4-6 to 2-10 to cement Offaly's new-found status as Leinster also rans, barely five years after they were, by a distance, the best team in the land.

It wasn't all doom and gloom though. McGee doubled up as manager of the Offaly under-21 team and they defeated hot favourites Kildare in the Leinster final that year. It was the first of three successive provincial finals they would reach in that grade, winning two. For the first time in years promising players were starting to emerge from underage teams. It gave McGee a mandate to promote exciting young talents like Gerry Carroll, Tomás O'Connor and Johnny Mooney.

The same day that the Offaly seniors lost to Wexford in Croke Park, McGee watched some of the minor game from the tunnel with Offaly also involved. One player towered over every other on the field in terms of class and pure footballing ability. It was obvious that he was special. He asked who he was. Matt Connor, he was told.

◆　　◆　　◆　　◆

Martin Furlong was still only 30-years-old and continued to play club football with Tullamore. Traditionally, the club has tended to produce good defenders though mounting match-winning totals always seemed to be a conundrum. At that level, they needed someone as streetwise as Furlong out the field. He was appointed captain and played full-forward in 1977. Tullamore beat Daingean in the county final and county chairman Fr Seán Heaney presented him with the Dowling Cup. Little did anyone know that another 23 years would pass before the captain of the county's premier club would feel the weight of that trophy again.

Their opponents in the Leinster Club Championship would be Longford's Newtowncashel, who were trained by McGee. Against his better judgement, given his already hectic schedule with Offaly, he took on the role when approached by the club earlier that year. When the county final against Longford Slashers came around, it clashed directly with Offaly under-21s' All-Ireland semi-final against Down in Newry. Efforts to shift the throw-in time came to nothing. McGee gave the team talk at three o'clock the day before the county final and made his way to Newry. Newtowncashel won their first county title the following afternoon.

By the time the first round provincial tie against Tullamore at O'Connor Park came around McGee was still involved but was phasing himself out. Tullamore's regular goalkeeper, Nicholas Whelan, was injured and couldn't play. Furlong was asked to fill in. The game finished in a draw but Furlong, in what was his first game between the posts for more than a year, pulled off a set of spellbinding saves and had clearly lost none of his natural flair for the position.

One evening a few days later he was at home when the doorbell rang. It was McGee. He came in and sat down. Furlong's six-year-old son Ken had left a dinky car idle and McGee nervously rolled it back and forth while putting it to him that he wanted him to rejoin the panel.

The National League was already up and running and Offaly had three games still to play against Galway, Dublin and Cork before the winter break. Daunting opposition for a man who had only had a single club game in goal since seemingly playing his final game for Offaly against Meath 17 months earlier. He was wary of going back in those circumstances. He told McGee that he'd think about it.

The following day he stopped into Noel McGee's barber shop on William Street. Noel was one of the few men that played with all four Furlong brothers and had the rare distinction of captaining both the Offaly hurlers and footballers. He was one of the biggest influences on Martin's life. As a boy he used to continually harangue Noel to get him a leather football. He eventually did, at a time when they weren't readily available.

Wednesday was a half day in Tullamore back then and when Furlong started working in Wakefield's as a teenager he'd go straight to Noel's barber shop on Wednesday afternoons and they'd hurl and kick football in O'Connor Park for the rest of the day.

Noel had a powerful strike and caught Furlong square in the chest with a shot one day, sending boy and ball flying into the goal. He chuckled at the good of it. He was a hugely popular figure in the town and beyond, a wonderful character. His barber shop hummed with talk of GAA matters on a daily basis. Furlong was never going to go anywhere else for counsel as he weighed up whether or not to accept McGee's invitation.

"I'd go back if I were you," Noel told him. "If I had to live my life again, I'd be in O'Connor Park every night of the week. It's only when you're not able to play that you'll regret not playing when you could."

He played in goal as Tullamore beat Newtowncashel in a replay that Sunday and returned to county colours seven days later in a one-point win over Galway, keeping a clean sheet and making a typically brave foray off his line to smother an effort by Maurice Burke. All-Ireland champions Dublin put four goals on Offaly a couple of weeks later at Croke Park but although Cork also beat them before the Christmas break, no goals went in this time. Furlong's inter-county career was back up and running.

By then all goalkeepers were expected to take kickouts. It's a task that has a very high premium placed on it nowadays but even back then it was a significant aspect of the game and wasn't an easy skill to master entering the latter part of your career.

"It was different because you had to try and build up power in your leg. It was not something you were doing for your formative years, if you like. Years ago the full-back or the corner-back used to kick out the ball and the corner-forward, if he was any way clever, went out as a third midfielder, between the half-back line and the midfield, getting under the ball. It's surprising that it took so long to cop onto the situation.

"You were more involved in the game. Before that all you could do was kick the goalpost to work off any tension or whatever you had. You could be standing there for 20 minutes and no one would take a shot and then some fella would take a shot from 30 yards... You could die of the cold there some days."

"An awful lot of them used to screw over my side, putting me under pressure!" says Eugene Mulligan of Furlong's earlier efforts. "As time went on obviously he worked on his kickout and he was hitting them pretty decently."

In June 1978 Offaly beat Longford at a canter and went to Portlaoise and overcame Laois more comfortably than the final two-point margin suggested. John Furlong penned a letter to his mother, who was visiting her sons in America, telling her how it was the best Offaly performance since 1973. It set up a Leinster semi-final against Dublin, bidding for their third All-Ireland title in succession.

There was no shortage of drama early on in the game. A Vincent Henry free for Offaly struck the post in the second minute and a significant portion of the upright broke off as a result, barely missing Dublin goalkeeper Paddy Cullen. A couple of minutes later Furlong controversially conceded a penalty after a clash with John McCarthy as both of them raced for a breaking ball. It seemed a harsh call by referee Séamus Aldridge. Both men were worse for wear following the collision.

"I think it was his fist or elbow got me in the butt of the chin," Furlong recalls. "It drove my bottom teeth into my top gums. I had top dentures from the time I was 17. I got my teeth out one time when I was in Wexford on holidays. I had to get a couple of teeth out and he took them all out."

Jimmy Keaveney stroked the penalty past Furlong but Offaly took control of the game for the rest of the half. They led 0-6 to 1-2 at half-time, though it was scant reward for their domination, even allowing for the penalty that kept Dublin in touch. Kevin Heffernan was no longer in charge of Dublin but, having passed the reins to player-manager Tony Hanahoe, the St Vincent's influence was still strong.

"I remember going onto the field at half-time and the Dublin players were going by me and I looked into their eyes, most of them, and they had a haunted look about them," remembers Eugene McGee. "This was not supposed to be happening. And, as well as that, the last person Dublin wanted in charge of Offaly was me, that's for sure. Heffernan especially. I had gone through Dublin club football with Vincent's for seven or eight years. Some of the dirtiest football ever played in Ireland between Vincent's and UCD. I would blame Vincent's of course but, lookit, it takes two to tango."

It was panic stations for Dublin when Offaly kicked the first four points of the half. Sitting on the bench was Kevin Moran, home for the summer having only signed for Manchester United the previous February. He wasn't listed on the match programme and Dublin didn't envisage a scenario where they'd need him against Offaly but he was sent in to his customary centre-back slot early in the second half with the champions sinking fast. He made a few trademark bursts upfield that paved the way for three Keaveney points and with 12 minutes to go Dublin were level.

Willie Bryan had been recast as a full-forward and won a free to allow Henry to restore Offaly's lead. Bobby Doyle kicked another equaliser before Anton O'Toole pounced on a defensive blunder and flicked a pass to David Hickey who placed McCarthy to score a sickening match winning goal in the dying minutes. Dublin survived the fright of their lives to win by three points.

"I met Aldridge a couple of years ago at some function or other," says McGee, "and he said, 'Jaysus, I think I was wrong about that penalty'. It was harsh but it happened so quickly nobody had time to think. Keaveney scored the goal and that was it. They would never have won it only for that. They should never have won that match."

The disappointment of losing was one thing for Furlong, the fact that his mouth was in ribbons as a result of the clash with McCarthy was another matter altogether.

"That was in July. I got my teeth back into my mouth so I could eat my Christmas dinner. I was on fluids for a while. I used to put hot water on the dentures thinking they'd soften them or whatever and I'd just force them in and force the shape of my gums around the dentures."

Although defeat was their lot, that Dublin game offered hope to the team, management and supporters that there was a movement in Offaly football once again. The team retained experience in the shape of Furlong, Mulligan, Kevin Kilmurray and Paddy Fenning and there was a core of exciting young players, none more so than the burgeoning talent of Matt Connor.

"I suppose my first real contact would have been watching him play with Walsh Island," says Furlong. "Matt won matches for Walsh Island on his own. I remember him one particular day and he was doing nothing. Next thing Matt went off down the field and gathered up a ball and came soloing up, laid it off, kept going, got it back, laid it off, kept going. And buried it in the back of the net. Just like that. Turned the whole game around.

"He was the best. The very best. Not because he was from Offaly, but he was the best forward I ever saw."

"He was just so good," says Bernard Brogan. "If Matt Connor was playing today, would he get on any county team? Absolutely. So, is he the best forward ever? He'd be there or thereabouts. He was so good, he had two feet, he was a big physical fella. He was very good on his feet, very fast.

"I know my son Bernard is very good as well. Would he be better than Bernard? As a footballer, probably yeah, he was. And Bernard's very good. But Matt Connor would have been more of an in and out the field player than Bernard would be. When you look at fellas like Mikey Sheehy and all that, they were on great teams, they had great players around them but when Matt Connor started off he was the scoring forward. He did most of the scoring."

Over the years there was little in the way of specialised goalkeeping training for Furlong. Matt inadvertently filled that void for him. They began to stay on after training with Matt rifling shots at him as he flung himself around the goal. He saved his fair share of them but sometimes wondered if it was worth his while at all; the power in Matt's shots was phenomenal and often left his palms raw.

Although Furlong was more than a dozen years Matt's senior, they became firm friends. Their personalities rhymed in many ways in that both were quiet and unassuming and carried their reputations lightly.

"We were very good friends, we used to have drinks together," explains Furlong. "We used to have a little bit of a competition. I was partial to a drop of brandy at the time and Matt liked a pint of Guinness and when we'd start taking penalties, if he scored I owed him a pint, if I saved he owed me a brandy. I think I owed him more pints than I got brandies anyway!

"Definitely, the after training sessions with Matt did help, no doubt about it. We used to have good battles. He'd be bursting his ass to score a goal and I'd be bursting my ass to save it."

If there was one marked difference between Furlong and Matt, however, it was their demeanour on the field. No player was foolish enough to take liberties with Furlong but with Matt they felt they could get away with it.

"That was one of my pet grievances with Matt, that he never stood up for himself. He allowed insignificant guys to pull him and drag him around the field.

"I gave out to him one day, we were playing Wexford. He was getting hacked around the place and I lit on him at half-time. I said, 'What the fuck are you doing Matt, don't take that shit!' Matt was a big guy, he was six foot one or two. I said, 'You've got to stand up for yourself'. That would not be in Matt's DNA now. His brother Richie would be a different kettle of fish. Richie would take him on, straight up."

Furlong wasn't one for dressing room outbursts like that too often but his status within the group at that stage of his career commanded the utmost respect.

"In the earlier days I suppose McCormack dominated the dressing room but, when McCormack had gone, Furlong came in as the inspirational leader," explains Mulligan. "He wasn't a man that would say too much but if he did say it he'd mean it and you'd listen. If someone was after rounding you or doing something he'd say, 'Come on lad, come again'. He'd never say, 'For fuck's sake, tidy up your game', or whatever. He was never negative as a goalie even if you were getting a roasting. Now, maybe off the field he might say to you, 'You better cop yourself on', or whatever. Martin was very inspirational. He was a very positive person."

Offaly looked to 1979 with renewed hope. They beat Laois and Meath to reach their first Leinster final in six years. Dublin were waiting for them. The previous year they had been denied a third All-Ireland title in succession in a memorable final as Eoin 'Bomber' Liston came of age for Kerry, boring all sorts of holes in their defence. Dublin, with Kevin Heffernan now back in charge, had been on the road for a number of years having reached five All-Ireland finals in succession. Offaly were the coming team.

"We were, not struggling then, we were sort of wobbling," explains Brogan. "If you look at our team, fellas like Jimmy Keaveney, Gay O'Driscoll and those guys. There were all 32 or 33 at that stage. Six of our team were near the end of their career and those games were being played at a fairly hot pace. The advantage we had in '74 was we had fellas who were 26, 27 with a lot of experience but those lads, in '78, were gone the other side."

The Offaly-Dublin games of that era were relentlessly physical. Unusually for a GAA fixture, there were clashes outside the ground as well that day. Hill 16 filled up early and 15 minutes before the throw-in about 150 Dublin supporters stormed the garda barricade.

Like the previous year, Offaly set the pace and Dublin clung on as best they could. The Offaly half-back line of Pat Fitzgerald, Richie Connor and Stephen Darby was impenetrable in the face of Dublin attacks. Dublin, going for a record sixth Leinster title in succession, only managed 0-3 in the first half, all from placed balls. The trouble for Offaly was they could only register 0-5 themselves despite their dominance. Things got ugly before half-time and Keaveney was sent off.

With the extra man, Offaly pushed on and held a 0-9 to 0-4 lead with 13 minutes remaining. Dublin would most likely need a goal to retrieve the situation; when Jim Ronayne had one disallowed their cause looked hopeless. Steeled by the resilience of their previous five glorious years, Dublin flashed over a succession of points to narrow the gap to the minimum with Offaly retreating fast but time was almost up.

A late Dublin attack amounted to nothing and Furlong saw Brian Mullins bang the ground in frustration and sensed he was resigned to defeat. But he wasn't done yet. Seconds later Dublin were awarded a free in the middle of the field and when Mullins reacted angrily referee Paddy Collins opted to throw the ball up instead. Dublin won it and Mullins came storming through the middle with Bernard Brogan outside him.

"We advanced straight on the goal. Furlong was on the other side of goal, going for Mullins. He gave it to me and I put it in the net. And that was the last kick of the game. He put the ball down, kicked it out and the whistle blew.

"That was amazing. We were beaten in that match. Like Offaly look back and say they left it behind them as opposed to us winning it. In that match we sort of stuck in. You don't get many matches where you win like that.

"I was working with a fella, an Offaly guy, and he was in the stand with an American visitor and he had a bet before the match and the American guy had actually paid the money across. He had bet on Dublin and the Offaly guy had bet on Offaly and he had paid the bet before I scored the goal."

The match was later immortalised in song through the Wolfe Tones' 'Fourteen Men'.

And there was 14 on, 14 was off,
Jimmy on the sideline having a gawk,
Heffo and the boys were working out a plan,
How to beat the Offaly lads without the extra man.

The front page of the following day's *Irish Press* led with Furlong bemoaning Offaly's misfortune. "I can't believe it... I didn't think fate could be so cruel to us." He also told the journalist, Seán Mannion, that he would give retirement serious consideration. If he did, he didn't ponder on it too long. Once the rawness of the defeat subsided, he reasoned that the team remained on an upward curve and his form was still good.

Others weren't so sure about the team's progress. A noisy constituency in Offaly weren't too enamoured with McGee and his regime. There was an element of arrogance to it, too: what would a Longford man be able to tell us about football? His existing selectors were voted out at a county board meeting though he would be retained with four new selectors foisted on him. They would be Noel McGee, Mick O'Rourke, Seán Cooney and Furlong, who was on holidays in Enniscrone at the time and picked up the paper one morning to learn he was an Offaly selector.

"They went on their own then and picked the team for the winter and the National League," recalls Eugene McGee. "I had no say because it was always four-one. It was a very delicate situation. After the league I made a decision that I was going to have to do something about this. I wasn't going to go through the championship with that carry on.

"There was a big tournament match that used to take place on one of the church holidays in May in Ferbane, usually it was Galway and Offaly and there'd be a couple of thousand at it. When we went to the dressing room before the match, I handed the lads the team sheet and I said, 'That's the team we're playing today'. Without any consultation.

"So, of course, they got into a huff and walked out and went on the far side of the field. Thankfully we won the match. So that night then, they wrote a letter to Fr Heaney, the four of them signed it, saying that because of what had happened they couldn't continue as selectors. Fr Heaney went around to each of their houses and dropped a letter in thanking them for their services, full stop."

A caretaker selection team was put in place for a while before McGee eventually enlisted the services of Seán Foran, PJ Mahon, Paddy Fenlon and Leo Grogan. Furlong had enough to be contending with as a player and combining it with a role in the management team, he reflects, wasn't the brightest of ideas. If there was any acrimony between him and McGee it subsided very quickly, though he was sympathetic towards his three fellow selectors who missed out on what was to follow.

"It probably put more pressure on McGee than anyone," says Furlong. "You couldn't keep on losing to the same team again. It was a hump we had to get over."

◆ ◆ ◆ ◆

Offaly were back in the Leinster final in 1980 with Dublin their opponents once more. They reached their sixth successive All-Ireland final the year before but suffered another trouncing at the hands of a Kerry team approaching the peak of its powers. Retirements were rife, Mullins was involved in a car accident that could have killed him. Their team was groaning and, this time, Offaly simply couldn't lose to them again and look forward to the following year with optimism.

Among the Dublin retirees following the 1979 campaign was goalkeeper Paddy Cullen. Heffernan couldn't settle on his successor and parachuted the previous year's minor goalkeeper John O'Leary into the panel ahead of the Leinster final.

"I got a phonecall on the Friday night to come training on the Saturday and I was told to bring my gear on the Sunday," he recalls. "I remember Tommy Drumm asked me on the way in to Croke Park would I like to be playing and of course I gave the standard answer, 'Oh I'd love to be playing'. Maybe he knew. I didn't know until half an hour later, Kevin Heffernan gave me the jersey and said, 'You're in today'."

As Furlong's inter-county career was coming towards its latter stages, another goalkeeping great was being unveiled. Later, Con Houlihan would write that "Martin Furlong is the more brilliant – John O'Leary is less liable to make a mistake".

The goalkeeping trade was changing and O'Leary had grown up in an era where they weren't a hunted species. Therefore, charging off his line a la Furlong wasn't an essential part of his artillery.

"His heritage would have been that a forward could come in and kill the goalkeeper and he turned it the other way: he'd come out and kill the full-forward when you could get away with both of them. I wouldn't have experienced that coming through at underage. So, by the time I got to the senior team it was kind of gone. The days of goalkeepers ending up in the back of the net was gone as an acceptable policy."

Early in the game Furlong's fearless instincts, for once, saw him come out worse for wear. A ball broke in front of the Offaly goal and he charged out as Dublin forward John Caffrey closed in.

"I would have overheard a discussion with David Hickey and Jimmy Keaveney talking about Martin Furlong and they would have had fierce respect for him," says Caffrey. "They were saying you went into his square and you paid the price. He was in charge of the square.

"The two of us went in, he went down and my knee collided with his head and he ended up wearing a bloodied bandage for the rest of the match. The ball broke loose and Bobby Doyle kicked it into an empty net."

Furlong was treated for several minutes and resumed the game, only realising that Dublin had scored a goal when he looked at the scoreboard. Undoubtedly, it was yet another case of concussion that he was oblivious to.

Dublin held a six-point lead at half-time. Offaly, and McGee, were staring down the barrel. Matt Connor was switched to centre-forward for the start of the second half. He kicked a couple of points and then applied a thunderous finish past O'Leary. In a role reversal of the previous two years, Offaly were now breathing on Dublin's shoulders and they kicked for home, eking out a critical two-point victory for the county's first Leinster title in seven years.

"His goal in 1980, that was the making of it," says McGee. "History would have been completely changed. It was a super goal by any standards. He had the option to pass the ball but he was confident enough to go and blast it."

The game was unmercifully robust, causing Houlihan to write in his much-loved *Evening Press* column the following day that "yesterday's game was not dirty: that is too mild a word – it was brutal." Furlong's bloodied face was splashed over the front page of the following day's papers. An excited Offaly fan rushed onto the field and embraced him at the final whistle, leaving her face smeared with his blood. "I'm not going to wash it, I'm not going to wash it!" she cried.

Making a play on a banner unfurled by Offaly supporters in the ground that day, Furlong told reporters after the game, "We flushed the Jacks and we will take Kerry in our stride." Having downed one of the finest sides in the history of the game, though admittedly well past their best, after three years of toiling, Offaly turned to face another behemoth. Kerry, however, were at the peak of their powers.

"I think we felt we had won not playing as well as we could against Dublin," says Furlong. "Playing against Kerry was a different kettle of fish altogether than playing against Dublin, a totally different type of game. It wasn't near as physical. They would play a pretty open style of football and we liked to think that we could play an open style of football and did. Dublin were notoriously strong and physical. Anyone that tells you Dublin play a lovely brand of football, they do, but Jaysus they can hurt you."

The game was something of an exhibition but Kerry were always in control. Three times they looked to have put clear daylight between themselves and Offaly but were reeled in. Their lead peaked at 11 points but finished at five – 4-15 to 4-10. Matt Connor proved he could mix it with the very best, scoring 2-9 of Offaly's total to bring his total for the year to a stunning 5-31. Gerry Carroll was Offaly's only other scorer on the day with 2-1.

The high-scoring nature of the game was aided by the handpassed goal, which was now becoming an epidemic. The majority of the goals in that game were handpassed efforts, a practice that was outlawed after 1980.

"It was depressing," says Furlong. "Why would you kick it? Why would you shoot when you could run in until you'd see the white of the goalkeeper's eye and just throw it one side of him? You were so helpless."

◆ ◆ ◆ ◆

Dublin were a spent force in Leinster after Offaly beat them in 1980. They didn't even get back to the provincial final in 1981 as Laois took them out at the semi-final stage. Laois had a decent side but lacked the wherewithal to beat Offaly in that era. A second successive Leinster title was secured and Offaly won a drab All-Ireland semi-final against Down to reach the decider for the first time in nine years.

The Offaly hurlers were also on the crest of the wave at the time. The previous year they had won their first ever Leinster title and retained it in 1981 to make for two successive provincial doubles. And this time both teams would be competing in the All-Ireland final.

Mickey Furlong packed his bags. His trips home were becoming more rare but with the two county teams that he played for both contesting All-Ireland finals in the space of a couple of weeks, and his kid brother involved with one of them, this was a trip that just couldn't be missed. With a much smaller family by comparison, Tom was a regular visitor to Ireland and the three Furlong brothers took their seats together in the Cusack Stand for the hurling final against Galway; John was too much of a creature of habit on big days to break rank from his usual crew. When Johnny Flaherty scored the match-clinching goal for Offaly late on, Mickey, Tom and Martin embraced as bedlam reigned around them.

"Next thing," says Tom, "Martin disappeared, he fell down on the ground in between the seats. 'Jaysus,' I thought, 'fuck me, I hope he's alright, that's all it needs now, Tom Furlong came home and hurt his brother before the All-Ireland'. Martin got up anyway and he was alright."

Remarkably, the double was on. Offaly is a small county by most comparisons and to split it between hurling and football and have two teams in All-Ireland finals in the one year was phenomenal, especially when set against the barren times that currently prevail. No county had ever won the All-Ireland double and Liam Currams, who was on both teams, was bidding for his own personal slice of history.

"The county was crazy," says Furlong. "People that never followed GAA was into it. It was huge. Everybody and their mother was into it. When you think about it now, Jesus Christ, a small county. That time the population was only 60,000 or 65,000 tops. It's mind-boggling to think that you were in two All-Irelands."

As reporters swept into Tullamore to gauge the mood among Offaly fans ahead of the football final, they were drawn to the Furlong brothers. John quoted Kerry's struggles to win All-Irelands in years ending in '1' as a favourable omen and another journalist asked Mickey if the double was on. "You'd better believe it," he replied. "The full potential of this Offaly team has yet to be realised but, with the first leg up, that time is now."

Mickey was half right, but Offaly's time to beat Kerry hadn't yet come. Disaster struck ahead of the final when Tomás O'Connor picked up a knee injury in a challenge game against Galway while Johnny Mooney broke his shoulder when falling off a trailer on the bog.

Suddenly an alternative midfield partnership was needed. In the end, the pair were patched up with the hope of getting a half out of each of them. That's how it transpired but they were nowhere near being right to take on Kerry, against whom limiting the variables was absolutely essential.

"Well, once Johnny Mooney fell off the load of turf I knew we were bolloxed, as simple as that," says McGee. "That again proved how thin the line is with a county like Offaly. It always is. One man can make a difference. If we had a full strength team in '81 we would have been very close, based on the scoreline."

Having been limited by O'Connor and Mooney's injuries, McGee set the team up to play a game of containment. It kept them competitive without ever really threatening to cause a shock.

"Gerry Carroll hit the crossbar midway through the second half," says Kerry's Mikey Sheehy. "That was a crucial moment in the game. I felt we were that little bit better than them but if that goal had gone in it could have changed the context of the game."

Kerry won by seven points in the end with only Jack O'Shea's late goal, arguably the greatest team score ever posted in Croke Park, finally killing off the Offaly challenge and wrapping up the four-in-a-row.

Furlong was helpless as the shot flew past him and into the top corner of the Hill 16 end goal. It didn't stain what had been an excellent season for him on a personal basis, however.

Once again, he was bewildered by the reception afforded to the team in Tullamore, similar to 1969, after coming home beaten. In O'Brien Park the crowd chanted "we want Furlong, we want Furlong" before he sheepishly emerged to the front of the platform to raucous cheers as Seán Lowry cradled his head in his broad chest.

A few months later he picked up his second All Star award, nine years after his first. In the 1981 championship he faced four penalties. He saved three of them. Earlier that year Sheehy lined up a penalty against him in an All Star game in New York. Furlong saved it to his right.

CHAPTER 16

SAVING GRACE

A FEW months after their historic All-Ireland success in 1981, the Offaly hurlers were presented with their medals at a function in the County Arms in Birr. On the same night, the footballers would get their Leinster medals and All-Ireland runners-up medals. When it was Eugene McGee's turn to speak, he took the opportunity to talk down the value of runners-up souvenirs.

"They only signify that you weren't good enough," he said.

Privately, McGee was adamant that Offaly's performance in the 1981 final was underestimated. For all the setbacks they suffered coming into the game with injury, not to mention the vast gulf in experience between them and Kerry in terms of contesting All-Ireland finals, they had been very competitive against the greatest team in the game's history and, in many respects, had turned a corner.

"It was completely misread by everybody, especially Kerry," says McGee of the '81 final. "They just assumed it was another easy Kerry victory. They won by seven points but they didn't analyse it. Only for Jack O'Shea's goal it would have been a so-called cliffhanger at the end.

"From the minute that match was over, I said, 'We're in business here', to myself. We were within shouting distance now because we had stopped this rampaging forward line scoring goals.

"I remember a tournament in Edenderry one Sunday night, six goals, and Furlong used to have a pain in his back. I remember one time we played them in Castleisland, the opening of a pitch, and there was six goals there as well. This craic went on all the time like. That's why '81 was so significant."

◆　◆　◆　◆

On November 15, 1981, Offaly went up to Roscommon and won an unremarkable National League game by four points. Afterwards, when they were in the hotel having their post-match meal, the All Star trip the following May came up. Martin Furlong, Richie Connor and Brendan Lowry were the only Offaly players chosen on the 1981 All Star team but others would be added to the party as replacements while McGee would also be going. The Kerry team, as All-Ireland champions, would travel in unison on the trip.

With closing the gap on them now their raison d'etre as footballers, Seán Lowry reckoned that the rest of the Offaly players couldn't afford to be left idle for a couple of weeks approaching the championship. He suggested a team holiday, but not the sort of jolly that would see them arrive back worse for wear: there would be a training regime drawn up for it too. Moreover, the wives and girlfriends would be included.

The players set off on an extensive fundraising drive and by the end of it had enough for a travelling party of 52 to spend a fortnight in Torremolinos. They trained hard every second morning. There was a social element to it as well and that was no harm. Lads could let their hair down as long as it didn't compromise their attendance at training. Twenty years later, when Armagh went to La Manga ahead of the championship in what turned out to be their All-Ireland winning year, it was seen as ground-breaking.

"It was a fabulous idea, a fabulous trip," says Seán Lowry. "Everyone was delighted with it. No matter how sick you were from the night before you'd get up and you'd go down. We had a great time. People got to know one another better.

"I'm not saying it helped to keep the women off our backs but it wasn't a coincidence that there was no fella missing from training afterwards and that when you came home in the evening your bag would be ready for you. Everyone was with us then at that stage and that was so important."

Furlong linked up with his brothers in America with the All Stars and training resumed seamlessly when he and the others returned home. At 35, he wasn't expected to do all the same training that the rest of the outfield players did but he did his share. Running up the hill in Rhode was torture.

Being a decade and more older than most of the players on the team and a settled family man with four young children, Furlong didn't have a huge amount in common with many of his teammates on the surface of things. But he gelled well with them nonetheless.

"When you're meeting as often and being together as often over that period from '77, you're talking about five years practically, near enough, living together between football and travelling and everything. There was no room for people not pulling. If you're not pulling, you're not winning. I depended on them and they depended on me."

The footballing landscape was different then. The championship was straight knockout and whatever was in Ulster and Connacht had, at best, an ability to frighten the genuine All-Ireland contenders on a given day without threatening much more than that. Not since Galway shocked Offaly in 1973 had a team from either province beaten Leinster or Munster opposition.

When Offaly were falling just short of Dublin while trying to burrow their way out of Leinster in the late '70s, Seán Lowry was never in any doubt that they would be coming back for another cut at them the following year given that the rest of the province wasn't up to it. Once they took care of Dublin in 1980, Kerry assumed that status in their minds.

"You knew then," says Lowry. "People say to me, 'It's so hard to train for an All-Ireland, it's so hard to train for a Leinster final, all the nights you're gone'. It's the easiest thing in the world to train for that. The hardest thing to train for is to play in a first round and know you're going to be beaten.

"That was the case for Westmeath and Laois that time and all the others. Laois were in the Leinster final in '81 but there was still no danger of them beating Offaly. I'd tell them that any time. We went to play Westmeath in Cusack Park in 1981 and they gave us a good run for their money in the first round but we hadn't even trained. That was their All-Ireland but if we were training to beat Westmeath we weren't going to play Kerry or Dublin."

That mindset was evident in McGee's approach. Johnny Mooney

went to America after the 1981 campaign and he was happy to wave him off, telling him he'd be flown home for the All-Ireland semi-final, so confident was he that Offaly would still be involved at that stage.

They beat Louth comfortably in the first round of the championship before labouring past Laois to set up another Leinster final meeting with Dublin. The legends of the '70s team were dropping out one by one and that game proved to be Bernard Brogan's last championship outing for Dublin as they suffered a chastening 1-16 to 1-7 defeat.

"Previous to that we were on the wane," he says. "We were trying to come back. It was traumatic. We didn't like being beaten but that Dublin team were beginning to wobble anyway."

Captain Richie Connor missed the game due to cartilage damage to his knee. Again, McGee's confidence was reflected in the fact that he was satisfied to send him for surgery when he might possibly have been patched up to play in the Leinster final. Having his best team available to face Kerry was all that mattered. Furlong was vice-captain and walked the steps of the Hogan Stand to lift the cup in Connor's absence.

Eyebrows were raised when McGee called Séamus Darby back into the panel following the Laois game after years in exile. He was parachuted straight into the team and hit 1-3 in the Leinster final. A hamstring injury ruled him out of the All-Ireland semi-final against Galway. Mooney returned to the team for the game and it was just as well: his performance was probably the difference as Offaly very nearly came unstuck as they eyed up Kerry in the final.

"I reckoned from the minute we lost the '81 final we were going to be back in the final and it wasn't false bravado," says McGee. "We knew Dublin were slipping at that stage and we beat them well in '82 so that proved the point, but the one that we nearly got caught was against Galway. Weeshie Fogarty gave them two frees and they got two 50s I think in the last 10 minutes and missed the whole lot of them."

Richie Connor returned to the side unexpectedly early for that semi-final and ended the game at centre-forward, where he did well. Seán Lowry had been shifted from full-forward and slotted in at centre-back in his absence for the Leinster final and coped comfortably with Brian Mullins, who was only feeling his way back into the game after his accident.

In the other semi-final Kerry had 10 points to spare on Armagh in yet another routine victory as they moved within one game of becoming the first team in GAA history to win five All-Irelands in succession. The fact that Armagh goalkeeper Brian McAlinden saved a penalty away to his right from Mikey Sheehy was barely a footnote.

◆　◆　◆　◆

A Kerry-Offaly final didn't have the same romantic appeal among the media as the Kerry-Dublin clashes of a few years earlier. However, Mikey Sheehy insists that that wasn't reflected in the mindset of how the Kerry players approached facing Offaly who, he says, were always afforded the same respect.

"The reason people might say that we didn't is because Dublin, being a city, it was the city slickers against the country boys. There was a big build up and there had been a ferocious tradition, even going back to the '55 All-Ireland final.

"The media seemed to build up the rivalry between Kerry and Dublin more than any other final that we would have played in against any team, be it Offaly, be it Roscommon, be it any team that you would play in a final, again because of the city slickers against the country boys. So it wouldn't have been a fact that you would take Dublin more seriously than Offaly."

Kerry had pucks of experience when it came to All-Ireland finals but this one would be different to any other ever played. All year there seemed to be rumblings about something or other. There was hassle about who would captain the team. Eventually the role went to John Egan.

As the final approached there were rows about whether Killarney or Tralee would welcome the victorious team home on the night after the All-Ireland final. A music group, Galleon, penned a song, Five in a Row. T-shirts were printed. Then there was hassle over what brand of jerseys Kerry would wear in the final, a saga that ran right up until the eve of the game.

None of this, of course, had anything to do with the Kerry players, but it didn't help them. Sheehy recalls Kerry's press night taking place about 10 days before the final. He thought it was too close to the game for a start. All the interviews took place on the pitch. It was a breezy evening and he began to feel cold and stiff as he stood yapping to press men. Then, Mick O'Dwyer put them through their paces.

"I'm only speaking for myself," says Sheehy, "but I felt tired and I just think the thing was going downhill from there.

"I won't say we were on a hiding to nothing but there was a pile of stuff that went on before that that was completely out of our control. Coming out on the Thursday before the game after training, Mick O'Dwyer lost the plot with some fella outside selling t-shirts which we had no control over. It was crazy stuff.

"I can remember even getting off the train in Dublin the day before the final and John Egan was captain, the late John. A guy from Sneem came over and myself and Seánie Walsh were getting off the train, 'Whatever you do, make sure you're down in Sneem on Monday night with the cup'. Again, you have no control over this kind of stuff."

There were other things, too. Jimmy Deenihan, their four-in-a-row captain and ever reliable corner-back, broke his leg a few months before the final. There was no sign of Pat Spillane's long-running knee problems coming right as he struggled through a madcap rehab programme.

There were signs of fatigue setting in with Kerry as well. They had a long league campaign that included a dog of a game with Cork the previous February before their rivals took them to a replay in the subsequent final, with Kerry eventually winning out. It took them a couple of games to shake off Cork in the Munster Championship too.

There was little pressure on Offaly by comparison. As a manager, the hoopla coming from Kerry was manna from heaven for McGee in terms of motivating his players.

Furlong chatted away to journalists at the Offaly press night. "Kerry might have the incentive, going for a record, but I wonder if they have the appetite," he told them. "It must be hard to keep going, the pressure is definitely on them. I think it would be a divil if they had to re-write the five-in-a-row song that's coming out," he added, in typical deadpan fashion.

The Offaly team had matured nicely over the years and had been fashioned with beating Kerry in mind. In front of Furlong, Liam O'Connor regularly seemed to have the measure of Eoin 'Bomber' Liston.

"Liam was tall and rangey," says Furlong. "As it turned out he was the right sort of a man to be marking Eoin Liston because he had the height for him anyway. He was able to get up there and knock the ball away or win it, you know. Liam didn't look to be a classy footballer or anything like that but, I mean, try and get around him just the same."

Seán Lowry had a lifetime of experience as a centre-back, a position he was settling back into nicely. At midfield Padraic Dunne was developing into an inter-county footballer of real substance with a tireless engine that allowed him to get up and down the field continually.

Richie Connor's duel with Tim Kennelly would be critical to the outcome. 'The Horse' had dominated numerous finals for Kerry from centre-back and halting his gallop was essential if Offaly were to be successful. Connor was probably the only player who could match him physically.

Naturally, much would depend on his brother Matt. However, with the emergence of Brendan Lowry, who had parked his soccer ambitions, over the previous couple of seasons, the scoring burden on him was eased somewhat. He didn't have his most influential game by his standards in the '82 final in terms of directly affecting the play, but he took such watching that it opened avenues for others, particularly Lowry.

"Everyone was afraid of him getting the ball and scoring," says Seán Lowry of Matt. "It gives the rest of the team a small little bit more. If you look at '82, and I always maintain it, the full-forward line we had was Brendan Lowry, Matt Connor and Johnny Mooney. Sure I mean, janey God, where would you get a forward line like that? I always think that's the best full-forward line, as good as what Kerry ever had."

Over the summer they had developed a simple but ultimately effective gameplan. The Kerry forward line thrived on one-twos, giving and going. The Offaly defenders would stick rigidly to their direct opponent in a bid to rob the Kerry attack of its fluency.

"Every night it was getting better and better and better," Lowry explains. "I used to come home and say to Nuala, 'We're getting better at this now. If we can crack this now, this is the one'. There was a lot of discipline in that back line."

The Sunday before the final, they went to do one last session on the hill in Rhode. Furlong took full part, two days before his 36th birthday, and felt in the shape of his life.

"That was a kind of a psychological thing," says McGee. "We had done that a lot. We said that we'd do it one more time before the big one. It wasn't really necessary but it was for effect really. He never looked like an athlete at all but he did a lot of that training.

"That hill was crazy. It was at least 400 yards long and straight up. It's still there. It was a brilliant thing. Apart from the element of sacrifice, it was practical. Don't forget, the runs were devised by Tom Donohue so they were scientifically devised. They weren't just picked out of my head. They were phenomenal for stamina."

After that session Furlong spoke to the players in the dressingroom. The previous year Offaly approached the final hoping that things might turn out well for them, this time their belief that they would win was unshakeable. He told them that they would be All-Ireland champions by the following Sunday. The players never needed any convincing about the validity of Furlong's statements.

"I just felt the determination was there, everybody was in good spirits, everybody was fit. Everything seemed to be right."

Offaly played Roscommon and Down in a couple of challenge games held in secret in the run up the final. Unlike now, those counties were back in training at that time of year with the National League approaching. Offaly won both games comfortably and Down manager James McCartan Snr approached McGee and told him, "You're going to win this final, you're just playing too well."

"You couldn't be going in hoping against that Kerry team," says McGee. "There's such a slight difference between hoping and knowing. Everybody says they know but they don't know. They actually are hoping."

Tom Furlong shared the confidence of his brother too. He travelled home for the game and the day before was coming out of the Brewery Tap and making his way over to his car in O'Connor Square when Mick Dunne of RTÉ spotted him. He was in town soaking up the last of the pre-match atmosphere and asked Tom for a few words. He happily obliged. Naturally, he asked Tom who he thought would win.

"Well," he replied, "I was just talking to my wife and she told me she had a dream that Offaly scored a goal in the last minute and beat Kerry. I'm going with that: Offaly's going to win with a last minute goal."

The mood in Offaly was different from 12 months earlier. Then, the hurlers had just won a historic first All-Ireland and the prospect of becoming the first county to win both titles in the one year sent the public into a frenzy as the football final approached. In 1982, the colours were out alright but it was as much for the sake of it than anything else. Few inside the county believed Offaly would stop Kerry.

One of the luxuries Offaly players had in the run up to big games at Croke Park was that they could sleep in their own beds the night before. That Saturday evening Katie Furlong prepared her husband's gear bag as she had done for years. Boots, socks, nicks, swimming togs and towel. He wasn't one for wearing gloves unless it was a wet day. The high-tech pairs available today that almost double the size of goalkeepers' hands weren't in vogue back then; a woollen pair was more than sufficient for Furlong. A peak cap to guard against the sun was also essential. So too was his drop of brandy.

Then there were his trademark knee pads. People assumed that he bad knees because of them, but he didn't. Goalmouths could be rather unkempt places back then and, given Furlong's all action, some would call it kamikaze, style of goalkeeping he tended to skin his knees rather badly and they'd never get a chance to recover. So he wore the pads.

A couple of days before the final Seán Lowry attended the removal of an aunt of his in Moate. Afterwards, a contingent repaired to the family home. Most were drinking half ones but Lowry sat in the corner sipping tea. A lot of players wouldn't want to expose themselves to the inevitability of chit chat about the game less than 48 hours in advance but that was never Lowry's way. He enjoyed interacting with supporters, feeling it was part of his duty as a county footballer.

"The biggest job I had," he says, "was stopping talking most of the time."

He was approached by a chap from Edenderry, Declan Carolan, who was known to the family. Not long after he started talking, Lowry could tell there was a different hum to what he had to say compared to the usual platitudes.

He told him how, as a youngster, the much celebrated Tipperary hurler Pat Stakelum was a hero of his. One day, years after Stakelum had finished playing, he saw him in Athlone Golf Club. He approached him and they talked away about hurling. He felt fortunate that he got to meet his idol and impress on him just how inspirational a figure he was in his youth. But he was in the minority in that respect, and that was the essential point he was making to Lowry.

"You'll never know all the people that are shouting for you," he told him. "You'll never meet them. There's going to be old women shouting for ye on Sunday and ye'll never meet them after, people in Australia and America will get up on Monday morning with their chest out because ye beat Kerry.

"You think you're playing for your family and your fans but there's people you'll never meet and they'll be as proud as punch."

It had a profound effect on Lowry. He felt it would be remiss of him not to share it with his teammates. He relayed the story to Richie Connor on the morning of the game. Connor told Lowry that he would have to impart it on the players and they agreed Lowry would do it last thing before they went out on the field.

"I didn't want them to get out of that zone because I can remember when I was told it how it affected me and this was serious stuff," Lowry explains. "I thought it was a fabulous story and I just said it would have a huge effect on people, which it did. But still, if you spoke to every one of the Offaly fellas in '82 some of them might say, 'I never heard the speech at all'. Liam Currams always said it was unbelievable altogether, the effect on him."

By the time Lowry relayed the story, Furlong had already taken his customary swig of brandy. He always brought it out with him too, just in case there was a lull in the match and he felt he needed a jolt. As the Artane Boys Band played Amhrán na bhFiann he would typically run through the Our Father, praying for a bit of spiritual guidance to come their way. Against this awesome Kerry outfit, Offaly needed it more than ever.

Before the ball was thrown in, Richie Connor met Tim Kennelly with a thump into the chest that creased him. The match was only a few minutes old when John Guinan nailed him with a shoulder unawares.

"After that he was only a shadow of himself," says Lowry. "'What's going on here? This never happened to me before'."

Offaly bossed the game for much of the opening half. Each of the half-backs got up to kick a point each. Brendan Lowry hit three. Johnny Mooney was cruising through the game having kicked one point and had a hand in four others. Offaly could feel somewhat short-changed by the fact that they only led by a point, 0-10 to 0-9, at half-time. It had been a terrific game of football and Offaly had shown that they could take Kerry on through their footballing ability without building their game plan around containment, which had essentially been foisted on them 12 months before.

Kerry were always likely to come with a big surge in the third quarter. Rain teemed down at half-time and changed the terms of combat somewhat. Kerry hit three of the first four points of the second half to go in front. They often devastated teams in periods like this. Another flurry of scores, or even a goal, would put the five-in-a-row within touching distance.

A John Egan point effort landed on the crossbar and Furlong dived on the rebound ahead of Eoin Liston, who landed on top of him. He got up and defiantly banged his chest three times in an effort to inspire his teammates.

A few minutes later Liam O'Connor made a crucial interception to deny John Egan possession in front of the Offaly goal. Furlong swept up the loose ball but his stray handpass only found Pat Spillane, who returned the ball to Egan. Stephen Darby grappled with him. When Egan hit the ground he looked at the referee PJ McGrath in anticipation of a penalty. With none forthcoming, he got to his feet and attempted to shoot again. As he did, Darby pulled him down. This time McGrath spread his arms for a spot kick.

◆　　◆　　◆　　◆

That All-Ireland final was Martin Furlong's 56th senior championship game for Offaly. By then, he was straining every last drop of experience he had accumulated over the years. He knew Croke Park and how it played.

"Croke Park wasn't a level field," he says. "If you were in the Hill 16 end, the side of the square on the Nally Stand was higher than the side of the square on the Cusack Stand and Hill 16 side. And if you were down the other end, it was higher on the left hand side than it was on the right hand side. I always felt the forward coming in from the high side had the advantage. You were sort of running up a hill like. It wasn't a hill but every inch counts at that stage."

His record at saving penalties was good. He didn't exude confidence in terms of how he carried himself as a person generally but in this setting he was sure he wouldn't be beaten. He had a simple but informed theory on penalty-takers.

"The pressure's on the other guy, isn't it? He's expected to score.

I had a philosophy of watching the ball. Fellas can throw shapes this way and that way. I always found that watching the ball was the best logic.

"A penalty-taker would normally kick the ball where he felt was his strongest point so if a left-footed guy is kicking it, nine times out of 10 he's going to try and put it to his right-hand corner. And a right-footed kicker is going to go in the other side."

Mikey Sheehy was right-footed, therefore he was most likely to strike to his left and Furlong's right, he reckoned.

"Very seldom I scored a penalty to my right-hand side," says Sheehy. "I got a good few of them for my club but I'd say 90 percent of them were that side."

Sheehy didn't fancy this penalty, though. He didn't believe that penalty-takers should be pre-ordained, feeling that a player's form in a match would dictate the likelihood of scoring too much. In the 1979 final he was in flying form and lamped one past Paddy Cullen. In '82, though, Mick Fitzgerald stuck to him like a leech and he couldn't work his way into the game.

"I wasn't playing well that day and I would have been quite happy if someone else wanted to take it. Fellas were saying to me, 'Why did you take it?' Fuck it, because nobody else wanted to take it! There was plenty of volunteers a week or two later when they were having a couple of pints inside in Tralee! But nobody would volunteer to take it.

"Jacko would have been a good kicker now. Egan would have been a fella who was good but John never wanted to kick a penalty. The rest of the lads didn't."

Furlong screamed at his defenders to watch the rebound as Sheehy lined up the kick. He struck it to the side Furlong expected him to, about four feet off the ground. Furlong advanced off his line and palmed it away. Pat Fitzgerald picked up the rebound and Offaly swept down the field. Soon, Johnny Mooney kicked a point and the sides were level.

"That was our chance," says Sheehy. "I felt when I missed that penalty, there was something in my head saying, 'We're going to lose this game'."

"I remember banging me fist, banging me fist, banging me fist," says Furlong. "It was a great feeling, Jaysus, to save a penalty in an All-Ireland. Not that you'd have thought about it at that stage. We were still in it."

A goal at that stage might have seen Kerry shift into turbo mode and blow Offaly away, as they had often done before. They still had the better of the game and moved four points clear in the final stages. But they weren't out of sight.

"I felt we were in trouble alright," says Furlong when they drifted four behind. "I don't think I'd ever say it was gone but we needed a score. Matt scored a couple of points from a couple of frees."

In Michael Foley's *Kings of September* McGrath insisted that both frees were fair awards, though it could certainly be argued that they were soft. "I thought mine was dubious enough," admits Seán Lowry. "But I'd say PJ McGrath thought that we were beaten. I remember I hopped the ball and it must have hit a divot or something and it went sideways on me. Someone kind of came across and I fell then but the ball went from me."

"That'll happen," says Sheehy philosophically. "We often got soft frees."

By then, Kerry were retreating fast as they attempted to hold their lead and ensure history and the five-in-a-row. The Offaly half of the field was largely a vast expanse left idle in front of Furlong. Rather than being in position to kick the insurance scores, Sheehy and Co had drifted back into defence.

"Micko got blamed then, that we went back defensive after missing the penalty. We didn't. It was just a subconscious thing. That's exactly what it was. Everybody went back and I could see it coming."

With seven minutes remaining Séamus Darby replaced John Guinan and went straight in at corner-forward. With a couple of minutes to go and Offaly two points down, they won a free around midfield after Liston barrelled into Pat Fitzgerald. He clipped the ball to Richie Connor, who transferred it to Liam O'Connor, up from full-back. His long and hopeful delivery was dropping between Tommy Doyle and Séamus Darby. Doyle appeared to mistime his jump, Darby peeled off him, caught the ball and arced a beautiful left-footed shot into Charlie Nelligan's top left-hand corner.

"That was a brilliant goal," says Furlong. "It was going away from Charlie Nelligan all the way. Charlie couldn't be blamed. It was a tremendous shot that dipped down to the corner of the net. Hardest shot for a goalkeeper to save."

"Fuck it, the finish was unreal," Sheehy adds. "It was a great goal. It was a historical goal and it'll be spoken about forever and ever."

Gerry Carroll had a chance to double Offaly's lead but kicked wide. Yet, Kerry still had time to retrieve the situation. Tom Spillane set off on a run down the Hogan Stand sideline but Seán Lowry stripped him of possession. Furlong raced out and collected the loose ball before directing a handpass towards Brendan Lowry only for Sheehy to intercept. He looped the ball back across goal. Seán Lowry waited for it to drop.

"I remember thinking if I catch it over my head and the Bomber comes in and drives it into the back of the net, it's all for nothing. Imagine all these things came into my head. I was catching it in my chest and just then, when it was still a good bit up, 'You're on your own Jack', someone behind me shouted.

"Paudie Lynch was nearby. Never came. Never jumped. Eoin Liston could have got there no problem. They were just shell shocked."

"When the head goes..." says Sheehy ruefully. "It isn't as though we didn't have our chances. We had two or three chances to level it. We had no pot at goal but we could have engineered a chance to do it."

The final whistle sounded with Lowry sauntering out of defence with ball in hand. The crowd soon engulfed the players. Furlong was chaired by Offaly supporters, pulled and dragged this way and that. He didn't mind a bit of it.

"It was like a lorry load of bricks was lifted off you. The elation. The relief. The relief that you finally got there and it was over. Ecstasy and relief, that'd be about right. You were so close to losing it and then to win it. Mind-boggling.

"The fact that we were such, such outsiders, to pull that win off against a team that was going for five-in-a-row, hard to beat that satisfaction."

In the dressing room afterwards he was interviewed by reporters. "We beat one of the best teams of all time," he told them. "We mustn't be too bad ourselves so."

As long as football is discussed, the debate will rage as to whether Darby pushed Doyle in the back before gaining possession. Again, McGrath always insisted that he made the right call. It's reasonable to conclude that if he had given a free out, the uproar would have been much greater.

"Who ever went for a ball that didn't get nudged or shoved or pushed?" asks Furlong. "Come on, let's be honest about it. Football is not played like that. It's a contact sport. Pushing and shoving you'd see anywhere, in any game."

Some Kerry players are adamant that it should have been a free out. Others are more magnanimous about it. Sheehy falls into the latter category.

"The goal was the goal. People say that there was a nudge. We often got away with nudges. It was innocuous enough."

When the Offaly team arrived back in Tullamore the following night to be greeted by thousands, they knew they'd achieved something special. Once again the local crowd chanted "we want Furlong".

"To be coming down the street with the cup... it's one of the greatest feelings of all time," he says.

On the Tuesday morning Tom Furlong put his suitcase in the boot of the car, intending to head to the Listowel Races to hook up with Mickey Moynihan and Brendan O'Donnell as he did every year. By Thursday, his mother advised him to take the suitcase out of the car – he still hadn't made it out of town.

The following day he finally resolved to make his way for Kerry. As he drove away from the family home on O'Moore Street he met Martin walking on the street. He was in ribbons.

"Where are you going," he asked Tom.

"Down to Kerry," he replied.

"Do you want company?"

"Why, what's the matter?"

"I have to get out of this fucking county, it'll kill me with brandy!"

They hooked up with Moynihan and the boys in Tarbert and were chatting in a bar when they noticed a young lad of about 10 or so peering around the corner at them. It was clear he recognised Martin. The lads thought maybe that he wanted an autograph. Eventually he approached them.

"Are you Martin Furlong?"

"I am."

"Well, Charlie Nelligan's a better goalkeeper than you!" he said, before scampering away.

They roared laughing at the good of it.

Bowing out at that stage would have made for a glorious ending to Martin's magnificent career. Again, with Noel McGee's words from years before still ringing in his ears, he still felt he had something to offer. And while the team had been on the road quite a while, its age profile was generally young.

However, they would never scale the same heights again. Kerry regrouped from absolute devastation to win a few more All-Irelands that Sheehy and others felt they wouldn't have had the appetite for if they had won the five-in-a-row.

"It took a long, long time to get that defeat out of our system, I'll tell you that," he says. "It took Micko longer than any of the players but it took us a long time to get over it. We were mentally scarred for a while. Then, in fairness, the majority of the team won in '84, '85, '86, which was a good achievement again.

"We were up a few years ago in the Bridge House in Tullamore. They had a reunion. We had a great night altogether. Typical Offaly.

We would compare Offaly with ourselves, country lads, enjoy the game and enjoy the craic.

"That night now, they gave us a fantastic night. We got a great ovation from the lads. We wouldn't have said it straight after the game but, in years after, if you wanted to be beaten by anybody, you'd be quite happy to be beaten by a team like Offaly."

CHAPTER 17

THE FINAL FURLONG

AS a winter full of celebrations and banquets rolled out in front of the Offaly players and as 1982 blended into '83, the accolades mounted up for Martin Furlong. Man of the Match in the All-Ireland final. Save of the Year from RTÉ for his block on Mikey Sheehy's penalty. Another All Star award. Tullamore GAA Club made a string of presentations to him on the night of its annual dinner dance. But the award that meant most to him was that of the Texaco Footballer of the Year.

In more recent years, the All Stars scheme initiated its own version of player of the year which is now considered the most prestigious individual prize in the game, but back then the Texaco award was the only show in town. Just one goalkeeper had won it before, Billy Morgan in 1973, and no 'keeper has won a footballer of the year award of any kind since.

The awards banquet itself offered something different to the All Stars, which was an exclusively GAA affair. The Texaco awards recognise all mainstream sports. The hurling award went to another goalkeeper, Noel Skehan of Kilkenny. Ollie Campbell was the recipient for rugby, Gerry Armstrong for soccer. Seán Kelly for cycling. The racing award went to Pat Eddery. Ronnie Delany was inducted into the hall of fame.

Barry McGuigan won the boxing award. Furlong stretched out his hand to shake it with his. McGuigan pulled back, though. He had recently beaten Vernon Penprase to win the BBBC Featherweight Title and his hands were still raw.

The star attraction, however, was snooker's Alex Higgins. He had been crowned world champion for the second time the year before. As the night dragged on, the Hurricane grew restless. "This is boring," he said to Furlong, "let's get the fuck out of here."

God knows what a night on the tiles in Dublin with Higgins would have brought with it. Furlong resisted the temptation.

"He was mad for action," he says. "I was too timid. I had a big interest in him. I had an interest in snooker because it was one of the few sports that was ideal for television. Unless you were sitting on the table you couldn't be any better. It was a tremendous television sport. That and darts."

That year's National League was a means to an end but Offaly maintained their dominance over Dublin, defeating them twice in the competition. In the Leinster Championship they had 13 points to spare on Wexford and romped to a 15-point win over Kildare to qualify for a fifth successive provincial decider. The Sunday before they were due to play Dublin in the Leinster final, Kerry were shocked by Cork in Munster as Tadhg Murphy, much like the previous September, hit a last minute goal to end their stranglehold on the province that stretched back to 1975.

Offaly were, certainly on paper, the best team left in the championship. Another All-Ireland was well within their grasp. Dublin had struggled through to the Leinster final and there was no indication that they were about to turn a corner.

The night before the game, Eugene McGee addressed the players in a manner that suggested they couldn't lose. The basic tenor of his speech was that they should go out and pummel Dublin into the ground.

"When you take on the like of Dublin or Kerry there can be no way that you can think you're going to have a handy day at the office," says Furlong. "In fact I think I might have mentioned it at the meeting that night. I had my nagging doubts that we were going to beat the crap out of them. That wasn't right."

Kevin Heffernan threw a tactical curve ball at Offaly. John Caffrey was named at right half-forward and started in the corner on Charlie Conroy but immediately reverted to a third midfielder role, a tactic very much in its infancy back then.

Caffrey's predicament is indicative of the inertia that seemed to be surrounding the Dublin team at the time. He had spent the previous summer in America and when he wasn't getting game time in '83 he told Heffernan he was off again. He hung around for the win over Louth in the semi-final and did well when introduced at half-time but soon left for Philadelphia. Heffernan flew him back for the Leinster final but his club in America had a ticket booked to fly him back the following morning. Few envisaged Dublin's summer lasting beyond that July afternoon.

"I would say that we caught them on the hop in '83, there's no doubt about it," says Caffrey. "They had been fairly convincing winners over us in '82.

"I got away with murder in the first half. Poor old Charlie wasn't a midfielder. Mullins was back then in '83 but he was carrying a leg. He wasn't nearly as athletic as he had been. Jim Ronayne was never the most athletic fella and they wanted me to play a line of three across the middle. I was the one doing most of the running and the donkey work."

The game was tight and edgy in the first half and Offaly looked to have weathered the storm with Dublin having spurned a number of opportunities but Joe McNally and Caffrey struck for two quick-fire goals before half-time to put the Dubs four points ahead.

They stretched it to seven after half-time, despite Furlong having saved a penalty from Mullins, before Matt Connor missed one at the other end. Connor got in for a goal to cut the deficit to three points entering the home straight. Offaly had found a winning kick from that juncture so many times in the past but, that day, it just wasn't there. Dublin closed out the game with the last couple of points. They won a scruffy All-Ireland against Galway the following September.

"I think we were a much better team in '83 than we were in '82," reflects Seán Lowry. "I remember we went down to play Sligo in a challenge match a couple of weeks before, opening some pitch or something, and God bless us, we were playing such free flowing football, such class football and everyone was playing with this abandon.

"We got off to a wrong start against Dublin. Everyone seemed to be in bother that day. You know where some fella might be in bother and you'd help him out, but that day we seemed to be all struggling with our men."

"We were too complacent," says McGee. "We thought we couldn't lose the match and we actually tried a couple of new things that day. I made that clear to the players. I take personal blame for that defeat."

McGee had toyed with the idea of quitting in a blaze of glory after the All-Ireland win and it was reported in the media at the time that he was on the brink of stepping down. Now, he felt he couldn't leave like this.

"Personal vanity didn't allow me to go in '82. I thought we'd win another one in '83. It appeared that Kerry were still on the wane and Dublin were cracking up so it looked an open door. The reason I stayed in '84 was for the centenary year."

The whole operation was grinding to a halt, however. Whether those in the inner circle realised it at the time was another matter entirely. Generally, the team was young in years but they had been on the road for quite some time. Furlong won his fourth All Star and third in succession for 1983 and committed to another year.

In the 1984 championship they managed to salvage a draw against Longford. Furlong would not be fit to play in the replay. Rheumatoid arthritis had set in and, at times, would restrict the movement in his arms severely, though that was kept a secret. Dinny Wynne got a long-awaited start in goal but had a poor first half. Laz Molloy, attending as a supporter, heard his name called out on the tannoy in Croke Park to report to the Offaly dressing room before the game. He ran back to his car, got his boots and, with Wynne struggling, was introduced for the second half.

Offaly got through to face Dublin in the semi-final the following Sunday and attempts to have the game postponed due to a lengthy injury list were knocked back. Furlong took the field for what proved to be his final championship outing at Croke Park. The teams had moved in different directions over the previous 12 months and Dublin won at a canter against 14 men with Brendan Lowry sent off early in the second half. Indeed, Offaly registered their only score of the second half in injury time and managed just 0-5 in total.

"The show was over," says McGee. "I knew it was over anyway because it was one of the first times I ever had to attack Matt Connor. There used to be an annual match there between Laois and Offaly in Clonbullogue for Fr Ramsbottom and we were pure shite in the first half.

"Matt Connor waddled around, didn't bother his arse, and I attacked him at half-time in the dressing room. Anyway, in the second half he gets out and blasts about three goals. He nearly took the head off the goalkeeper. The dust rising in the goals when he hit it was unbelievable. He tore the whole team apart.

"It was very seldom that I ever said anything to him or had to say anything to him but it was a sign of frustration on my part as well. You wouldn't normally have to do that."

Later that year came another representative honour for Furlong. The Compromise (now International) Rules series between Ireland and Australia was instigated for the first time. There would be three Tests, the first of which was in Páirc Uí Chaoimh. Furlong was chosen in goal. However, the arthritis laid him low again. He woke up in the team hotel on the morning of the game and couldn't raise his arm. An emergency call was sent out for Charlie Nelligan to replace him but he couldn't make it. Furlong took an injection from Dr Con Murphy and played.

"I had to play with one arm hanging down beside me. The Australians were big strapping hoors. It was a fairly rough and tumble match. We were horsed out of it."

The goalkeepers were rotated over the three Tests with Nelligan and John O'Leary also featuring as Australia won the inaugural series 2-1. Playing for Ireland completed a nice set of representative honours for Furlong with club, county, province and country, though the hybrid concept is something he's cooled on since.

"It has done nothing for GAA. All it has done for Australian Rules is that they could find a few players that could adapt themselves to it. But, I mean, what has it done for the GAA? Nothing."

◆   ◆   ◆   ◆

Whatever chance the Offaly team had of resurrecting itself rested largely on the shoulders of Matt Connor. By 1984 he was widely considered to be one of the greatest players to have played the game and, while still only 25, appeared to have his best years ahead of him yet. However, a cruel turn of misfortune meant that playing football was taken off his agenda. Indeed, he had a whole raft of extensive adjustments to make to his life before football even entered the equation.

Working as a garda in Tullamore, he dropped into the station for a while on Christmas morning 1984, as was the tradition. On the way home to Walsh Island his car spun out of control and hit a tree, leaving him paralysed from the waist down.

"It was the next day I heard about it," says Furlong. "I cried. I cried that night in the bed. I went to see him in Dun Laoghaire, an eye opener. And bad and all as Matt Connor was, there were people in there so much worse. There were people in beds they couldn't get out of and never would get out of. They used to rotate the bed. They were strapped into it but so they would get time off their back, if you like. That was just mind-boggling.

"I mean, my best buddy, as far as I was concerned, was in there and that was Matt. It's not what you wanted to see. I cried my eyes out that night too."

Eugene McGee was no longer Offaly manager by then having stood down and been replaced by John Courtney. His ties to Offaly and the Connor family remained strong, however, having married Matt's cousin, Marian.

"There's young people talking about Matt Connor who never saw him playing," he says. "What would he have been if he had played for another five years? Even with a bad Offaly team, he would have been the greatest superstar of all time because he would have got better, all those great players get better up until 30. So we only saw a glimpse of him.

"My memories of Matt Connor are primarily of training sessions. I saw him up close hundreds and hundreds of times and his contests with Furlong. We'd be playing backs and forwards a lot and Matt Connor would be scoring goals and Furlong would be getting angrier and angrier because he didn't like being beaten. It was very serious stuff.

"I think the greatest goal I ever remember him scoring was against Ferbane one Saturday evening. He walked through the whole bloody team and put a banana shot into the goals and people were gasping. Just couldn't understand that this had happened. Anyone who was at that match will never forget it. They won against the odds again, as usual.

"He did incredible things that time. We were lucky, we were privileged to see him. And like all great sportsmen around the world, his manner and demeanour matched his brilliance. That's a big factor. All the great players, Seán Purcell, Christy Ring and all these people, their demeanour matched their ability. They were modest beyond belief. Matt Connor was so modest it was unbelievable."

Mick O'Dwyer later commented that if he was able to call on a footballer of Connor's talents, Kerry might well have won 10 All-Irelands in succession.

"It was a tragedy, what happened him," says Mikey Sheehy. "We probably hadn't seen the best of him, and what we'd seen up to then... When Matt was going well he was unmarkable, very similar to the Gooch or Peter Canavan or Bernard Brogan or Maurice Fitzgerald.

"He's as good a player as ever put on a county jersey. Just pure class. Played the game as it should be played, Matt, and a lovely guy on and off the field. No ego with Matt. An exceptional talent, the kind of player who comes along once in a blue moon. I'd rate him as high as any player I've ever seen."

Shortly after the accident, the Matt Connor Trust Fund was established, with Furlong and McGee among those who served on the committee. In April 1985 benefit games were held for him in Tullamore, the All Stars against the Rest of Ireland in both hurling and football. Star players from all corners of the country played in front of a packed O'Connor Park.

"It wasn't going to be a big job because of the esteem that Matt was held throughout the country," says Furlong. "I mean, there's not anyone that could ever say a bad word about Matt Connor because he never pulled a stroke on anyone.

"You wouldn't hear Matt behind a newspaper. But his presence. You didn't have to hear him. His presence was enough. Just to be there.

"I have to say, I never saw Matt Connor feeling sorry for himself. I don't know what way he felt when he was at home or if he ever said, 'God, why me?' or whatever but I never, ever, ever, from that day to this, did I ever see Matt Connor feeling sorry for himself. Never met the man in bad humour. Never, ever."

Offaly faced into the 1985 championship with their chances of progression greatly diminished. Another championship meeting with Dublin beckoned, a Leinster semi-final, this time played in Tullamore. Ahead of the game, Furlong was interviewed along with John O'Leary by Micheál Ó Muircheartaigh. He indicated he'd retire if Offaly lost.

Offaly managed to be much more competitive than they managed 12 months earlier but Dublin were never in grave danger. They had a flattering six-point lead in the final minute when Furlong made a point-blank save from a Joe McNally effort. The rebound fell to Barney Rock, whose effort was blocked by Mick Fitzgerald before McNally finally finished to the net. Furlong turned to the umpires and argued that it was a square ball. They shook their heads. He smiled wryly at them and took the kickout. It was his last act as an inter-county footballer.

"After almost 20 years in the county colours, he is as much a tiger as ever – but he wasn't very busy yesterday," wrote Con Houlihan in the following day's *Evening Press*.

Ó Muircheartaigh cornered Furlong on the field after the final whistle, expecting that he might announce his retirement there and then.

"I denied it, which I thought afterwards was very unfair to Mícheál Ó Muircheartaigh."

The following Friday he sat down to pen a letter to John Dowling, secretary of the Offaly county board, who was making waves in GAA administration and would be elected incoming president of the Association within two years.

> *Dear John,*
>
> *This is to inform you of my decision to retire from inter-county football and to thank all the officers of the county board, past and present, for the courtesy shown to me down through the years.*
>
> *I would like to take this opportunity to wish all the Offaly teams of the future the best of luck in the years ahead and, to yourself, a special thanks and I hope that you soon attain the highest honours the GAA can bestow on you.*
>
> *Yours in sport,*
> *Martin Furlong.*

That same month, John Egan, who was within minutes of becoming Kerry's five-in-a-row captain in 1982, and Roscommon's Dermot Earley also announced their retirements. Furlong's inter-county career had started 19 years earlier and his 62 championship appearances was a Leinster record.

He also resolved to quit football completely as his 39th birthday approached. "My philosophy was if I wasn't fit to play for the county I wasn't fit to play for the club," he says. Ideally, that would have involved winning a fourth county title with Tullamore and, perhaps, a fairytale run through the club championship but it wasn't to be. By now he was back in goal for the club and a few weeks later Gracefield knocked them out of the championship in Daingean.

Naturally, he was very emotional at the final whistle. Those present recognised that one of the truly great footballing careers had come to a close, none more so than Pat Fitzgerald and Offaly manager John Courtney, who pulled him for a photograph as he made his way off the field. It meant a lot to him.

His career was glory laden, yet he has regrets. He played a bit of minor hurling for Offaly and is sorry that he didn't play more hurling with the club. When the Team of the Millennium was selected in 1999, he was shortlisted as one of the candidates for the goalkeeping position, though lost out to Kerry's Dan O'Keeffe.

As brilliant as he was, he felt he could have extracted more from himself. He gave up cigarettes shortly after he retired and didn't take a drink for some 13 years.

"I would have trained harder. I would have took better care of myself, eating right and drinking right and that sort of stuff. Not smoking.

"I read Donal Óg Cusack's book, there's goalkeeping coaches involved now and I'm saying, 'Jesus, that would have been lovely'. I would love to have had the current facilities."

The cabinet in his house groans under the weight of the various trophies and honours bestowed on him. He remains the most decorated player to have represented Offaly in either code.

"I'm very proud of that fact," he says, "but I would have no qualms if somebody beat it."

CHAPTER 18

NO MUD ON THAT NAME

ONE evening early in 1988, Tom Furlong put a call through to Bagnall's in Tullamore, near neighbours of Martin in Clonminch. Martin didn't have a phone in his house at the time so he'd often use theirs. Tom and Yvonne had bought a bar up by the Catskill Mountains for the sum of $160,000. It would hold a summer licence only but required a bit of work to get it up and running. Tom wanted someone he could trust with experience of the trade. He asked Martin would he come over for a few months and help him get the place started. Although he had toyed with the idea of moving to New York back in 1973, he had never really imagined leaving Tullamore. Tom said he'd ring back the next evening for his response.

"I was taken aback," says Martin. "I had to stop and gather myself. That was out of the blue, totally out of the blue. There was absolutely no talk about it previous to that. Didn't even have an idea that he was interested in buying a place. There wasn't much sleep got that night, I can tell you that."

He had to weigh things up quickly. He took a step back and wondered what he'd be leaving behind and the risk factors associated with it. He was a selector with the Offaly senior footballers, managed by Mickey McBrearty, at the time. By then he was supplementing his job as a rate collector with Offaly County Council with a bit of wood-cutting on the side.

One evening he was in Clonaslee cutting down a Norwegian spruce with a colleague from Walsh Island, Jody Nolan. As he went to hook up the near fallen tree he didn't notice another rotten one that was resting against it. As it fell it hit him on the back of the head and left him sprawling on the snow-covered ground.

By the time he got home that evening he was disoriented, feeling like his head was half full with water. He went to casualty in Tullamore General and was soon transferred to the Mater in Dublin where several tests were run. Fortunately, it didn't amount to anything serious and he was allowed home after a week. He continued to work at that job for some time afterwards and was glad of the extra income to supplement his Council job, which was effectively part-time. But experiences like that underlined how it wasn't the most attractive career to pursue.

Back in the '80s Ireland was an economic wasteland as young people left the country in droves. He thought of his four children. Joan was 17 at the time, a year older than Ken. Mark and Tom were 11 and 10 respectively. Would they have to leave the country in time to come too? He reckoned there was a strong likelihood that they would and reasoned that giving them a head start in America would be in their best interests. These are the things that he and Katie pored over long into the night after he came back from Bagnall's with his brother's startling proposal.

"Myself and herself were sitting there at the fire drinking tea and talking it around. At about two or three o'clock in the morning she said, 'Twenty years from now we could be sitting here looking into the same fire and saying, "I wonder what would have happened if we'd went to America?"'

And that was it. He took Tom's call the following evening and told him he'd take the job. "I was surprised when he said he would and then when he told me he was bringing the whole shebang, that was a tremendous challenge for somebody," says Tom.

It was a huge decision that, naturally, would bring quite an amount of upheaval with it. The household was settled and peaceful as it was. None of the children had ever been to America before.

"As kids, going to bed at night you'd be messing or playing around the room or whatever and you'd be told go to sleep and Ma would come down and say, 'Go to bed'," explains Ken. "I remember one night she banged the wooden spoon at the bottom of the bed and it broke and she started laughing and that was the end of that. She wasn't the strong one but Dad would open the living room door and let down a roar and that was usually the end of it. If he had to come down there was serious trouble.

"I suppose it was a happy house. You could sense the love in the house but there was no going around doling out hugs and kisses to everybody. We'd go to bed at night, we'd kiss Mam and Dad good night. We weren't ones for a bullshitting show and still wouldn't be."

Martin would play football or hurling out in the back garden with them but the competitive edge he gleaned in that type of setting with his brother Tom as a youngster many years previously wasn't blunted. "If you won, you deserved to win," smiles Ken.

A critical aspect to the decision to go to America was that if it didn't work out, he had a job to come back to seeing as he was able to take a leave of absence from the Council. Much less straightforward, however, would be telling his mother that he would be the third of her sons to leave for America. And, not only was he going, but he was taking her beloved grandchildren too.

"That did not go down well," Martin admits. "It broke her heart. She wasn't pleased that I was taking her grandchildren away from her because she had been very good to them. She was very close to Katie as well. Katie was the daughter she never had. They got on like a house on fire. I guess John wasn't pleased either but he didn't say a hell of a lot."

Martin left on his own on May 1, 1988. Joan was sitting her Leaving Certificate the following month and once all the children had completed their schooling for the year they and Katie would join him at the end of June.

He wasn't the only Furlong brother coming to Tom's aid in the Catskills. After he had retired from MaBSTOA, Mickey went with his son Michael to Florida to help him buy a house in 1987. With more time on his hands to play golf, he reckoned there was nowhere better than Florida to do it. He got back to Hazlet and was shovelling snow from his drive when he yelled, "May, we're moving to Florida!"

He was keen to come on board with Tom and Yvonne and, given that it was a fledgling business, his affable nature was bound to be a huge asset.

"Howeya Sarsfield!" was his famed catchphrase that he'd fall back on to greet people whose names he couldn't recall. "I feel like 10 men, nine dead and one dying," he'd often say when asked how he was, one of his many stock phrases that lost nothing through repetition.

Every summer for years afterwards he'd come to May looking for the green light to spend a few months working for Tom in the Catskills. In later years he'd put the money he'd make up there towards his daughter Eileen's education.

That first year, the bar opened on Memorial Weekend in late May with Mickey working the day shift and Martin there at night. Yvonne was a big presence too, while the plan was for Tom to continue his work in the Transit Authority up to the age of 50 to maximise his benefits. When mulling over what to call the bar, all sorts of names were thrown around. John 'Kerry' O'Donnell suggested keeping it simple. "Why don't you call it Furlong's?" he said. "There's no mud on that name." Furlong's it was.

"Mickey was a great asset," says Tom. "A lot of people from his time would be coming up to the Catskills at that time. He knew them all. You'd go into Mickey in the morning and there'd be about eight guys in there maybe and they'd all have out the paper for the horses and all that. He'd do a bit of singing and dancing.

"If myself and Yvonne had to go to a wedding or something like that on a Saturday there used to be great fenagling with the money. He'd say to Yvonne, 'Room one rented'. 'How much did you get for it?' 'How much do you think?' '$60?' 'Yeah, that's right, $60 and $20 for myself!'"

Tom's son Tommy was part of the New York minor football team at the time and was about to go to Ireland and play against Dublin in the Leinster Championship when Mickey, then in his late 50s, challenged him to a sprint outside the pub. He was giving up more than 40 years to the teenager and beat him not once, but twice.

Given that Mickey had left Ireland when Martin was just eight years of age, having already spent a couple of years in Dublin at that stage, it was an opportunity for the brothers to connect with each other as men for the first time. Mickey got home to Ireland as often as he could over the years though once his playing days ended and his family expanded, those opportunities became much fewer. But while that brotherly bond was strengthening, the move to the US wasn't working out quite so well for the rest of his family.

Given that they were in or near early adulthood, Martin had told Joan and Ken that if they couldn't settle in America they were free to go home. Having moved over in the summer, the whole experience had something of a holiday feel for Ken initially. But that changed when it came to going to school. The family was fractured somewhat by the fact that while Martin worked in the bar upstate in East Durham, Katie and the three boys stayed in Tom and Yvonne's place in Nanuet, 90 miles south, where they attended school. Ken had a girlfriend back home and had maintained the relationship as best they could. Mickey used to tease him about "Dear John" letters coming in the post.

"It was the culture shock of the school, the teachers, the subjects, the pupils," Ken explains. "While a lot of it was the same, nuances and little things were different about it. Even the fact that a friend of Tommy's used to pick us up in his car. We were only 16 and you'd load into the back of the car and he might be early or late and there was a lot more freedom in that part of it. On Saturdays there would have been games and after it you'd be out on a Saturday night and that was alien to me."

When they went up to East Durham to visit one weekend, Martin immediately noticed that Ken wasn't himself.

"What's up with your man?" he asked Katie.

"Ah, he'll tell you himself," she replied.

Later on, they talked it out and Ken confirmed he wanted to go home.

"I was disappointed to tell you the truth but, at the same time, that was the deal I had made with them. If they didn't like it they could go home. I said, 'Are you sure that's what you want to do?' and he said, 'Yeah, that's what I want to do'. So I said, 'Ok, you'll have to give me two weeks till I get things together'. It was like a switch. He was back to being like himself again. So I booked him a ticket and off he went. I was sorry to see him going, very sorry.

"He was going home to my mother and John so she was going to be very happy. What I didn't know at the time was that Joan wanted to go too. She didn't want to hit me with a double whammy. So she held until the following spring.

"She said she missed her friends. They still meet a couple of times a year, the same girls. Of course my mother, she was highly delighted then. She had her little girl back."

When the family was leaving, friends of theirs concluded that the kids would settle into the way of life over there much more quickly than a couple in their early 40s. But it was very much the opposite. Martin and Katie adjusted to driving on the other side of the road, the trunk instead of the boot, dollars and cents instead of pounds of pence, the tipping culture and all the other myriad changes that go with living in America seamlessly. They knew after a few months that they'd be staying and within a year had bought a house in Nanuet.

Of course, one niche that he could never quite compensate for in America was that left by the GAA. He managed the Offaly football team in New York for a few years and got a kick out of it, but it wasn't quite the same. Still, once he was involved, he stuck by the same principles that governed his playing career back home.

His nephew Tommy, a corner-back on the team in those days, remembers him reading the riot act to a player who stood on the Offaly jersey while towelling himself down. He was reminded in no uncertain terms how better men had worn the jersey before him.

"That used to drive me fucking mad. I stopped all that shit. Stopped them throwing the jersey on the ground.

"It's not the same out here but at the same time it was the best it could be. We had a great bunch of lads here at the time. The number of Offaly lads that were here and togged out and training was great. It filled a gap but it never filled it adequately."

Margaret would happily have taken all the kids back but Mark and Tom were that bit younger and the option that Ken and Joan had to go home wasn't there for them. They too found it difficult to settle but in time adjusted well and made good careers for themselves.

The bar did a very good trade that first summer but Martin had to find work for himself once the licence expired as the winter approached. Yvonne fixed him up with a job in the Three Counties bar, owned jointly by two Irish couples, on 231st Street and he stayed there for several years, working the day shift from 8am to 6pm.

However, his status and that of his family in America was illegal for the first few years. After going home to Ireland in February 1990 for the first time since leaving, he was pulled aside by immigration officials when returning at JFK Airport. They asked numerous questions and he managed to blag his way back in. But the experience frightened the life out of him.

The following year Margaret came to America to visit and spent much of the summer there. She had made several trips over the years and John had come a couple of times too but by now she was well into her 80s and slowing down. Tom felt that by bringing her out, at least they could look after her and it might give her a lift. He gave her a couple of the rooms over the bar to herself and adapted them to her ever growing needs. But by the time it came to sending her home she would have been too much for John to handle on his own. Tom took her home in a wheelchair and thought it unlikely he'd see her alive again.

"She had rheumatoid arthritis and that was slowing her down so when she came home she went into the nursing home on Arden Road," he says. "I paid for her, then she found out she could get her hair done, I was getting bills for this and that but I didn't mind. Then the doctor called me and told me she wasn't doing good. I tried to get it out of him, what it was. I think what happened was she couldn't feed herself and she didn't want the nurse to be feeding her so then she just stopped eating and that was it. She was dead in three weeks."

Mickey and Tom came home for the funeral but Martin couldn't take the chance given that his illegality still hadn't been resolved. "That was hard," he says. "I couldn't chance it because I wasn't legal. The other part of it was we had a house here. If I went home and I couldn't get back, Katie was here with two kids and a mortgage. She would have understood my predicament."

Two years earlier, Connecticut congressman Bruce Morrison had written the Immigration Act of 1990. The bill included a provision called the Morrison visa program whereby 40,000 visas each year for three years were allocated to countries that had been disadvantaged by the 1965 immigration legislation. Irish immigrants were allotted 40 percent of the visas available. The applications had to be filed in Virginia and Martin drove down to apply for the whole family.

"We were going around to every mailbox and post office we could find stuffing envelopes into them because that time you could put in as many applications as you wanted whereas now you can only put in one."

Enough of them landed in the right channels and they were all granted. He had to go back to Ireland in August, 1992, four months after his mother passed away, for an interview in order to complete the process.

His brother John was only too happy to see him. With both his parents now gone and his three brothers in America, he was somewhat isolated in Tullamore, albeit he had a loyal circle of friends. Those who knew him best conclude that his mother's passing took a lot out of him.

"Now and again you'd see an oul' tear coming to his eyes and he'd say, 'The bloody smoke'. But you'd know well it wasn't," says Sonny Lloyd, one of his closest friends. "He didn't like talking about her. It didn't help him when she died because he really had no one to go back to. After all, he never had to hardly polish his shoes. She did everything for him. He had no one to go home to and when you go home then you're looking at the walls. She was there always to make him a cup of tea or something when he'd go home. I believe she wouldn't go to bed until he came in, or she wouldn't sleep."

Way back when he was at death's door, his mother made daily trips on her bicycle to the old St Vincent's Hospital at the opposite end of town to visit him. The roles were reversed at the end when she was in the nursing home situated on the same site and he tipped up and down.

John's illness as a teenager had repercussions for his general health for the rest of his life and he perhaps didn't lead a lifestyle that was conducive to containing that. His diet could have been better; he certainly had a weakness for fry ups. A few months after his mother died he wasn't feeling particularly well and complained of pains in his chest. His heart was weakened by his illness and he had an irregular heartbeat. He went to the doctor but didn't quite get to the bottom of it. One evening he was playing snooker in Tullamore GAA Centre when he collapsed having suffered a heart attack. The hospital was only across the road but it took some 45 minutes for an ambulance to arrive. The delay effectively sealed his fate.

Mickey, Tom and Martin rushed home from America but their brother, as they knew him, was, effectively, no more.

"He was brain dead when I saw him," says Tom. "He was on a ventilator and it was going up and down and he was going up and down and there was no sign of him doing anything."

Mickey and Tom nipped out for a short while to Paddy McCormack's pub in town and had something to eat. They then went to visit their parents' grave. While they were running those errands, the doctor had stressed the need to Martin for John's bed to be freed up. John wasn't going to recover and he pressed for the ventilator to be switched off. Martin frantically called various different spots where he thought his brothers might be but to no avail. When they finally got back to the hospital they met Rosie Fitzpatrick, wife of John's long-time friend, Martin, in floods of tears. John was gone.

"I mean we were after coming 3,000 miles," says Martin, still bitter at the manner in which it was handled. "Another hour or so wasn't going to make a big difference. He could have waited. I know in my heart and soul they would have liked to have been there with him when he was dying."

"We knelt down and said a decade of the rosary and made arrangements for the funeral," says Tom. "It was very difficult because you looked down and there was a brother of yours dead. It's natural to see your mother and father die before you. But to see your own brother lying there. That was an awful belt in the cajones."

His death, at just 58, came barely six months after that of his mother. Too close to be a coincidence, Tom believes.

"He was very close to my mother. She had been by his side all his life. She learned the sign language off him. She only had to start two letters of the word and he'd know what it was and she'd be onto the next one. They were inseparable. He'd go down town and have his few jars and all that. She might give out to him now and again but that was her John."

"John did have, all things considered, a great oul' time," Martin reflects. "He made the best of it. He enjoyed the games and he enjoyed his darts and his snooker and he enjoyed his pints. He enjoyed his arguments. He got a good kick out of life. He was a very proud Offaly man and a blue blood. He was Tullamore to the hilt."

Misfortune meant that John wasn't able to scale the athletic peaks that his three brothers did, but he achieved plenty to make them as proud of him as he was of them nonetheless.

"He was well respected," says Tom. "Of course, people used to love taking the piss out of him and get him going and get him into an argument or something like that. They'd get over that and John would get over it.

"If I went with John to a football game or a hurling game at home, everybody knew John. It wasn't me they knew."

CHAPTER 19

FALLEN TOWERS, FALLEN TOWER

AS a boy, Mark Furlong had a tendency to pick up bee stings from time to time. It was compounded by the fact that he had an allergy to them and had to be rushed to hospital each time, which saw Martin and Katie presented with a hefty bill. The family had no medical cover.

Working in a bar, as Martin was at the time, could be lucrative insofar as tips were concerned but it didn't bring much beyond what he walked out the door with in his pocket. There was no pension or health coverage or benefits to go with it. He considered a change of career and got chatting to a customer about his predicament in the bar one day. "Why don't you try Pat Donaghy?" he suggested to him.

Pat Donaghy was a Tyrone native and owner of Structuretone, a prominent construction company. He was a founder member of the Celtic Golf Club, of which both Tom and Martin had been presidents in the past. Martin knew him reasonably well and called him up wondering if he might have anything going. "Let me see what I can do," he said. A couple of days later he called back and told him to report to Ed Walsh on 26th Street for a chat. He did just that and was hired as a labourer. After a few years a position came up driving a truck for the company, dropping off tools, gang boxes and the like from job to job around the city, and he got it.

"It was easier on the body, harder on the mind, if you like," he says. "Driving in the city is stressful. The one thing I was hoping was that I would get out of it without having knocked down or hurt or killed somebody." He managed to avoid that misfortune and others.

One morning early in September 2001, he made a drop off at the World Trade Centre, as he often would. At times he could find himself down there three days running but mightn't wind up back there again for a couple of weeks. Structuretone did quite an amount of work in the twin towers.

"We always had work going on there," he says. "There was a hundred and something floors there. We did an awful lot of work for financial people and lawyers and all of that."

Martin had scheduled time off for the second week of September. On September 8, Ken, his wife Paula and their family arrived out on holiday for a couple of weeks. They rented a spot together by the beach in New Jersey. On the Tuesday morning, Martin was disturbed while shaving by Katie, who told him that a plane had hit one of the towers.

"I went out to look and I still had shaving cream on my face. One side of me was shaved and the other wasn't. It was unbelievable to watch and the next one went into it then."

Three of his Structuretone colleagues perished. Among them was Sligo native Kieran Gorman. He had been working near the top of the south tower when it was struck. He was married with two children and his wife, Anne, was expecting another. The family had only returned from a holiday back home two days before. The 35-year-old wasn't due to resume work for a few days after he came back but was called in earlier than expected. Like Furlong, he was a former inter-county goalkeeper, having played for Sligo back in the '80s.

"Big gentle giant," he says of him, "lovely, lovely fella. I knew him well, knew him very well. I knew his buddy that was down on the ground, Fintan Henry. He was also from Sligo and he escaped."

There was a Tullamore link to the tragedy too. Yolanda Dowling, a magnificently talented classical singer who was the daughter of Mickey's old teammate Christy and niece of former GAA president John, was coming towards the end of her time working for Aon Corporation in the south tower and was lost.

If Ken hadn't booked that holiday when he did there's no guarantee that Martin would have been down there when the attack occurred. But there's no guarantee that he wouldn't have been either. Only days before he was there at the same time of the morning making a routine drop off. His fortune at avoiding it is not quite something that he's pondered every day since, but the thought that he could possibly have been wrapped up in one of the most horrific events in modern history did play on his mind.

"To a certain extent, yeah. I wouldn't play that up though. It was an awful tragedy, an awful tragedy. It was mind-boggling. When you think of it, who in the name of Christ would think of doing what they did? It wasn't one plane, it was two planes, three planes... how they got away with it... how they pulled it off... how they even thought of doing it... mind-boggling."

Structuretone worked on the recovery and the poisonous taste in the air at Ground Zero wrapped itself around his throat on the occasions that he was down there.

"It did bring the city to its knees. It took it a while but it came back. I never thought it would come back to the way it is, I really didn't. I mean business-wise. Construction-wise. Attitude-wise. I mean, it was the first time America was ever attacked on its own soil. It was a huge culture shock. It rattled the people big time. To see the destruction that was done was just mind-boggling. They said the air was clear down at Ground Zero. It wasn't clear. You could feel it in your neck once you passed Canal Street. You could taste it. The dust was so fine. So fine. It just got through everything. It was like an itch. A dryness in the back of your neck. There was no way was that air right."

He believes that exposing workers to that environment will carry repercussions for years to come.

"There's fire fighters dying now and cops and I'm sure there's steel workers but you don't hear about them, or labourers. It's cops and firemen you hear about. I'm sure there's electricians as well. I still think that there'll be a certain amount of people will not want to work in those towers."

It became commonplace for Americans to hang the national flag outside their home following September 11 and Furlong was no different. He was 13 years in the country at that stage and it had been good to him and his brothers too. For the Furlongs, though, another seemingly indestructible unit was soon to unexpectedly fall as well.

◆　　◆　　◆　　◆

After John's death in 1992, the old family house on O'Moore Street was left idle. Beside it was Mahon's field, a large site close to town that, as the Celtic Tiger cleared its throat, was never likely to be restricted to grazing cattle. In 1996 the Flanagan Group started work on a new hotel, which was badly needed in the town, on that site. Sadly, the old house had to go.

The following year the Tullamore Court Hotel was opened. To mark the hotel's first anniversary in November 1998, the idea of calling the bar after the famous family that grew up nearby was floated. They were always reluctant heroes but Mickey, Tom and Martin flew home for the official opening of the Furlong Bar. A montage of pictures was created by Martin's former club and county teammate Paddy Fenning. It was a huge event as more than 1,000 people packed the hotel.

Jody Gunning, a long-time teammate of Martin's and well-known broadcaster on local radio, had a roving microphone and he interviewed the Furlongs and famous football personalities from all over the country. The likes of Paddy 'Hands' O'Brien, who thwarted Mickey Furlong with Meath back in 1954, was there. Mickey's Offaly minor teammate from 1947, Monaghan native Tommy Moyna, made the trip. TJ Gilmore too. Old teammates came home from all over the country and overseas. Joe McDonagh, GAA president at the time, was the keynote speaker.

Micheál Ó Muircheartaigh was master of ceremonies and recalled his time sharing digs with Mickey on St Brigid's Road all those years before. He read riveting citations on the Furlong brothers that had been penned by local GAA historian John Clarke. The formalities ended with Mickey belting out Boolavogue, having typically introduced it as the "Furlong national anthem".

"It was a great night and it was late when I left," recalls Ó Muircheartaigh. "It was the following day when I missed my coat. I rang up and it was very noisy. I said to the receptionist, 'You must have a wedding today?' She said, 'No'. I said, 'Why all the noise?' And the way she put it, 'Last night didn't finish yet'. And that would be typical Furlong, wouldn't it?"

When Mickey was walked through the montage of pictures a shot of the Offaly 1954 team was pointed out to him. He looked at it ruefully.

"We should have won the All-Ireland that year," he said. "Meath beat us by three points, a lot of easy goals went in that day." At the time of the bar opening, Offaly were the reigning All-Ireland hurling champions while the footballers had won the National League earlier that year for the first time – two teams that Mickey had represented with distinction. "I was never more proud to be an Offaly man than I was this year," he said.

"Out in this field, right where this hotel is, is where I started off. It's very emotional.

"I see a lot of guys here that played football with me, like Des Garland and I met Seán Foran in there and the 'Hooper' Farrell and Mick Casey of course, the great Mick Casey, best footballer that ever stood on a football field, by the way.

"And," he smiled, "I met a lot of guys whose wives I know!"

The opening fell a day before the sixth anniversary of John's death and he wasn't forgotten in all the excitement on what was a poignant evening for the family too.

"It's fabulous," said Mickey. "When I came back this week and I saw the house gone, it was very sentimental but when I walk in here now, and any time I come back, it'll be like walking into the house, seeing the pictures on the wall. It's unbelievable."

But, sadly, there would be no further visits to Tullamore for Mickey Furlong.

◆   ◆   ◆   ◆

Mickey may have left his drinking days long behind him but he didn't banish all of his bad habits. The quality of his diet still left something to be desired and he required a quadruple bypass in the mid '90s. He was also diabetic.

"He'd go to a buffet and he'd fill it up like a volcano on the plate and say, 'Ah Jaysus, I'm not feeling too good today!'" smiles his daughter Mary. He'd joke further by claiming he was on a diet by virtue of the fact that his tipple of choice by now was Diet Coke rather than the regular version.

In 2002, he had an irregular heartbeat and required a jump start to get it back in sync. Not long after that, he settled in to watch the US Masters on television one afternoon. Pádraig Harrington had made a good start to the tournament and was still hanging in come the third round. Mary's son Michael had a baseball game and she wondered would he come and watch it. He'd usually go at the drop of a hat but wasn't feeling particularly well and was by now engrossed in the golf.

"Harrington's doing well in the Masters, and I'd like to see if he wins it. Would you mind if I didn't go?"

"No problem, Dad," she replied. "It's no big deal."

May made him a sandwich and left him to watch the golf, presuming his ailment was no more than something minor like a flu. Although he wasn't one for milking it when under the weather, the following day he still wasn't well and May asked her neighbour, who worked as a nurse, to stop by. They decided to take him to hospital, presuming he'd be right as rain in no time.

"I was sitting in the front of the ambulance," says May, "he was in the back, they were working on him and they said, 'Oh he'll be ok, he'll be ok'. We didn't think he was that sick but the doctor did say he was a very sick man."

Mary joined her mother at the hospital and went to check on her father as she returned from getting a cup of coffee. It was then she realised the gravity of the situation. His eyes were flickering as the medical staff swarmed around him. She was whisked away along with her mother and placed in the hospice room, which didn't fill her with optimism either.

"I called my husband and I started crying, 'There's something wrong with him'. Oh my God, it was just the realisation that something was wrong with him and what do I do. My husband was like, 'Don't worry about it, just stay with your mom, I'll call everybody'. It was a kind of a blur. I remember when the doctor came in to tell me that he had passed away. The phone rang and it was Eileen, she was getting married in a couple of weeks, and she said, 'How's Dad?' and I said, 'He died'."

He was only 72. That he went fast is a consolation of sorts to the family.

"I feel God took him," says May. "He always said that 'I hope God takes me, and I go fast'. And He did, He did take him fast. It was hard on us."

There were tell tale signs in the run up to his death that might well have made it avoidable. In the end, it's believed that he suffered a massive heart attack having essentially bled to death internally. He had been on a drug called coumadin, which is commonly referred to as a blood-thinner though, strictly speaking, its primary function is to prevent blood clots from forming. A few weeks earlier it was found that his blood levels were low when he underwent a routine test. In that context, he ought to have been weaned off the drug for a period. Instead, by remaining on it when he may have had an infection of sorts, it hastened his demise.

May had helped him to the toilet the night before he died and noticed that he passed a lot of blood. It was only then he revealed that that had been the case for about a week. There was a suggestion later that his illness may have been instigated by a bleed through a polyp. While he lay in bed at home that night he said to her, "You know, I'm not going to take that medicine any more."

"He knew that it was something to do with the medicine that was making him sick," she says.

The family are philosophical about that aspect of it, however. They believe in fate and that it was simply Mickey's time to go. Kicking up a fuss in the aftermath wasn't their style, nor his either. "You have that fate to get you through sometimes," says Mary. "You just have to believe that it was his time."

His death left a massive void. The night before, he and May had been planning a trip to Ireland with Mary and her fiancé Peter, and would also take in his native Germany. When Eileen, his youngest, was married a few weeks later, her brother Michael and May led her up the aisle. Martin did the honours for Mary on her wedding day a number of months later. Each of his seven children learned Boolavogue following his death and sang it in unison at both weddings.

Back in 1982, Mickey had been hit by a car in Hazlet when crossing the road on his way home from work. He believed he was saved by the fact that he jumped prior to the impact before going through the windscreen. He was very badly injured, suffering a broken ankle and a small fracture to his spine while his head was gashed in several places.

When the police came to review the scene they asked where the other vehicle involved in the accident was, struggling to believe that the damage to the car that hit him was inflicted by one individual and, moreover, that he had survived. Most would have been wiped out by it. The fact that Mickey wasn't franked the toughness that set him apart as a player, but also added to the sense of shock when he later slipped away so quickly. It's still palpable in Martin's voice when he talks about it today.

"Couldn't believe it," he says. "I was just after coming in after playing golf one Sunday. Couldn't believe it. You always felt he was indestructible anyway. What he went through and getting hit by a car and came back from it. You would have felt that, Jaysus, he would have lived to his mid-80s anyway. You really would. And he should have."

Tom was driving from his regular winter retreat in Florida back up to reopen the bar for the summer season when his son Tommy finally reached him on the phone after a number of hours and gave him the heartbreaking news. Mickey was buried in Palm Bay, Florida and Tom delivered a moving eulogy at the funeral and again at a memorial service held in New York. "It was kind of getting the better of me at that stage," he says. "It was very emotional."

"In the end, he ended up doing more good for others through AA and other ways," says Mickey's son Johnny. "I had many people that approached me at his memorial services that knew him from the Catskills. They told me of the impact he had on them through his words of encouragement and the gentle way he had about him in his later years long after he quit drinking. He was always helpful, with an attentive ear. He possessed a great deal of compassion and empathy. People sensed that, which allowed them to open up to him. That is mostly what I choose to remember about him. I think, in the end, that is probably how he would want to be remembered."

After Martin had moved to America he developed a wonderful relationship with Mickey, having only been exposed to each other sparingly for most of their lives up to then. He was always fiercely proud of his little brother's string of achievements and they'd chat on the phone at length on a regular basis, conversations which Martin still misses to this day.

"Katie will tell you that," he says. "I miss his oul' phonecalls. I'd call him, he'd call me, whatever. 'How's it going there, lad?' He was a great oul' chat."

Mickey and May's relationship had come through the mire and been strengthened considerably for that. The two of them were richly enjoying their golden years together and were counting on many more of them. They had already bought a plot in the cemetery and would regularly sit there and talk. "This is our second home," he'd tell her.

"The last years, I'm glad we got them," she says. "We could go over to the beach and, I swear to God, we could spend five hours on the beach, the two of us sitting together. We didn't need anybody else and just to chat, the kids were all gone, the two of us and he'd say, 'You know Mother, we'll never go back'. He loved Florida. I was lucky I got those years.

"He used to look at the kids and he'd say, 'You know Mother, we didn't do too bad', and I'd say, 'No, we didn't'. We had our rough years and I used to say to him, 'How did we make it, the two of us?' He'd say, 'You know Mother, because we had a lot in common'. We had a lot in common, the two of us. We both came from Ireland, we loved each other deep down. We went through the rough years and just to survive what we did, we had to love each other. There had to be love there because that's what holds it together.

"I remember he said, 'Mother, if anything ever happens to me I want you to just find yourself somebody else'.

"But I wouldn't want anybody else because I would be looking for somebody like him."

And there was only one Mickey Furlong.

CHAPTER 20

BACK FROM THE BRINK

THE business in Furlong's up in the Catskills was brisk for a long number of years. After the first summer of 1988, they carried out an overhaul of the bar and accommodation and stayed open for the hunting season too. Tom continued his work in the Transit Authority for the first couple of years but when Yvonne got cancer, which she successfully overcame, he had to retire earlier than he had planned, on his 46th birthday in 1989, to help run the bar.

"Yvonne had the most presence there," says Tom. "I took a back seat because she knew how to run it. She was in the business, that's why I got the place. She'd worked as a barmaid and she'd worked as a waitress down town and then she was a banquet manager for nine years. She'd book weddings and all sorts of things. She'd have Joe Dolan in for a show. She'd have Johnny McEvoy in for a show down town."

Naturally, the bar had a strong sports theme to it. There was a picture of the 1960 Offaly minor team on which he starred and another of him from his American football days, the sole of his right boot pointing skyward and his tongue out in typical Furlong style as he nailed another field goal at practice. He got a couple of seats from Gaelic Park and after the Cusack Stand in Croke Park was demolished in 1993, a couple of the old wooden benches with the steel arm rests made their way out to East Durham too.

There was a picture of Babe Ruth alongside the Cavan and Kerry footballers ahead of their historic All-Ireland final in New York in 1947. The Offaly teams on which Martin starred also had a presence, along with a ball from the 1971 All-Ireland final.

'Whitey' Ford, the old New York Yankees pitcher, would often stop by and so too would Cathy Moriarty, one of the stars of Martin Scorcese's *Raging Bull*. "She was a good laugh, she had a good throaty laugh," says Furlong.

Initially there was live music every night of the week in the bar and they became more ambitious in that regard as time went on. From Séamus Moore, the JCB man, to Bagatelle, who they put on outdoors at the Irish Cultural Centre nearby.

"That was a two-day festival, Saturday and Sunday. It rained Sunday, screwed it up. Black 47, I gave them their opening shot there in the Catskills. We built a huge stage. With the sound system you could hear the bands three miles away."

And, of course, they had the matches from Ireland every Sunday. Sure enough, they'd get their biggest crowds come All-Ireland final day and you could double it again if Offaly were involved, as they often were during the bar's best days. For the finals, though, they'd show them in the fire house a couple of hundred yards down the road to maximise the crowd and justify the outlay on broadcasting the games. Offaly's hurling success in 1994 was particularly memorable. The place was heaving and the bedlam that broke out following Johnny Dooley's critical goal with five minutes remaining hadn't yet subsided when Pat O'Connor's immediate follow up strike nearly sent it into orbit.

When the bar shut down for the winter Tom and Yvonne often headed for Florida. Then, in 2010, they thought they'd have a go at keeping the place open all year round. On reflection, it was ill-conceived and doomed to failure. There simply wasn't enough footfall up there in the winter time to maintain the bar at that stage.

"It was too late to even consider that there was a business there in the winter time," he says. "There wasn't a business there."

Even if there was, events would take a turn to ensure that running a bar wasn't within Tom and Yvonne's gift any longer.

◆   ◆   ◆   ◆

One evening in January 2011, Tom sat up watching television in his home in the Catskills, about three miles from the bar, after Yvonne had gone to bed. A strange feeling came over him.

"I just felt like I was losing my feelings. The dog knew something was wrong. I think I got to the dog and I said something like, 'Go get mammy, go get mammy...' He was only a pup, only 18 months old, and he went in and he got the bed clothes off her and she thought that he wanted to go out to have a pee.

"So she got up and opened the door and let him out but he wouldn't go out. So she came up and said something to me about having a coffee. Then she saw I was hanging off the side of the chair. I was kind of out of it. I told her, 'I think I'm having a stroke'."

She called an ambulance and got a couple of the bar staff to come up too. In a relatively isolated location in difficult mountainous terrain in the depths of winter, the ambulance took quite some time to arrive and, as most people are aware, swift action is critical in limiting the effects of a stroke. He eventually reached Albany Medical a couple of hours after the stroke first hit him. He was out of it by then and would be for quite some time to come.

He was down in Martin's house one Christmas a few years earlier and stepped out for a walk with the dogs and his brother when he felt a tightness in his chest and decided to go back to the house. Martin carried on but thought better of it and cut his walk short. By the time he got back to the house an ambulance had been called. In stark contrast to his brother John back home years before, medical intervention was swift.

At the hospital they couldn't make up their mind whether he had suffered a heart attack or not until another one suddenly came on. He was transferred to Westchester Medical and a quadruple bypass was immediately performed. He'd only had himself checked out a few years previously and there was no cause for alarm then. He bounced back from that experience well but a stroke is often a by product of that type of surgery.

The outlook was grim following the stroke. Yvonne grew restless with the treatment Tom was receiving and eventually had him transferred to Benedictine Hospital in Kingston. Working there was an oncologist called Dr Paul Donovan, from Dublin, who had aided her with her successful cancer treatment years earlier. Tom knew him for years from when he had been training in Mount Sinai Hospital on 98th Street and Fifth Avenue and used to go to Murphy's bar nearby.

Although he didn't work in the area specific to Tom's illness, he spearheaded his bid to recover nonetheless and is afforded hero status in the eyes of the family, particularly Yvonne, as a result. If Dr Donovan told her that dressing as a clown would be beneficial to Tom's recovery she'd have raided the nearest circus.

He was severely disabled by the stroke and for those initial few months that he lay in hospital he had lost all movement on his right hand side. His mobility on the left side wasn't hectic either. The ability to talk also largely deserted him. He only has the odd memory of the first few months he spent in hospital and was often in a state of delirium, transposing himself back to the days spent in the fields while down in Wexford as a youngster for example.

"She keeps telling me things that happened but I don't remember them. I remember she came into me on her birthday, which would be February 20th, and I remember saying to her, 'Happy birthday' and I thought that was a tremendous achievement, that I was able to say it. That was it then, I don't remember anything again until one day I woke up, I was on the crane. I couldn't figure out where the hell I was but I knew I was in a crane. I'd be like that then, I was in and out."

He suffered numerous transient ischemic attacks (TIAs), which are effectively mini-strokes that often follow after a major one. He was on and off life support several times and on a couple of occasions a code blue was called as medics came running from every direction to tend to him. Twice Yvonne was advised to pull the plug.

"The second time, they were really, really talking to me," she says. "They said to me, 'The quality of life and the quality of living, that's not what it should come to with this man'. They said he wouldn't be able to walk, he wouldn't be able to talk ever again. 'He's going to be on a trach and on a feeding tube', because that's what he was on.

"And they said, 'You're not going to be able to take him home and he'll go into one of these homes because you wouldn't be able to afford to keep him in a private'. A private is $10,000 a month. They told me

I should pull the plug and I'll never forget it. I remember Martin was there and I remember our son walking down the hall, he was so upset.

"I remember there was somebody else there, another type of doctor, and he said, 'He's not going to pull out of that'. He was in critical intensive care and who arrived? Donovan. Donovan arrived on the scene and, by Jesus, there was no mention of pulling the plug."

His health insurance allowed him 100 days' cover and Yvonne reckoned initially that he'd be fine at that but they flew by and he was still in hospital. When he was released he was required to be out of the system for 60 days before his cover could kick in again but a setback that would restore him to hospital never seemed too far away once he got home. The countless scans on top of the care he received didn't come cheap either. The medical bills mounted up. They tried to keep the bar going but it was too much. Furlong's closed after 23 years.

Slowly but surely Tom began to make progress. It wasn't all smooth and he continued to have his setbacks and TIAs from time to time but he took them in his stride, so to speak. With the help of the physical therapist at the hospital, Micheal Keane, a Kildare native who had a natural and affable manner of cajoling him into action, he slowly learned to walk again. Nothing like he used to, but good enough to salvage his pride and a bit of independence.

"Of course, he related to Tom, he was mad about football, mad about hurling, he loved all that stuff and he wasn't soft with Tom," says Yvonne. "First of all he was in the wheelchair. He used to lift him. Tom Furlong never saw a toilet for seven months, he never saw a bit of food for seven months and he never saw a drop of water for seven months. I used to keep creaming him with the vaseline and stuff. Everything was being fed through the stomach. He was the best patient, he never looked for everything.

"But Mike would say, 'Straighten up boy, straighten up'. He used to go into when he was playing against such a one and how it didn't hold him back, 'Get going boy'. He was some character. He was powerful. He had Tom in front of him and he used to kick his legs out to walk, back and forth. He was unreal, he was unbelievable."

Dr Donovan was in no doubt that his athletic past played a key role in the astonishing extent to which he has recovered. His mind suffered no long term ill effects and his memory, which is impressive by any standards, is fully intact. Initially he stopped reading altogether but over time he got back into it to a voracious degree and regularly thumbs through books from start to finish in a matter of hours, a critical aid to his brain activity.

Having suffered his initial stroke in January 2011, he was fit to attend the Offaly Association, New York banquet by the following November and was toasted by all present. He was back living in the Catskills by then but it didn't lend itself to him leading the best quality of life. The mountainous terrain and harsh winters effectively left him housebound much of the time. For a number of years prior to that, he and Yvonne would spend the winter in Florida before returning to reopen the bar. He thought the way of life and climate down there would suit him much better.

Friends rallied around in numbers both in America and back in Ireland once news of his illness emerged. A few of them helped identify a place for him in Boynton Beach, where he had lived with Yvonne previously, and they moved there in April 2012.

"If he had continued to remain up in the Catskills, I think he would have died," says Joe Wrafter, his long-time friend and teammate who left Tullamore for New York a couple of years before him. "He was totally isolated up there, totally isolated, and he could be going days on end without really seeing anybody. You're looking out there at a miserable winter, cold, and he wasn't getting out and any damn thing.

"At least down in Florida he's able to get out in the sun and meet people and stuff like that. If you had seen him a few times up in the Catskills and you see him now, it's nothing short of a miracle. It's tremendous the way he's come back from the whole thing. He looks well right now and he's moving pretty good. His mind is good, very active. He needs to stay active like that and if he does stay active I think he'll be fine."

After his quadruple bypass he was to take an aspirin every day. But he had a bleed on the brain as a result of the stroke and it left a residue. Continuing to take aspirin would leave him susceptible to a further bleed. He has setbacks now and again and, sadly, one of them forced him to miss his nephew Tom's wedding in New York in December 2012.

While the physical therapy he had worked well in terms of getting him back on his feet again, there was a tendency to overdo it which left him susceptible to further TIAs. He has learned to cut his cloth accordingly as a result. He has his good and bad days but now accepts that he has hit a glass ceiling in terms of the progress he has made with his recovery. He won't ever get back into the shape he once was in but he's made his peace with that fact.

He can get up and go to the toilet independently. His right foot shifts a little bit along the floor compared to the left. He uses a walking frame when he ventures out and occasionally needs a wheelchair. But all of that is a far cry from being bed-ridden for months, unable to move, talk or eat. Resilience is a quality that flows through each of the Furlongs. Tom drew on it like never before in the last few years and found that he had it in spades.

Martin, at stages, had pretty much resigned himself to losing another brother and being the last link in the chain. He pays tribute to Yvonne and Dr Donovan for the role they played in restoring Tom to the condition he's in today.

"He wouldn't be alive only for her," he says. "Him and her. The doctor first and her second in the sense that he kept him alive at that time and then the nursing that she gave him after. I'd give her a thousand out of a thousand for that."

Yvonne tends to his every need. Every few months she'll throw a party in the condominium they live in, on occasions such as Thanksgiving or New Year's Eve. He looks forward to them and enjoys them immensely, feeding off the company of others. Living in Florida has its downside as they don't get to see their son and grandchildren as often as they'd like but they managed to get up to Tommy for

Christmas in 2013 and Martin and Katie joined them all for dinner on Christmas Day, events which the family treasure and appreciate now more than ever.

"Do you know what it is?" says Yvonne. "We can laugh. I kid him. Even if I get mad at him, you couldn't stay mad at him because he'd look up at you with a big smirk on his face. He'd be laughing. If I'm going around here saying, 'I've got to do this, I've got to do that', he just has a big smirk and I look over at him, 'What are you laughing at?' We never really stay mad at each other."

It's not how Tom Furlong imagined it would be at this stage of his life but he's managed to find happiness in his existence, something that would be beyond many people dealt a hand like his.

"I had the support of my wife through thick and thin and she's looked after me in a great way," he says. "Everybody's saying, 'Poor me', I don't think it's poor me. I'm very happy that I'm able to get up and go to the bathroom. Sometimes I'm bad on words but I'm happy that I'm as good as I am and I know I'm not going to get any better. I've had three strokes because I pushed myself on rehab. Now I know I can't push myself because it is what it is.

"But I'm happy. I'm happy now."

EPILOGUE

"I'M blessed, I'm blessed, I'm blessed," Martin Furlong says repeatedly when he reflects on the opportunities he had, and took, to be successful as a footballer compared to his brothers. "Absolutely blessed. If they had stayed at home, if they hadn't emigrated, if John hadn't been sick he could have added to the thing. I'm very blessed."

Nowadays he can watch the big GAA matches from the comfort of his own home rather than having to go to a bar or some other place on a Sunday morning. The All-Ireland finals are particularly poignant. He was a player on All-Ireland final day in Croke Park seven times over the course of his career. When he hears Amhrán na bhFiann ahead of the throw-in, his eyes fill up.

"That's when I would have been saying my prayers and I envision what's going through players' minds and how they're dealing with it. It's always very emotional because it's only in latter years you realise what you have achieved. All the great footballers that never won an All-Ireland and it just opens your eyes and brings it home to you how lucky you were. It's a Godsend.

"But you keep everything in context. Katie, I wouldn't be anywhere without herself. She lived through the whole thing, trying to keep me on the straight and narrow. We have a great relationship, thank God, and I think our move to America, at the time, gave us a new outlook on life and a whole new set of challenges. I think it was good for us. Very good for us."

He won his All-Irelands in two different eras and, perhaps if they operated in a different time, the Offaly '82 team would have won as much as the side that went a decade before them. "Comparisons should not be made," he says. "Not in our county anyway."

The two groups of players certainly have one common trait: an extremely tight bond. Eugene Mulligan took a trip to New York a few years back with his wife and called Furlong from Times Square to let him know he was in town. Within minutes he picked them up in his truck and gave them an in-depth tour of down town. Other teammates have enjoyed his hospitality in New York over the years and he looks forward to catching up with them every time he comes home. The bond is apparent every time they meet up. It's warm enough even to melt the Iron Man's heart.

"Martin was at my daughter's wedding in New York," says Paddy McCormack. "The very minute we met we put our arms around one another. You know what I mean? We're big buddies. Even the whole '71/'72 team like. You love to see them."

"I'd say he's one of the most popular men in Offaly," says Mick O'Rourke. "Without a shadow of a doubt like. When he was home in the summer, 14 or 15 turned up to play golf with him. We went for a bit of grub and the place was packed. Fellas just heard Martin was there and wanted to see him. A real legend.

"Martin is a different cut of a fella. Martin will go in there and sit down there with a young lad of six or an oul' lad of 80 and he wouldn't want anyone to know he was even there."

He's retired now, though he still does a few odd jobs down at the local golf club in the mornings. He enjoys life's simplicity, like taking his dog, Hughie, for a walk around the block in Nanuet and sipping a glass of Pinot Grigio with Katie in the evenings. He comes home once or twice a year and now that he's finished with Structuretone may spend some more time back in Ireland. Not too much, though.

"I'd like to, in one way, spend a couple of months over there in the summer time, see the matches and that sort of thing but then I'd be missing out on my golf tournaments here. I like the summers here. I'd hate to be at home in Ireland in the middle of July and it pissing rain."

Sadly, there aren't many marquee Offaly games to entice him home more often. Since that glorious day in September 1982, Offaly's footballing highlights have been few. They didn't win their next Leinster title until 1997 and haven't won another since. They've regularly frequented Division Four and will be back there once again in 2015. Success seems further away now than it ever was, maybe even more so than when Mickey Furlong was starting out. Back then Offaly had no winning tradition. The one they forged during Martin's career is being eroded with every passing year. Despite enjoying such great days in both codes in the past, the county simply isn't geared towards emulating any of that now.

"The longer it goes the harder it gets now. We're dragging ourselves up by the boot laces. It's hurtful. It'd be nice to see them back competing anyway. We just don't seem to be competing. I feel that some of the bigger counties have moved ahead of Offaly in facilities and preparation and that sort of thing.

"I don't know do lads realise what they're missing by not being successful. I don't know the mindset of younger people today. To be part of a team that would win a Leinster now at this stage would be fantastic I'm sure, it'd have to be. I'd like to see them getting back there, at least to win a Leinster in the next couple of years."

His son Ken played championship football for Offaly and was part of the panel that won that Leinster title in 1997 and the county's first National League a year later. He played for Offaly until 2000, meaning that a Furlong had represented the county at senior level for seven successive decades. The tradition continues with Martin's grandchildren now showing promise.

"I wouldn't say you knew you were special," says Ken of growing up as his father's son. "You weren't different to anyone. It's hard to explain it really. If I used the word privileged I'm wrong but there was a little bit of privilege.

"I know we have a weird life in that I came back from America when I was 17 but it's our normal and having Dad as Dad, he's just my Dad.

"It's pretty much normalised and it is what it is. A wrench when you're leaving. It's great when you're going to see them but it is what it is. It has been for a long time. Very rarely have we missed a week of talking to each other."

Like that, Tom is somewhat separated from his own family given that he and Yvonne live in Florida while their son Tommy rears his family in New York but he's more than content with the life he has, despite its limitations.

"I tried my hardest to get back but I find that I hurt myself by trying too hard and I'm happy now being able to go down the street to Finegans and be able to watch a game from Ireland," he says. "I'm happy that I have come so far and if I die tomorrow, I had a good life. I have no regrets.

"That's why I often said when I was younger, 'Don't leave anything behind you because you'll be wondering what if'. There was questions of whether to come to America or not, but I couldn't leave the what if. I had to see it to get it over with.

"My mother and father had a tough time together early in their marriage. None of us know how hard it was but thank God everything worked out alright and I know my father, even though he didn't say so, he was proud. Mickey was his pride and joy but I think Martin too was up there with his All-Irelands and all that. And I think he was proud of me too when I made my name in far away lands. He knew John was a good man, a good tradesman and that was what my father always believed in – a man being able to support himself. So I think, all in all, he was proud of his family."

Tom and Martin's two brothers are long gone now. Mickey and John would be octogenarians if they were still alive. Not everybody is privileged to live that long but the family feel that they, at least, ought to have made greater inroads. "I know my father loved John dearly and his death was a big shocker," says Michael Furlong, Mickey's eldest son.

It ran both ways. Years ago, a group from Tullamore were taking a trip to Killarney for a Munster final when one of them, Pat Heffernan, put a question to John: Who's the greatest footballer your ever saw? Such topics will always arouse great debate but John's view on these matters generally carried more weight than most. His response was awaited with interest.

"Ah, I can't say, I can't say," he replied.

Heffernan pushed him for an answer.

"No, no, I can't tell you," John insisted.

Later, Heffernan told Noel McGee about the exchange and wondered why John wouldn't elaborate. McGee smiled. "He won't tell anybody," he said, "but he thinks Mickey was the best player he ever saw."

John's opinion may have been influenced by nepotism to some degree but that particular episode sums the Furlongs up neatly nonetheless: their immense talent is surpassed only by their humility.

ACKNOWLEDGEMENTS

WHEN thanking people for their assistance in bringing this book to fruition, I must begin and end with the Furlong family and its various strands. I'm not old enough to have seen Mickey, John, Tom or Martin Furlong play but the family's standing in Tullamore, Offaly and beyond is something that wasn't lost on me when I was growing up.

Naturally, my familiarity with Martin was most acute. When the *Kerry's Golden Years* video was released I watched it repeatedly and was mesmerised by that great side. The highlight of the video, of course, was always the 1982 All-Ireland final. Even though I was barely five months old when that game was played, I later took immense pride and satisfaction from the fact that Offaly beat the greatest side in history in what is surely the most famous game of Gaelic football ever played and, moreover, that a man from my immediate locality played a central role. There was almost a mythical quality to Martin Furlong for me though as, by the time his achievements and reputation began to resonate with me, he was living in America, where two of his brothers had already made their home.

In more recent years I have got to know Martin on a personal level. Some say you should never meet your heroes and, in several instances, with good reason. Not with Martin Furlong, however. A more consummate gentleman you will never meet. Time spent in his company is always time well spent. He carries his array of honours and achievements with a level of grace and humility that I find incredible.

With that in mind, giving me the all clear to write this book is something that compromised him somewhat, as Martin is not one who ever wishes to see his name up in lights. I had come at him from various different angles in a bid to persuade him to participate in a book in recent years and finally succeeded when he was on a visit home last October. Whatever misgivings he may have had, he remained true to his word and the hospitality shown to me by him, his wife Katie and sons Mark and Tom when I spent quite an amount of time in their home in Rockland, New York last January is something that I'm extremely grateful for.

But there is much more to this book than Martin Furlong. While he is the best known of the four brothers, his siblings have compelling tales behind them too. The more I became aware of this, the more I felt it would be remiss of me not to commit their story to print. Sadly, in the case of Mickey and John, both have long since passed away and the book is the poorer for the fact that there is no direct contribution from them. However, I spoke to a range of people whose lives they touched and were much the better for it.

As well as spending time in Martin's home in New York, I also visited Tom in Boynton Beach, Florida and enjoyed an enthralling number of days in the company of him and his wife Yvonne. Again, the welcome which I was afforded went beyond the call of duty. As well as being a man of immense sporting talent, Tom carries an outstanding memory. He filled in several gaps for me in relation to the family history, enabling me to add more colour to the story. His stoicism in the face of the health problems he has endured in recent years is both humbling and inspirational.

There was also an evening spent in Melbourne, Florida, at the home of Mickey's daughter Mary. There, I chatted for hours with her, her sisters Michelle and Aggie and mother May, giving me a valued insight into that leg of the family. Mary has been a constant sounding board for me throughout this project and I'm particularly grateful to her for her help, guidance and encouragement.

Martin's eldest son, Ken, is someone who I see regularly through our mutual involvement in Tullamore GAA. He was always keen that this book be written and by dropping it into conversations on occasions it kept the aspiration alive within me when I felt like writing it off. Long before I ever started work on this book, his sister Joan had uncovered a treasure trove of information on her grandfather's volunteer past, making my job in detailing that aspect of the family story immeasurably easier. Special thanks also to Mark, who has been a very helpful conduit between Tullamore and Nanuet.

As anyone who knows me will be aware, I come from quite a large family and the encouragement given to me by them in terms of my work over the years and during the writing of this book is something I'm very appreciative of. I know that my dear mother Liz will be particularly pleased at the fact that she will see more of me now that I have completed it. My sister has a burgeoning photography business and I'd like to thank Paula Nolan Photography for my picture byline.

Like the Furlongs, there are strong connections to America within my own family. Over the years my uncle John Mooney, his wife Mary, my cousins Karen and Colette and their own families have made New York like a home from home for me. My almost annual visits there have become a yearly highlight. Their kindness and hospitality while I spent a couple of weeks at their home in January is something I deeply appreciate, not to mention the various lifts here and there that John afforded me, as well as his witty one-liners.

I also spent a night with my uncle Colman Mooney, my cousin Kate and her husband Dan while on my travels across Florida.

In writing any book, it is vital to have people who you can bounce things off and get ideas from. In that regard, I'm hugely grateful to Damian Lawlor and Paul Keane, two accomplished authors in their own right, for their feedback. Thanks also to my sports editor in the *Irish Daily Mirror*, Neil Fullerton, and colleague Michael Scully for affording me the leeway to concentrate on writing this book at times over the past number of months.

I am also blessed to have a close circle of friends from Tullamore that I have known all my life. Thanks lads for your loyalty and unwavering interest in my endeavours.

Offaly people tend to be unapologetically clannish by nature and I'm no different in that regard. Therefore, I knew I was placing this story in safe hands when PJ Cunningham from Ballpoint Press came on board as the publisher. It piqued his interest from an early stage and, given the esteem in which the Furlong family are held in Offaly, a laborious pitch wasn't required on my part. Thanks also to Joe Coyle for the fine work he has done in designing the layout of this book.

The Irish and Local Studies section of the Offaly County Library in Tullamore is something of a hidden treasure that I only stumbled across in the course of working on this book. It's a terrific facility which supplemented my research to no small end.

Following consultation between the Furlongs and myself, it was decided that Dóchas, the Offaly Cancer Support Group, would be the beneficiary of proceeds from this book. I would encourage anyone to call in to their base on Offaly Street in Tullamore; it will do you nothing but good. Their income is generated solely from fundraising and anything they glean from the sales of this book will be money well spent.

Outside of the Furlong family, there are many people that I interviewed in the course of working on this book and I thank them all for giving me their time. They are as follows: Martin Fitzpatrick, Mick 'Mickser' Casey, Paddy Cullen, John O'Leary, Ted O'Brien, Fr Rory O'Brien, Eamonn Fox, Paddy Fenning, Paddy Molloy, Séamus O'Dea, Pat Donnellan, Gabriel Hayden, Pat Heffernan, Eugene Mulligan, Alo Kelly, Billy Dowling, Eric Philpott, Willie Bryan, Paddy McCormack, Mick O'Rourke, Bernard Brogan Snr, Brian McEniff, Christy Dowling, Peter Nolan, Joe Bracken, Brendan Hennessy, Joe Wrafter, Mickey Moynihan, Sonny Lloyd, Micheál Ó Muircheartaigh, Dolores Sheeran, Norman Allen, Dollie Spain, Tim F Hayes, Mick O'Connell, Donie O'Sullivan, Mattie Kerrigan, TJ Gilmore, Seán Lowry, Eugene McGee, Mikey Sheehy and John Caffrey.

There are various people who helped me in many different ways, mostly through chasing down contacts as well as providing other bits of information. No one was more helpful than Paddy Fenning in that regard, but thanks also to Dave Hannigan, Michael Foley, Diarmuid O'Donovan, Jim O'Sullivan, Fintan Lalor, Mickey Whelan, Nicholas Furlong, Liam McAuliffe, Pat Gilroy, Jacqui Hurley, John Harrington, Charlie McCarthy, Jim Crowley, Mark Wilson, Bernard Brogan Jnr, Paddy Herbert, Roy Malone, Colm Keys, Gordon Manning, Martin Donnellan, Adrian Fitzpatrick, Kevin Nolan, Dr Paul Rouse, Mick Foy, Mick O'Brien, Miriam O'Callaghan, Damian Fox, Martin Breheny,

Ciarán Murphy, Michael Gilmore, Paul Caffrey, Enda McEvoy, Kevin Corrigan and Alan Aherne.

To conclude, thanks most of all to the Furlongs for trusting me to detail the story of their incredible family. I hope I've done it justice.

Pat Nolan
July 2014

INDEX